Careers in the Arts: Fine, Performing & Visual

Careers in
the Arts: Fine,
Performing & Visual

SALEM PRESS

A Division of EBSCO Information Services, Inc.

Ipswich, Massachusetts

GREY HOUSE PUBLISHING

Publisher's Cataloging-In-Publication Data
(Prepared by The Donohue Group, Inc.)

Title: Careers in the arts : fine, performing & visual.
Other Titles: Careers in--
Description: [First edition]. | Ipswich, Massachusetts : Salem Press, a division of EBSCO
        Information Services, Inc. ; [Amenia, New York] : Grey House Publishing,
        [2017] | Includes bibliographical references and index. |
Identifiers: ISBN 978-1-68217-320-6 (hardcover)
Subjects: LCSH: Arts--Vocational guidance--United States.
Classification: LCC NX163 .C375 2017 | DDC 700.23--dc23

First Printing

PRINTED IN THE UNITED STATES OF AMERICA

CONTENTS

PUBLISHER'S NOTE

Careers in the Arts: Fine, Performing & Visual contains twenty-seven alphabetically arranged chapters describing specific fields of interest in this industry. Merging scholarship with occupational development, this single comprehensive guidebook provides students planning to pursue a career in the arts with the necessary insight into potential opportunities, and provides instruction on what they can expect in terms of training, advancement, earnings, job prospects, and working conditions. *Careers in the Arts* is specifically designed for a high school and undergraduate audience and is edited to align with secondary or high school curriculum standards.

Scope of Coverage

Understanding the wide net of jobs in the arts and entertainment industry is important for anyone preparing for a career within it. *Careers in the Arts* comprises twenty-seven lengthy chapters on a broad range of occupations including traditional and long-established jobs such as Actor, Architect, and Musician, as well as in-demand jobs: Multi-media Artist, Cinematographer, and Graphic Designer. This excellent reference also presents possible career paths and occupations within high-growth and emerging fields in this industry.

Careers in the Arts is enhanced with numerous charts and tables, including projections from the US Bureau of Labor Statistics, and median annual salaries or wages for those occupations profiled. Each chapter also notes those skills that can be applied across broad occupation categories. Interesting enhancements, like **Fun Facts**, **Famous Firsts**, and dozens of photos, add depth to the discussion. A highlight of each chapter is **Conversation With** – a two-page interview with a professional working in a related job. The respondents share their personal career paths, detail potential for career advancement, offer advice for students, and include a "try this" for those interested in embarking on a career in their profession.

Essay Length and Format

Each chapter ranges in length from 3,500 to 4,500 words and begins with a Snapshot of the occupation that includes career clusters, interests, earnings and employment outlook. This is followed by these major categories:

- **Overview** includes detailed discussions on: Sphere of Work; Work Environment; Occupation Interest; A Day in the Life. Also included here is a Profile that outlines working conditions, educational needs, and physical abilities. You will also find the occupation's Holland Interest Score, which matches up character and personality traits with specific jobs.

- **Occupational Specialties** lists specific jobs that are related in some way, like Set Designer, Animators, and Photographer. Duties and Responsibilities are also included.

- **Work Environment** details the physical, human, and technological environment of the occupation profiled.

- **Education, Training, and Advancement** outlines how to prepare for this field while in high school, and what college courses to take, including licenses and certifications needed. A section is devoted to the Adult Job Seeker, and there is a list of skills and abilities needed to succeed in the job profiled.

- **Earnings and Advancements** offers specific salary ranges, and includes a chart of metropolitan areas that have the highest concentration of the profession.

- **Employment and Outlook** discusses employment trends, and projects growth to 2020. This section also lists related occupations.

- **Selected Schools** list those prominent learning institutions that offer specific courses in the profiles occupations.

- **More Information** includes associations that the reader can contact for more information.

Special Features

Several features continue to distinguish this reference series from other career-oriented reference works. The back matter includes:
- Appendix A: Guide to Holland Code. This discusses John Holland's theory that people and work environments can be classified into six different groups: Realistic; Investigative; Artistic; Social; Enterprising; and Conventional. See if the job you want is right for you!
- Appendix B: General Bibliography. This is a collection of suggested readings, organized into major categories.
- Subject Index: Includes people, concepts, technologies, terms, principles, and all specific occupations discussed in the occupational profile chapters.

Acknowledgments

Thanks are due to Allison Blake, who took the lead in developing "Conversations With" and to the professionals who communicated their work experience through interview questionnaires. Their frank and honest responses provide immeasurable value to *Careers in the Arts*. The contributions of all are gratefully acknowledged.

EDITOR'S INTRODUCTION

An Overview

The Arts includes a wide range of sectors and career paths, comprised of both the groups that produce and promote live performances and events, as well as the artists, performers and entertainers. Also included are those who manage, represent, and provide the artistic, creative and technical skills necessary to the production of live performances and artistic shows.

The professional and related occupations associated with the Arts, which includes Artists, was projected to increase 17% 2008 to 2018, approximately 7% higher than the U.S. work force overall. Of the artist occupations, museum technicians and conservators was projected to increase the most between 2008 and 2018 (26%), followed by curators (23%), landscape architects (20%), interior designers (19%), architects (16%), writers and authors (15%), and actors (13%). The artist occupations with little or no projected growth are radio and television announcers, floral designers, and fashion designers. Artist occupations likely to increase at the average rate of the labor force are fine artists, including painters, sculptors and illustrators; music directors and composers; producers and directors; and commercial and industrial designers.

Some artist occupations, such as actors, dancers, and singers, are expected to increase in both growth and competition. Some occupations are projected to have more favorable competition for job-seekers. Employment for landscape architects, for instance, is expected to increase at a much faster rate than the average labor force, and competition for those new jobs is likely to be good, affording at least a "rough balance" in the number of available jobs and job-seekers. Although jobs for floral designers are likely to decline, the competition is expected to be in rough balance or even "favorable" for job-seekers—meaning that the floral design industry will experience a rough balance between those seeking jobs and jobs that are available. Between now and 2018, however, no artist occupation is expected to face "good to excellent" competition, in which job openings are more numerous than job-seekers.

Many factors influence growth and competition within artist occupations. Certain industries are crucial to determining growth or decline in employment rates for some of the artist occupations; other occupations are dependent on different variables entirely, including geographical regions or the overall state of the economy. For the professional-and-related-occupations group, the top three occupations with the fastest projected growth in employment by 2018 are within the engineering, technology, and healthcare sectors. Although seemingly unconnected to artist professions, these fast-growing industries have a strong impact on artists' occupations.

Design

The field of design is both large and multi-faceted. In consequence, the projections vary widely among the different design occupations, which include graphic design, fashion design, floral design, interior design, and commercial and industrial design. Despite the projected decline in expected jobs for floral designers—mainly due to competition from simple floral arrangements from grocery stores that require fewer arrangers—the competition in this sector is expected to be "good," as people leave these positions due to low wages and minimal advancement. Commercial and industrial designers are projected to grow at the average rate, mainly due to off-shoring. While there is an increase in demand for the development of upgraded and high-technology products, the increase in design work being performed overseas will offset the industry's growth. Interestingly, employment of interior designers is expected to grow faster than average, primarily due to the healthcare industry.

With a rapidly aging U.S. population, there is growing demand for healthcare facilities, and interior designers will be needed to ensure pleasant surroundings for patients. The hospitality industry is also an important driver of interior-design employment. Graphic designers strongly depend on advertising and computer-design firms. As the demand for Internet advertising and interactive media increases, so will the demand for graphic designers.

Fine Artists

Similar to graphic design, some of the occupations under the category of "fine artists, art directors and animators" rely on advertising companies for employment growth. A surge in demand for multimedia artists, animators, and illustrators—especially those who are computer- and technology-savvy—is projected for 2018, due to companies' demand for advertising in online and digital formats.

While employment for multi-media artists and animators is expected to grow at a faster clip than for the labor force as a whole, craft artists and fine artists (including painters, sculptors, and illustrators) are projected to grow at the average rate. Illustrators in particular may even see a decline in employment due to staff cuts by newspapers and magazines.

There are few strict educational qualifications for fine artists, arts directors, or animators to enter the workforce; however, the majority of these artists hold some level of higher education—teaching certificates, bachelor's degrees, and often master's degrees.

Writers and Authors

The increase in the usage of multimedia technologies and online media also affects writers and authors. Companies' need to reach an increasingly technology-savvy consumer is growing, as is their dependence on disseminating information online, and skilled writers are needed for online publications, websites, and newsletters to attract customers. Further, like fine artists and animators, their education levels are relatively high—obtaining typically a bachelor's degree and often post-graduate education.

In addition to relying on the expanding technology sector, writer employment hinges on the advertising and public relations sectors, which themselves are growing. Writer employment also depends on publishing companies, which, conversely, are shrinking. These two factors result in writer occupations growing at the average rate.

Dancers, Choreographers, and Actors

Dancers and choreographers are an example of an occupation category whose outlook relies on the U.S. economy as a whole and not on other industries. Dance companies rely on contributed income and audience attendance—factors that are influenced directly by the state of the economy. A weak economy results in limited funding from private and public sources.

Jobs for dancers and choreographers are expected to grow more slowly than average. In addition, competition is keen; therefore, regular employment is a challenge in this field. Likewise, competition for acting jobs is extremely intense, though the outlook for actors in 2018 is not as bleak as for dancers and choreographers.

Actor employment is projected to grow as fast as the U.S. labor force, due to greater demand for satellite TV and cable, as well as major studio and independent films. Stage actors, like dancers, are subject to fluctuations in the economy as they, too, rely on live entertainment venues, ticket sales, and contributed income.

Dancers, choreographers, and actors share similar training and education characteristics: a college degree is not necessary, yet specialized training, classes, and instruction are essential.

Architects

The healthcare industry, environmental concerns, and geographic region-specific factors are all drivers of architect employment, which is projected to grow at faster than the average rate for all occupations. Architects (excluding naval architects) are essential in building healthcare facilities, nursing homes, and retirement communities. The population of the Sunbelt states— Arizona, California, Florida, Georgia, Louisiana, Nevada, New Mexico, and Texas—is growing, and people need places to live and work. "Green" design, also referred to as sustainable design, remains in demand. All these factors come into play when determining the employment outlook for architects.

Unlike some artist occupations, architects are required by most states to hold a professional degree in architecture from a college or university accredited by the National Architectural Accrediting Board (NAAB)—typically a five-year program. Architects are then expected to complete a training period of typically three years before they can take a licensing exam. Landscape architects must hold a degree from an accredited school as well as pass the Landscape Architect Registration Exam, required in 49 states.

Other Cultural Sector Occupations

The Occupational Outlook Handbook groups archivists, curators, and museum technicians together and defines them as workers who "preserve important objects and documents, including works of art, transcripts of meetings, photographs, coins and stamps, and historic objects" at institutions such as museums, governments, colleges or universities, and historic sites. Although the employment rate for this group is projected to grow by nearly 20 percentage points, the rate for archivists would increase by only seven percentage points.

According to BLS, the bulk of the increase is expected to occur within the curator and museum technician fields due to continued public interest in arts, science, and history. However, competition is keen for all these occupations as the skills necessary to perform the jobs are very specialized and require high levels of education—often graduate-level or higher. In addition, archivists and curators tend to remain in the same position for long periods of time and turnover is relatively low.

A report on employment projections from Georgetown University Center on Education and the Workforce entitled Help Wanted: Projections of Jobs and Education Requirements through 2018, notes that Americans' college completion rates are falling short of the projected need for educated workers. By 2018, more than 75 percent of jobs that fall under the five fastest growing industries will require a postsecondary education. And yet, according to the study, the U.S. will have a shortfall of three million degrees by 2018. Artist occupations, fall within the BLS category known as "professional and related occupations." These jobs typically require high levels of education or specialized training. In 2003-2005, for example, 55 percent of the nation's artists had a bachelor's degree or higher level of education—nearly twice the rate as U.S. workers as a whole. This tendency toward higher education may give artists an advantage in coming years.

—Editors of Grey House

*Artists in the Workforce: 1990-2005. Research Report # 48. National Endowment for the Arts. Washington, DC 20008.

Carnevale, Anthony P., Nicole Smith and Jeff Strohl. Help Wanted: Projections of Jobs and Education Requirements Through 2018. Georgetown University Center on Education and the Workforce. June 2010. http://cew.georgetown.edu/jobs2018/

Actor

Snapshot

Career Cluster(s): Performing arts
Interests: Creativity, performance, speaking, artistic expression
Earnings (Yearly Average): $52,000
Employment & Outlook: Higher than average growth expected

OVERVIEW

Sphere of Work

Actors are artistic professionals who perform on stage, television, or on film using their bodies and voices to bring the artistic visions of writers and directors to audiences around the world. There are many different kinds of actors, from stage and screen stars, to those who specialize in background or voice acting, to stunt actors whose work blends the line between acting and athletic performance. The success of elite actors, who can earn tens of millions for a single role and

can become internationally famous, creates an alluring mystique around an industry in which most struggle to earn a living from their craft and are forced to pursue acting as a part time or supplementary profession. In an industry known for being highly competitive, individuals seeking careers in acting need to be comfortable in competitive environments and should be passionate about acting as a form of self-expression and art as well as a potential career path.

Work Environment

Depending on the job, actors may be required to perform in a wide variety of environments. Some acting jobs take place indoors, on a stage or in a studio, while other assignments may require actors to perform some of their work in outdoor environments. Travel is a common requirement for acting work, with actors traveling to different auditions and shoots, sometimes requiring long periods living and working in different destinations. Some acting roles require little physical exertion while other roles require strenuous and even potentially dangerous physical activity and stamina is important as both film and stage roles may require long periods of standing, walking, speaking, and other activities. Irregular and overtime hours are common for actors during the height of a production though, when not actively working on a film or other production, actors may be required to spend little time working though they may be asked to participate in promotional activities to advertise their most recent project.

Profile

Working Conditions: Work Indoors and Outdoors

Physical Strength: Light to strenuous work

Education Needs: None

Licensure/Certification: Required in some areas

Opportunities For Experience: Part-Time Work, Understudy positions, Student employment

Holland Interest Score*: AE

* See Appendix A

Occupation Interest

Acting is both a career and a form of artistic expression and those seeking to become actors should be ambitious enough to compete for roles and have a strong, personal interest in the art of performance. Those seeking to become actors should also have interest in social interaction and collaboration, as actors typically work with other actors, directors, and designers to realize a production.

A Day in the Life—Duties and Responsibilities

A day in the life of an actor can vary greatly depending on the actor's specialty and the nature of a specific job. Before being cast, actors must participate in the casting process, which can involve studying potential roles, preparing for auditions, and performing in auditions for various roles. If an actor is cast in a role, he or she will begin preparing for the performance, which involves practicing lines, familiarizing oneself with stage directions, and doing background research for a role, such as perfecting an accent, memorizing a backstory for a character, or studying materials relevant to their character or the production. Those working in musical theatre or film may spend a portion of each day working with a musical director or other singers/musicians to practice aspects of the production's musical components. Actors also spend time in meetings with directors, producers, and other production managers. During a production, actors participate in table readings and various types of rehearsals. Depending on the production, actors may also need to meet with individuals form the costume department as well as set designers, stunt coordinators, and other professionals responsible for determining how an actor needs to move, where they need to positions themselves, and the environmental variables that will be included in each scene. In film productions, actors may spend time filming their scenes, an activity that can take minutes, hours, or days depending on the complexity and length of the scenes and how long a specific actor features in each scene.

Duties and Responsibilities

- Memorize lines and stage directions
- Participate in group readings and/or rehearsals
- Meet with directors and stage/filming managers
- Practice lines and/or stage movements with other actors
- Attend casting calls and other types of auditions
- Work with costume and set designers and consult with stunt supervisors
- Perform on camera or on stage for various audiences
- Meet with agents and representatives for various production companies

OCCUPATION SPECIALTIES

Voice-Over Artist

Voice-over artists, or voice actors, are actors who specialize in audio performances that may appear in commercials or in a variety of television and film productions. Many professional vocal actors practice performing in different accents or types of voices while some actors known for live-action roles are asked to perform in voice-only roles, such as in animate films or television productions.

Stunt Actor

Stunt actors bridge the line between athletic performance and acting, performing in action sequences either as a stand-in for an actor featuring in a production or as an independent character required to perform certain physical stunts during a performance. While stunt actors may be required to memorize lines and perform in roles similar to other actors, they also typically study the physical and technical skills needed for various types of performances, which may include driving vehicles, performing aerial stunts, or dealing with pyrotechnics and other practical special effects.

Actor Musician or Actor Dancer

Actor musicians are actors who also have skill in musical or dance performance. Some actors in this subfield specialize in performing in musical theater, either in live venues or on film. There are a number of films and television series that incorporate singing and dancing and specific films or television productions that are designed to showcase a performer's singing and/or dancing talents.

Background Actors

Extras are actors who work in bit parts for stage and film productions often appearing in the background of crowd scenes or in a variety of other non-speaking roles. While many beginning actors work as background actors before landing more significant roles in various productions, some actors specialize in background acting, supplementing other careers with occasional acting work.

WORK ENVIRONMENT

Relevant Skills and Abilities

Communication Skills
- Collaborating with other actors, directors, writers, and stage professionals.
- Delivering speeches, imitating or emulating emotional responses.

Interpersonal/Social Skills
- Working with other actors, directors, cinematographers, and stage managers.
- Accepting and adjusting to critical interpretations of a performance.

Organization & Management Skills
- Studying lines and stage directions.
- Managing a shooting and rehearsal schedule.

Research & Planning Skills
- Preparing and performing in auditions and casting meetings.
- Researching information necessary for a role.

Technical Skills
- Reading, writing, using equipment for special effects performances

Physical Environment

Actors may work in a wide variety of environments, from indoor sound stages to on-location shoots that may occur outdoors and even in extreme environments. Depending on the production, actors may shoot many scenes in different locations and may need to travel to different national or even international areas for a single production. Stage actors typically perform indoors, in theaters or studios. Those working in films or television productions that make use of computer generated imagery may need to work in special studios designed for motion-capture filming or with green screens for adding effects later.

Human Environment

Acting is a collaborative process in which the actor must work with a variety of other individuals to realize a specific production. Actors meet with costume and set specialists, stunt performers, directors, choreography specialists, script and film specialists, and other actors to practice and perfect their performance. Actors there need to be comfortable engaging in daily, at times intimate, interactions with other professionals involved in various productions and, those who interact well with their fellow actors and members of a production crew are likely to have more success in the industry.

Technological Environment

Actors may use a variety of digital technology in their work, including digital scripts, stage directions, and other tools to help actors learn and practice their parts, to working with highly complex CGI (computer generated image) equipment for scenes or productions involving computer animation. Motion-capture performance, for instance, requires actors to wear specialized suits during filming, which allow animators to change or alter the appearance of the actor with visual effects. In some cases, an actor may be asked to work with puppetry and other types of practical effects equipment.

EDUCATION, TRAINING, AND ADVANCEMENT

High School/Secondary

While there are no specific educational requirements for those seeking to become actors, secondary or high school students looking to become actors can often participate in acting/drama classes offered at many high schools to prepare for a future in the industry. In addition, an introduction to history, arts, performance, and linguistics is helpful for those looking to pursue acting as a career.

Suggested High School Subjects
- English
- English Literature
- World Literature
- World Languages
- Drama
- Public Speaking
- History of Film/Art
- Dance
- Singing/Choral

Famous First

The Screen Actors Guild (SAG now SAG-AFTRA) is one of the world's largest labor unions and grew out of the 1929 actors strike conducted by the nation's first actor's union, the Actor's Equity Association (AEA). A group of producers organized SAG to negotiate with studios on behalf of actors who were underpaid and often forced to work long hours. By 1938, an estimated 99 percent of actors were believed to be members of the organization and SAG become one of the most powerful labor unions in the world, lobbying successfully on issues including pay for extras, union rights, working hours, and contract negotiation guidelines.

College/Postsecondary

Actors can earn degrees in the dramatic arts at either the undergraduate or graduate level. A number of colleges and universities offer Bachelor of Arts degrees in drama or performance and there are some institutions that offer masters and doctorate-level degrees in acting or related arts. Collegiate level education in public speaking, English, literature, and the history of the performing arts is also a benefit to those seeking careers in the field and aspiring actors might also consider training in another performance arts discipline such as cinematography, directing, stage management, and/or script and screenwriting, as a way of increasing their opportunities to work in the field.

Related College Majors
- Film History
- Drama
- Directing
- Choreography
- Digital Cinematography
- Cultural Studies
- Screenwriting/Script Writing.
- Master of Arts

Adult Job Seekers

Adults looking to become actors do not necessarily need to pursue an education in drama or performance and can begin by searching for and participating in casting calls for actors in either background or featured roles. Some adult actors might consider auditioning for roles in local or community theatrical productions and many actors transition from working as stage or community actors to working in television and film roles.

Professional Certification and Licensure

There are no licenses or certification requirements for working as an actor though many states have specific rules and regulations regarding using school age or child actors in a production.

Additional Requirements

Depending on the specifics of a role, actors may be required to perform certain physical or technical activities and so might to train in new skills for a specific role. For instance, an actor in a film set in a marine environment might need certification for diving or other types of skills used in marine exploration. In general, acting requires coordination and stamina and some acting roles might require a performer to gain or lose weight or to participate in a physical training regime for the role. Learning a role also requires excellent reading comprehension to be able to read and comprehend one's lines, script directions, and other written materials related to a specific role.

Fun Fact

The early Christian church condemned theater, but during the Middle Ages, the English church used "Miracle Plays" to spread the message of the Bible during a time of mass illiteracy. Their success led to a number of non-religious productions.

Source: http://www.stagebeauty.net/th-women.html

EARNINGS AND ADVANCEMENT

The average member of the Screen Actors Guild (SAG) earns $52,000 per year, but this average is skewed due to the extremely high earnings posted by major film stars against the vast majority of background, local, community theater, and part-time actors, who often participate in the field without earning a living wage. The vast majority of actors may earn less than $1000 annually and the Bureau of Labor Statistics (BLS), estimates the average hourly wage for all actors at $18.80 as of 2015, with the lowest-paid 10 percent earning less than $9.00 per hour and the highest-paid 10 percent earning in excess of $90.00/hr. While the vast majority of actors work only part time, those able to perform in a wide variety of roles or who have experience that allows them to fill different roles in a production, will have greater success making acting into a career.

Metropolitan Areas with the Highest
Employment Level in this Occupation

Metropolitan area	Employment	Employment per thousand jobs	Hourly mean wage
Los Angeles-Long Beach-Glendale, CA Metropolitan Division	14,560	3.55	N/A
New York-Jersey City-White Plains, NY-NJ Metropolitan Division	8,270	1.28	$57.53
Chicago-Naperville-Arlington Heights, IL Metropolitan Division	2,020	0.57	N/A
New Orleans-Metairie, LA	1,350	2.42	$22.37
Baton Rouge, LA	1,120	2.87	N/A
Albuquerque, NM	1,000	2.66	$16.37
Salt Lake City, UT	650	0.99	$16.98
Baltimore-Columbia-Towson, MD	640	0.49	$25.92
Boston-Cambridge-Newton, MA NECTA Division	630	0.36	$20.68
Washington-Arlington-Alexandria, DC-VA-MD-WV Metropolitan Division	460	0.19	$28.10

Source: Bureau of Labor Statistics

EMPLOYMENT AND OUTLOOK

The BLS estimates that the acting field, as a whole, will grow by more than 10 percent annually between 2014 and 2024, constituting faster than average growth in comparison to the average 7 percent growth for all careers in the US. Job prospects vary, however, according to one's field. The proliferation of animated film and television productions, as well as extensive use of CGI in film, has created more demand for voice acting, while opportunities for stage acting and other types of live performance have declined. The expansion of the television marketplace, due to the growth of streaming television services, has also increased opportunities for all facets of television acting and production. Despite faster than average growth and an increase in opportunities, acting is a highly competitive field with many individuals competing for even small roles in a production.

Employment Trend, Projected 2014–24

Actors: 10%

Total, all occupations: 7%

Entertainers and Performers, Sports and Related Workers: 6%

Note: "All Occupations" includes all occupations in the U.S. Economy. Source: U.S. Bureau of Labor Statistics, Employment Projections Program

Related Occupations
- Dancers and Choreographers
- Musicians and Singers
- Screenwriters
- Film and Video Editors and Camera Operators
- Producers and Directors
- Multimedia Artists and Animators
- Digital Effects Designers
- Announcers

Related Occupations
- Military Training Production Actor

Conversation With . . .
NICK SULFARO

Actors' Equity Association union member
Boston, Massachusetts
Professional actor, 6 years

1. What was your individual career path in terms of education/training, entry-level job, or other significant opportunity?

When I was about 8 or 9, my mom put me into a community theater children's program. The first day went horribly. Everything about the attention being put on me was really uncomfortable. But I fell in love with it pretty quickly. I went to a high school with a really good program and an excellent director who encouraged those of us who were good to go into this professionally. I went to Emerson College in Boston and got a Bachelor of Fine Arts in Acting. Right out of school, I booked a show at an Equity (union) theater and I just kept doing that. I made a point of trying to make this a profession, which usually defaults to commercial theater because that's where you can make money. (The stage actor's union is the Actors' Equity Association.)

I supplement my income with other jobs. I work for a company coaching kids auditioning for college theater programs, and I teach drama and direct shows with high school and college-age students. I also do freelance scenic design work.

Something I'm battling is the starving artist trope, which I'm over. It's another reason I joined the union: I'm skilled and I have training and I should get paid for it.

Later this year, my husband and I are moving to New York. The thing that's great and terrible about New York is that there's a lot more work available, but there's also a much larger pool of very good actors.

2. What are the most important skills and/or qualities for someone in your profession?

I don't like saying "thick skin," because you're allowed to be sad if you don't get a part. But you have to keep at it, so perseverance is imperative. You have to *need* to do it. If there's something else you think you can do, you probably should.

You have to have a good sense of self. It's something that I'm trying to get better at. If you see yourself as someone you're not, you're going to constantly be battling yourself and the people in the room trying to give you a job and you're not going to get the job.

3. What do you wish you had known going into this profession?

Really practical things. I think every kid should be required to take a personal finance class, and part of that should focus on taxes. At Emerson, the emphasis was on the craft, not the job. With so much emphasis on the craft, there's no practical application: how do you take that and actually make a living?

People say this a lot, but I wish I had known it was going to take this long.

4. Are there many job opportunities in your profession? In what specific areas?

There are definitely more actors than there are jobs. If you're a film actor in LA, it's even harder than it is to be a theater actor in New York. In LA, there's a lot of commercial work and voice-over work, a lot of smaller stuff, but even more so than in New York, you have to have representation to get an audition.

5. How do you see your profession changing in the next five years? What role will technology play in those changes, and what skills will be required?

The screen acting world is enormous with the rise of made-for-Netflix shows and made-for-Hulu shows. Already the on-camera scene in New York is bigger.

It's going to be harder to get people into seats and to convince them to sit in a room with us when there's so much technology everywhere.

Theater performances are being filmed live and broadcast on PBS and a channel called BroadwayHD. It's something I think is really great and it's something I have a problem with, because theater is not meant to be filmed. The size of what you do and how it's done is meant to be seen by someone who's in front of you.

Technology also offers the chance to do interesting things in terms of style in the theater, really incredible things that 20 years ago just weren't possible.

6. What do you enjoy most about your job? What do you enjoy least about your job?

The people. I love that theater is a community and it's a collaborative art form. It's the only art form where you need two people. You can sing to yourself, you can paint for yourself, but theater has to be witnessed. There has to be an audience. I just love what I do. As difficult as it can be, I recognize that it's an extreme privilege.

What I like least is that there's no job security—you don't always know if you're going to have a job or what kind of job you're going to have. And the fact that I have to have supplemental jobs.

7. **Can you suggest a valuable "try this" for students considering a career in your profession?**

So much of what's important in acting is knowing yourself, but also knowing other people. Try people watching and creating stories in your head about who is this person and where are they going and what are they doing? Creativity is like a muscle that you have to work out. Try to be an assistant director and you'll learn a lot about acting by watching. Act in plays—do it wherever you can.

MORE INFORMATION

SAG-AFTRA
5757 Wilshire Blvd. 7th Floor
Los Angeles, CA 90036-3600
323-954-1600
www.safaftra.org

Actors Equity Association (AEA)
165 West 46th Street.
New York, NY 10036
212-869-8530
www.actorsequity.org

National Endowment for the Arts (NEA)
400 7th Street, SW
Washington, DC 20506-0001
202-682-5400
www.arts.gov

Casting Society of America (CSA)
1149 N. Gower Street, Suite 110
Los Angeles, CA 90038
323-785-1011
www.castingsociety.com

Micah Issitt/Editor

Architect

Snapshot

Career Cluster: Building & Construction, Architecture & Construction

Interests: Design, drawing, drafting, computer technology, communicating with people

Earnings (Yearly Average): $74,520

Employment & Outlook: Faster Than Average Growth Expected

OVERVIEW

Sphere of Work

Architects design and sometimes oversee the construction of a wide array of buildings and other structures. They plan homes, offices, government buildings, schools and educational complexes, and other buildings and complexes according to safety, function, and budget specifications, as well as the needs of the client. Once an architect creates the blueprints for the project, he or she may coordinate with construction crews during all stages of the project to ensure that it is built to plan and stays within budget. About one-fifth of licensed architects are self-employed, a higher than average percentage compared to other careers,

while the remaining 80 percent work for larger firms, construction companies, and government agencies.

Work Environment

Architects spend most of their work days in an office setting, where they meet with clients, draft blueprints and reports, and coordinate with contractors, engineers, and other architects. They may frequently visit work sites to review the progress of a particular project, monitor the types of materials used, and meet with contractors and workers. Building sites can present physical risks, such as exposed wiring and exposure to dust and debris. Architects may work long hours at the office, drafting blueprints and drawing models.

Profile

Working Conditions: Work Indoors
Physical Strength: Light Work
Education Needs: Bachelor's Degree, Master's Degree
Licensure/Certification: Required
Opportunities For Experience: Apprenticeship, Military Service, Part-Time Work
Holland Interest Score*: AIR

* See Appendix A

Occupation Interest

Architects must be comfortable taking a leadership role in construction, renovation, or preservation projects. They take the general ideas and needs of a client and use both creativity and spatial design expertise to transform those ideas into a reality that construction contractors can execute. People who seek to become architects should be attracted to careers that combine both engineering knowledge and imagination.

Historically, architects drew blueprints by hand. However, today they use innovative computer technologies, such as 2-D and 3-D drafting, modeling, and design tools and software, almost exclusively to design and draw blueprints. The profession attracts individuals able to work independently as well as collaborate with others.

A Day in the Life—Duties and Responsibilities

Prior to the project's initiation, an architect meets with clients to establish the budget, project objectives, and client requirements. Using this information, the architect begins pre-design activities, such as conducting environmental impact assessment studies and feasibility reports, preparing cost analysis and land-use studies, establishing design requirements and constraints and, where necessary, helping in the selection of construction sites. Once pre-design is complete, the architect works with his or her staff to prepare blueprint drawings and generate ideas to present to the client. It is not unusual for several plans to be presented before the architect and client agree on a final version, so architects should be prepared to design and execute multiple drafts of a plan for any project.

When the client approves of the architect's proposals, the architect begins the construction phase of the project. He or she develops final construction plans, which include structural systems and other design components such as electricity, plumbing, heating, ventilation, and air conditioning, ventilation (HVAC), and landscaping. The architect may also be responsible for choosing building materials and awarding construction bids on behalf of the client. Once the crews have been organized and building begins, the architect may coordinate consistently with these groups at the construction site to ensure that the project is proceeding according to schedule, budget, and design specifications. He or she may also spend time with local government officials to ensure the project complies with building and fire codes, zoning laws, and other ordinances. Finally, the architect may make changes to the plan (and, if so, coordinates with the construction contractors regarding these changes) as asked by the client.

Duties and Responsibilities

- Referring to building codes and zoning laws
- Working with drafters to prepare drawings for the client
- Developing detailed drawings and models
- Presenting designs to the client for approval
- Translating the design into construction documents
- Selecting a builder or contractor
- Supervising the construction of the building

OCCUPATION SPECIALTIES

Marine Architects

Marine Architects design and oversee the construction and repair of marine craft and floating structures, such as ships, barges, submarines, torpedoes and buoys.

Landscape Architects

Landscape Architects plan and design the development of land areas for projects, such as recreational facilities, airports, highways, hospitals, schools and sites that are planned for residential, commercial and industrial development.

School-Plant Consultants

School-Plant Consultants formulate and enforce the standards for the construction of public school facilities. They develop legislation relative to school building sites and school design and construction.

Architectural Drafters

Architectural Drafters prepare detailed drawings of architectural designs and plans for buildings, according to the specifications, sketches and rough drafts that are provided by architects.

Landscape Drafters

Landscape Drafters prepare detailed scale drawings and tracings from rough sketches or other data provided by a landscape architect.

Sustainable/Clean Energy/Green Building Architects

Sustainable/Clean Energy/Green Building Architects design buildings that use clean energy technologies to meet new environmental standards.

WORK ENVIRONMENT

Physical Environment

Architects spend most of their time in an office environment, whether as part of an architectural firm, a home office, or the headquarters of a developer or construction company. A significant amount of time may be spent at building sites, supervising the construction process and discussing the project with contractors. Some architects also spend time at local town and city halls and offices, securing permits and filing compliance reports with government officials.

Relevant Skills and Abilities

Communication Skills
- Speaking effectively
- Writing concisely

Interpersonal/Social Skills
- Being able to work independently

Organization & Management Skills
- Coordinating tasks
- Managing people/groups
- Paying attention to and handling details
- Performing duties which change frequently

Research & Planning Skills
- Creating ideas
- Using logical reasoning

Technical Skills
- Performing scientific, mathematical and technical work

Human Environment

Architects work with a wide range of clients, which includes homeowners, but more often developers and building owners. They may work on a daily basis with construction workers, general contractors, and other professionals (such as plumbers, electricians, and interior designers). Some architects work closely with public officials, including fire marshals, health and building inspectors, and environmental officials, ensuring compliance with local and state laws, regulations, and ordinances.

Technological Environment

Architects predominantly work with computer modeling tools and software to create blueprints and construction plans. They must be familiar with computer-aided design and drafting (CADD) and building information modeling (BIM) technologies as well as other 2-D and 3-D systems. They must also understand the construction tools and materials necessary for the project, as well as have an understanding of building methods. A thorough comprehension of how to execute environmental impact statements related to any project is increasingly a necessity.

EDUCATION, TRAINING, AND ADVANCEMENT

High School/Secondary

High school students interested in becoming architects should take courses that will help develop their spatial design capabilities. These classes include geometry, algebra, physics, industrial arts, drafting, and computer science. It is also useful for students to study history to gain a better understanding of period architecture and art. Because communication with clients and contractors is a critical aspect of the architectural design and building processes, students are encouraged to take courses that build verbal and communication skills.

Suggested High School Subjects
- Algebra
- Applied Math
- Applied Physics
- Arts
- Blueprint Reading
- College Preparatory
- Computer Science
- Drafting
- English
- Geometry
- Graphic Communications
- History
- Industrial Arts
- Mathematics
- Mechanical Drawing
- Physics
- Trigonometry

Famous First

The first woman to receive a patent for her architectural design was Harriet Morrison Irwin. She designed a two-story hexagonal house in 1869 and it was characterized by a central hallway which connected all the rooms. The house design was not only accepted, but built on West Fifth Street in Charlotte, North Carolina. Harriet Morrison Irwin was also the sister-in-law of General Stonewall Jackson.

College/Postsecondary

Most states require that architects have a professional-caliber degree in architecture in order to receive their licenses. These degrees are considered to include the five-year Bachelor of Architecture degree and the two-year Master of Architecture degree. Advanced degrees increase the individual's competitiveness as a candidate for employment and can help them specialize in certain fields of architecture. Some schools offer graduate-level degrees in "green" or environmentally sustainable architectural design.

Related College Majors
- Architectural Drafting
- Architectural Environmental Design
- Architecture
- Drafting, General
- Engineering, General
- Landscape Architecture
- Naval Architecture & Marine Engineering

Adult Job Seekers

Architects who complete their degree training must then complete internships working under the direction of an established architect. These internships can lead to full-time employment. Experienced architects may apply directly for open positions. All architects are advised to join a professional trade association or organization, such as the American Institute of Architects (AIA).

Professional Certification and Licensure

Architects are required to become licensed in order to practice architecture. This license is gained by obtaining a professional degree, completing an internship, and passing the Architect Registration Examination (adopted by all states and administered by the National Council of Architectural Registration Boards, or NCARB).

Additional Requirements

Architects are expected to have strong computer skills, both for office management and writing proposals and for 2-D and 3-D CADD and BIM usage. Additionally, architects should have exceptional communication skills, visual design acuity, creativity, and spatial intelligence (necessary in engineering and drafting).

Fun Fact

The world's most complex architecture is a 9-foot tall, 2,000 pound series of columns made from cardboard created by Swiss architect and programmer Michael Hansmeyer.

Source: http://www.fastcodesign.com

EARNINGS AND ADVANCEMENT

Salaries vary according to the type of firm and its geographic location. Architects with well-established private practices generally earn more than salaried employees in architectural firms. Architects starting their own practices may go through a period when their expense is greater than their income.

Median annual earnings of architects were $74,520 in 2014. The lowest ten percent earned less than $44,940, and the highest ten percent earned more than $121,910.

Architects may receive paid vacations, holidays, and sick days; life and health insurance; and retirement benefits. These are usually paid by the employer.

Metropolitan Areas with the Highest Employment Level in this Occupation

Metropolitan area	Employment	Employment per thousand jobs	Hourly mean wage
New York-White Plains-Wayne, NY-NJ	9,650	1.79	$40.72
Chicago-Joliet-Naperville, IL	3,630	0.97	$37.06
Washington-Arlington-Alexandria, DC-VA-MD-WV	3,500	1.47	$41.90
Los Angeles-Long Beach-Glendale, CA	3,280	0.81	$42.69
Boston-Cambridge-Quincy, MA	3,000	1.67	$42.74
Dallas-Plano-Irving, TX	2,520	1.13	$38.87
Houston-Sugar Land-Baytown, TX	2,470	0.87	$40.96
Seattle-Bellevue-Everett, WA	2,280	1.53	$36.54
Denver-Aurora-Broomfield, CO	1,910	1.44	$36.37
Philadelphia, PA	1,780	0.96	$38.75

Source: Bureau of Labor Statistics

EMPLOYMENT AND OUTLOOK

There were approximately 107,500 architects employed nationally in 2012. One in five architects was self-employed. Employment is expected to grow faster than the average for all occupations through the year 2022, which means employment is projected to increase 15 percent to 20 percent. Employment is affected by the level of activity in the construction industry and the cyclical changes in the economy. Competition will continue to be keen for jobs in the most prestigious firms, which offer good potential for career advancement. Prospective architects who gain experience in an architectural firm while they are still in school will have a distinct advantage in obtaining an intern-architect position after college graduation. The demand will be higher for architects who are skilled in "green" or sustainable design, which puts an emphasis on the use of environmentally friendly practices and materials.

Employment Trend, Projected 2012–22

Architects, except landscape and naval: 17%

Architects, surveyors, and cartographers: 15%

Total, all occupations: 11%

Note: "All Occupations" includes all occupations in the U.S. Economy. Source: U.S. Bureau of Labor Statistics, Employment Projections Program

Related Occupations
- Civil Engineer
- Construction Manager
- Drafter
- Landscape Architect
- Marine Engineer & Naval Architect
- Mechanical Engineer
- Surveyor & Cartographer
- Urban & Regional Planner

Related Military Occupations
- Marine Engineer

Conversation With . . .
JORDAN ZIMMERMANN

Associate
Arrowstreet, Boston, Massachusetts
Architect, 7½ years

1. What was your individual career path in terms of education/training, entry-level job, or other significant opportunity?

I grew up around my dad's design/build landscape architecture firm in Memphis. I didn't gravitate towards the plant science aspect of his work, but I shared the same talent and interest in design of the built environment. Interior design and architecture were the natural alternative avenues for me. I received a Bachelor of Science in interior design from Murray State University in Kentucky. One of my professors, Mr. Michael Jordan, was an architect who gave us an assignment to design an airport. This was a pivotal project for me, as I realized I loved designing both the exterior and interior of buildings—and developed the opinion that neither can be designed in a vacuum. After graduation, I worked for an architecture firm in Memphis before attending Washington University in St. Louis for a master's degree in architecture. There, I studied design not only in the Midwest, but also spent a full semester in Helsinki, Finland, and another in Seoul, South Korea. My now-husband brought me to Boston, where I have found a meaningful and growing career in architecture.

2. What are the most important skills and/or qualities for someone in your profession?

Architecture requires a natural eye for design and interest in science, art, and history. More important, it requires the ability to work collaboratively with clients who don't always understand design. Every day is a new challenge. Years ago, I thought everyone was silly, telling me not to pursue architecture unless I wanted to work excessive overtime for a small salary. However, they were mostly right. If you're truly passionate about it, though, you'll pursue it anyway–like I did.

3. What do you wish you had known going into this profession?

I believe I was prepared for working as an architect. Graduate school was the toughest part. I wish I had known that working smarter and with very clear intentions, instead of working longer hours, would have gotten me further in school. I had amazing professors at Washington University, but I spent too much time guessing what everyone else wanted me to do instead of focusing on my own interest in projects. In the real world, you are challenged with so many practical constraints. I always wish I could go back to some of those school projects now and not worry about the constraints.

4. Are there many job opportunities in your profession? In what specific areas?

You can use your architecture license to design any building type you can imagine. Many architects become experts in specific areas, such as health care or student life buildings. Others are more generalists. Some architects are best in design roles, creating concepts and programming for buildings. Others function in a technical role—they figure out the details such as how to keep water out of the building. Integration of sustainable design is a growing area in the industry. Boston and other coastal cities are facing the reality of rising sea levels and vulnerability to flooding. Architects play a role in the future of coastal development. There are a lot of opportunities and challenges in this area.

5. How do you see your profession changing in the next five years? What role will technology play in those changes, and what skills will be required?

3D modeling has changed the industry significantly in the past ten years. We are now able to 3D print practically anything, from scaled study models to full-size building elements. This has changed the design process and has advanced full-scale building techniques.

6. What do you enjoy most about your job? What do you enjoy least about your job?

You cannot possibly master every building type in one career. My colleagues with thirty years of experience still have opportunities to learn. It's exciting and exhausting at the same time. What I enjoy least is the inconsistency of work load. Both the industry and individual firms are either overwhelmingly busy or depressingly slow. It's the nature of project-based work that's dependent on the market.

7. Can you suggest a valuable "try this" for students considering a career in your profession?

In order to understand architecture, you need to understand the history of it. Books like *Ten Books on Architecture*, *Devil in the White City*, and *The Eyes of the Skin* are good recommendations. It's important to read about the past but also be aware of current design progress and leaders around world. *ArchDaily*, *Dezeen* and other publications are easily accessible online. More specifically, Harvard University has a career discovery summer program that gives students a taste of design studio without a long-term commitment. Other schools may offer something similar.

SELECTED SCHOOLS

Many colleges and universities offer programs related to the study of architecture; a number of them also have schools or programs specifically devoted to this field. Some of the more prominent undergraduate programs in architecture are listed below.

Cal Poly, San Luis Obispo
San Luis Obispo, CA 93407
Phone: 805.756.2311
www.calpoly.edu

Cornell University
Ithaca, NY 14850
Phone: 607.254.4636
www.cornell.edu

Pratt Institute
200 Willoughby Avenue
Brooklyn, NY 11205
Phone: 718.636.3600
www.pratt.edu

Rhode Island School of Design
2 College Street
Providence, RI 02903
Phone: 401.454.6100
www.risd.edu

Rice University
6100 Main Street
Houston, TX 77005
Phone: 713.348.0000
www.rice.edu

Southern California Institute of Architecture
960 E. 3rd Street
Los Angeles, CA 90013
Phone: 213.613.2200
www.sciarc.edu

Syracuse University
900 South Crouse Avenue
Syracuse, NY 13244
Phone: 315.443.1870
www.syr.edu

University of Texas, Austin
Austin, Texas 78712
Phone: 512.471.3434
www.utexas.edu

University of Southern California
Los Angeles, CA 90089
Phone: 213.740.1111
www.usc.edu

Virginia Tech
Blacksburg, VA 24061
Phone: 540.231.6000
www.vt.edu

MORE INFORMATION

American Institute of Architects
1735 New York Avenue, NW
Washington, DC 20006-5292
800.242.3837
www.aia.org

Association of Collegiate Schools of Architecture
1735 New York Avenue, NW
Washington, DC 20006
202.785.2324
www.acsa-arch.org

Association of Licensed Architects
22159 North Pepper Road, Suite 2N
Barrington, IL 60010
847.382.0630
www.alatoday.org

National Architectural Accrediting Board, Inc.
1735 New York Avenue NW
Washington, DC 20006
202.783.2007
www.naab.org

National Council of Architectural Registration Boards
1801 K Street NW, Suite 700K
Washington, DC 20006
202.783.6500
www.ncarb.org

Society of American Registered Architects
14 E. 38th Street
New York, NY 10016
888.385.7272
www.sara-national.org

Michael Auerbach/Editor

Art Director

Snapshot

Career Cluster: Arts, Business, Management & Administration, Media & Communications

Interests: Advertising, Art, Media & Communications

Earnings (Yearly Average): $85,468

Employment & Outlook: Slower Than Average Growth Expected

OVERVIEW

Sphere of Work

Art directors work in a variety of industries, including advertising, theatre, film, video games, and publishing. While these fields involve different media, the essential task of an art director is the same: an art director oversees the aesthetic direction of a project from its conception to completion. The art director typically does not play an active role in the creation of the various elements of a project; rather, he or she works closely with artists and writers to reach a shared goal.

Work Environment

Depending on the industry and the size of the project, an art director can expect to work with varying numbers of artists and writers on a particular project. No matter what the industry, the art director has executive control of the work. All artistic decisions must be made with the art director's consent and approval before being made public. In a large advertising firm, an art director may report to an executive creative director. Art directors usually work during standard business hours. Long hours may be required to meet deadlines.

Profile

Working Conditions: Office Environment/Studio Environment
Physical Strength: Light Work
Education Needs: Bachelor's Degree
Licensure/Certification: Usually Not Required
Physical Abilities Not Required: No Heavy Physical Labor
Opportunities For Experience: Internship, Part-Time Work
Holland Interest Score*: AES

* See Appendix A

Occupation Interest

Working as an art director appeals to individuals with creative vision who are able to articulate and carry out that vision in an effective manner. Those drawn to this occupation have a firm grasp of the history of their media, are aware of cultural trends, and have creative minds. They can imagine the final product, whether it's an advertising campaign, a book, a magazine, or a film; and they can coordinate the various tasks and elements involved in the creative process. Art directors have strong people skills and work with a team to realize an idea. Those with an undergraduate degree in advertising, art history, or graphic design, or previous experience as a visual artist, actor, or filmmaker would be suited to the field. Successful art directors should be problem solvers, have strong communication skills, and must be well organized.

A Day in the Life—Duties and Responsibilities

An art director's daily duties vary by industry. Art directors commonly work for film, advertising, and publishing companies.

In large film productions, an art director meets with the prop master and costume and set designers to develop the overall "look" of a movie. He or she reports to the film's production director. The art director is often responsible for scheduling and hiring individuals working in construction, sound, and special effects and ensuring that the set construction and location are ready for filming. The art director also often manages a portion of a film's budget. Art directors for smaller productions may be required to take on more responsibilities and tasks.

In an advertising agency, an art director collaborates with one or more artists, such as graphic designers, illustrators and animators, and copywriters to develop the overall concept for a project. The art director organizes face-to-face or virtual meetings to discuss the relationship between the textual and visual components of an advertisement and any related promotional material. Suggestions may be made from one department to another, with copywriters and artists exchanging ideas about visual and textual aspects of the advertising campaign. During these conversations, the art director acts as facilitator and executive decision maker. Once aesthetic decisions have been made, the art director may supervise the work itself.

An art director working in publishing performs a similar job function to that of an advertising art director. He or she works closely with writers, editors, and designers to establish an aesthetic approach for the layout of a book or magazine. The art director typically has the final say on matters such as the typeface of a book, the visual details of the book interior, and the jacket design that best fits the work.

Duties and Responsibilities

- **Working with and directing copywriters, assistants, artists, illustrators, cartoonists, and designers**
- **Performing duties as graphic designer, illustrator, or artist**
- **Reviewing portfolios of photographers, illustrators, artists, directors, and producers**

WORK ENVIRONMENT

Physical Environment

Art directors working in advertising or publishing usually work in an office setting. A large creative department may have separate studio spaces for the various creative personnel who work there. Artists and directors working in theatre or film work predominately in offices, but also spend time on the set.

Human Environment

While art directors do not usually hold the top position in any industry, they have considerable control over their specific projects, acting in a guiding, executive role with the various artists, assistants, and writers they supervise.

Skills and Abilities

Communication Skills
- Translating concepts into concrete ideas

Creative/Artistic Skills
- Being skilled in art, music, or other expressive forms

Interpersonal/Social Skills
- Working with and directing a team of creative individuals

Organization & Management Skills
- Balancing art requirements with business goals
- Identifying and coordinating tasks

Technological Environment

Art directors interact with clients and colleagues using standard telecommunications tools (email, phone, video conferencing) and in face-to-face meetings. Computers play a large role in their daily activities. Art directors should have familiarity with graphic and photo-imaging software, as they may make adjustments to a project or need to demonstrate a compositional idea. (Art directors in the film industry may be familiar with even more sophisticated graphic technologies depending on their field.)

Experience with web design and computer code can also be valuable as more companies expand their efforts in Internet and social media marketing.

EDUCATION, TRAINING, AND ADVANCEMENT

High School/Secondary

Students aspiring to become an art director should pursue a rigorous college preparatory program, with an emphasis on coursework in the arts, such as theatre, media arts, computers, drafting, art history, visual art, and English. Students particularly interested in the financial and administrative aspects of art direction may also find advanced courses in arts management and economics helpful.

Interested students should research and apply to postsecondary schools that offer a relevant major. Some professional organizations provide career workshops for high school students, as well as scholarships for postsecondary studies in art direction.

Suggested High School Subjects
- Arts
- Audio-Visual
- Business
- Drafting
- English
- Geometry
- Graphic Communications
- Humanities
- Journalism
- Literature
- Mechanical Drawing
- Photography
- Psychology
- Speech

Famous First

The first modern photographic print in a publication appeared in the *New York Daily Graphic* in 1880. It showed a shantytown in the city. The print was produced by means of the halftone process, which uses tiny dots of different sizes and gradations to create the optical illusion that the viewer is seeing shades of gray along with black and white.

College/Postsecondary

At the university level, students should consider a major in visual art, film studies, art history, English, theatre, art administration, or advertising, depending on their industry of interest. An aspiring art director should major in art administration or pursue summer internships in an industry relevant to his or her interests.

Related College Majors
- Art Administration
- Art History
- Commercial Art & Illustration
- Graphic Design
- Media Studies
- Theater Arts

Adult Job Seekers

Art direction is a highly competitive field; most employers hire those with experience in the industry. Entry-level positions that may lead to a career in art direction are often unpaid or low paying. Young adults may opt for internships to make connections in a particular industry. Artists may easily enter the field and advance to an art director position.

Professional Certification and Licensure

No certifications or licenses are needed to become an art director. In the film industry, however, some art directors do pursue specialized certificates, particularly if they are serving in the capacity of creative director or a similar role.

Additional Requirements

Owing to the competitive nature of the field, most art directors are extremely motivated, hardworking, efficient, organized, and creative individuals. Successful art directors are excellent communicators and comfortable working collaboratively. Working well under pressure can be a deciding factor for future success, as art directors commonly serve a central role on film productions or advertising campaigns where Art directors held about 32,000 jobs nationally in 2012. Employment is expected to grow slower than the average for all occupations through the year 2020, which means employment is projected to increase approximately 9 percent. Job growth in traditional print publications will slow but will be replaced with new opportunities in electronic and Internet-based publications.

EARNINGS AND ADVANCEMENT

The path of advancement most often is receiving a similar job in a larger, more prestigious corporation, agency or organization. This usually results in increased responsibilities and earnings.
Median annual earnings of art directors were $85,468 in 2012. The lowest ten percent earned less than $45,410, and the highest ten percent earned more than $173,236.

Art directors may receive paid vacations, holidays, and sick days; life and health insurance; and retirement benefits. These are usually paid by the employer.

Metropolitan Areas with the Highest
Concentration of Jobs in This Occupation

Metropolitan area	Employment[1]	Employment per thousand jobs	Hourly mean wage
New York-White Plains-Wayne, NY-NJ	5,940	1.15	$62.83
Los Angeles-Long Beach-Glendale, CA	2,830	0.73	$57.01
Chicago-Joliet-Naperville, IL	1,650	0.45	$38.67
Boston-Cambridge-Quincy, MA	1,010	0.59	$45.34
San Francisco-San Mateo-Redwood City, CA	970	0.96	$59.28
Minneapolis-St. Paul-Bloomington, MN-WI	730	0.42	$39.45
Seattle-Bellevue-Everett, WA	630	0.45	$48.69
Washington-Arlington-Alexandria, DC-VA-MD-WV	590	0.25	$40.97

[1]Does not include self-employed. Source: Bureau of Labor Statistics, 2012

EMPLOYMENT AND OUTLOOK

Art directors held about 32,000 jobs nationally in 2012. Employment is expected to grow slower than the average for all occupations through the year 2020, which means employment is projected to increase approximately 9 percent. Job growth in traditional print publications will slow but will be replaced with new opportunities in electronic and Internet-based publications.

Employment opportunities may be found in areas such as advertising and public relations agencies, specialized design services, direct marketing agencies, motion picture and video industries, and publishers. Art directors should expect strong competition for available openings.

Employment Trend, Projected 2010–20

Total, All Occupations: 14%

Arts, Designing, Entertainment, Sports and Media Occupations: 13%

Art Directors: 9%

Note: "All Occupations" includes all occupations in the U.S. Economy. Source: U.S. Bureau of Labor Statistics, Employment Projections Program

Related Occupations
- Advertising Director
- Graphic Designer
- Medical & Scientific Illustrator
- Motion Picture/Radio/TV Art Director
- Multimedia Artist & Animator
- Photographer

Conversation With . . .
PATRICK CALKINS
Art Director
30 years in the profession

1. **What was your individual career path in terms of education, entry-level job, or other significant opportunity?**

   At the age of fifteen, I found out what a commercial artist was at 'career day' at my high school. I knew immediately that it was what I wanted to do. I showed my high school portfolio and was accepted at The Burnley School of Design in Seattle and studied figure drawing and illustration, graphic design, lettering and typography, advertising design, industrial and sign design, and printing.

   After graduation I got an assistant art director job at a start-up ad agency. It was a beginning, and I created some real-world portfolio pieces. I then took the advice of my art school teachers who said, "If you want a variety of opportunities to work in this field go to Los Angeles or New York." I chose New York. I got a non-art job and went back to art school at the Parson's School of Design, and added to my portfolio. I applied to a magazine company for a beginning job in the art department and was hired. I learned a lot about how magazines were designed and put together. Again, I built up my portfolio and found a better job with more pay and was on my way. At one point I bought a good camera and studied photography so I could illustrate a magazine story or do an ad with my own photos.

2. **Are there many job opportunities in your profession? In what specific areas?**

   Every magazine has an art director, an assistant art director, and sometimes an associate art director and/or a junior designer. Art departments change personnel as experienced artists move up and change jobs. Advertising agencies always have art departments. Freelancing is also a possible way into the industry. Webpage design is a basic design course offered in any modern art school along with graphic design, animation, video game design, film and video plus sound and technical studies. Pretty much all of it is hands-on practical application. When a student graduates, he or she would have a digital media portfolio. It would show a variety of disciplines from print media to animation and video to sample web pages complete with sound and music.

3. What do you wish you had known going into this profession?

When I started out I didn't know anything about photography. That includes composition, artificial versus natural lighting, exposures and flash, color versus black and white, studio and location shooting and other technical subjects. Today, anybody can take a photo with their phone or digital camera but learning the art of photography is very important to an art director.

4. How do you see your profession changing in the next five years?

I think the future of graphic design and related careers will be within the internet where everything will be online. Printed media will become less and less of a factor so learning digital design for the web would be an advantage. At the present time tablet computers are outselling desktops by an increasing margin yearly. Mobility is the key here which means you could also work from home. Another change is that many editors and writers are learning how to design pages which only makes it harder to find art jobs. The smart art director should learn to write.

5. What role will technology play in those changes, and what skills will be required?

Apple Macs are still the industry standard but now the design program is an all Adobe package called the Indesign Suite. It includes the Indesign publishing graphics system in combination with Photoshop and Illustrator. If you want to be in this industry you need to learn these programs inside and out to even compete.

6. Do you have any general advice or additional professional insights to share with someone interested in your profession?

A solid design education is essential to get a foothold in this industry. But that is not the only thing that makes a great art director. Learning is an ongoing endeavor and should be pursued every day. Know what's going on in the world. Learn world and American history, study all the arts and sciences. Get familiar with popular culture and not just American culture. The more you know, the more resources you can draw on to make intelligent design decisions. I learned this definition of design when I was 18 and never forgot it. "Design is the logical selection and arrangement of visual elements for order plus interest."

7. Can you suggest a valuable "try this" for students considering a career in your profession?

Start with a written story or an editorial from a local newspaper or a school newsletter. Read it a couple of times and visualize what the writer is trying to say. Come up with an idea or two and sketch it out or compose a photo and put them together to create one article. You could also pick a product or service and compose an advertisement. Lastly, why not design your own business card and stationery? It can be a good way to show what you can do and you can hand out your work. Working in an art department is a creative and fun way to earn a living. Good luck.

SELECTED SCHOOLS

Many large universities, especially those with schools of art and design, offer programs in the arts. The student can also gain initial training through enrollment at a liberal arts college or community college. Below are listed some of the more prominent institutions in this field.

Art Center College of Design
1700 Lida Street
Pasadena, CA 91103
626.396.2200
www.artcenter.edu

Carnegie-Mellon University
5000 Forbes Avenue
Pittsburgh, PA 15213
412.268.2000
www.cmu.edu

Massachusetts Institute of Technology
77 Massachusetts Avenue
Cambridge, MA 02139
617.253.1000
www.mit.edu

Parsons The New School for Design
66 5th Avenue
New York, NY 10011
212.229.8900
www.newschool.edu/parsons

Pratt Institute
2000 Willoughby Avenue
Brooklyn, NY 11205
718.636.3600
www.pratt.edu

Rhode Island School of Design
2 College Street
Providence, RI 02903
401.454.6100
www.risd.edu

Rochester Institute of Technology
1 Lomb Memorial Drive
Rochester, NY 14623
585.475.2400
www.rit.edu

Savannah College of Art and Design
342 Bull Street
Savannah, GA 31402
912.525.5100
www.scad.edu

Stanford University
450 Serra Mall
Stanford, CA 94305
650.723.2300
www.stanford.edu

University of Cincinnati
2600 Clifton Avenue
Cincinnati, OH 45221
513.556.1100
www.uc.edu

MORE INFORMATION

The Advertising Club of New York
235 Park Avenue S., 6th Floor
New York, NY 10003-1450
212-533-8080
www.theadvertisingclub.org
Grants & Scholarships:
www.theadvertisingclub.org/winners

AIGA (American Institute of Graphic Arts)
164 5th Avenue
New York, NY 10010
www.aiga.org

Art Directors Club, Inc.
106 West 29th Street
New York, NY 10001
212.643.1440
www.adcglobal.org

Art Directors Guild
Headquarters Office
11969 Ventura Boulevard, 2nd Floor
Studio City, CA 91604
818.762.9995
www.adg.org

Association for Women in Communications (AWC)
National Headquarters
3337 Duke Street
Alexandria, VA 22314
703.370.7436
www.womcom.org

Mark Boccard/Editor

Art Therapist

Snapshot

Career Cluster: Health Care; Human Services

Interests: Art, creative thinking, encouraging others to express themselves

Earnings (Yearly Average): $41,775

Employment & Outlook: Average Growth Expected

OVERVIEW

Sphere of Work

An art therapist is a recreational therapist who specializes in the use of art in conjunction with psychotherapy to help treat a variety of psychological, physical, and emotional issues. Most art therapists have a background in art or are art enthusiasts who take satisfaction in helping people (or are trained caregivers). They believe in the value of painting, drawing, sculpture, and other artistic activities to alleviate pain and stress, aid in the recovery of a mental illness or trauma, or otherwise help people lead more fulfilling lives.

Work Environment

Art therapists work in offices or treatment/therapy rooms in a variety of medical and mental health institutions. They also work in counseling centers at schools, recreational rooms in prisons, senior citizen centers, domestic violence shelters, and other locations where therapeutic services are rendered or required. They interact mostly with patients or clients, and may also collaborate regularly with other therapists and health care professionals, as well as social workers or teachers. Most therapists work during regular daytime hours, although evenings and weekends may be part of their schedules, based on client needs.

Profile

Working Conditions: Work Inside
Physical Strength: Light Work
Education Needs: Bachelor's Degree
Licensure/Certification:
  Recommended
Physical Abilities Not Required: No
  Heavy Labor
Opportunities For Experience:
  Volunteer Work, Part-Time Work
Holland Interest Score*: ESI

* See Appendix A

Occupation Interest

Art therapists must be passionate about helping people and comfortable around those with special needs. They need to be creative and imaginative thinkers to apply their knowledge and skills to specific cases. While a high level of artistic ability is valued, it is not necessary. More importantly, the therapist needs to be able to encourage others to be expressive and believe deeply in the importance of art in healing and personal growth. Other necessary qualities include patience, empathy, and excellent communication skills.

A Day in the Life—Duties and Responsibilities

Art therapists work with individuals by appointment or with groups of patients in regularly scheduled workshops or sessions. A mental health organization might offer an art class every day or once a week that is attended by a select group of patients. An art therapist may also arrange to meet with patients individually in his or her office or studio. They may specialize in the needs of a targeted population, such as children, the elderly, or the terminally ill, or those with emotional or mental health concerns.

Art therapists are not art teachers, although in some situations they do work on developing artistic skills and techniques; rather, they are more concerned with the process of creativity and their patients' ability to express themselves. Some of their projects may require little artistic prowess beyond the ability to scribble or cut and paste.

The art therapist's first task is to assess the needs of the patient and devise a treatment program. In many cases, an art therapist receives patients by referral and is provided with a relevant diagnosis and set of goals to use as a springboard. He or she then selects activities that work towards fulfilling those treatment goals. For example, to treat depression, an art therapist might have a patient draw or paint about events that are deeply seeded in the unconscious. Similarly, an art therapist might arrange for children who have been traumatized by war to make paper dolls to help lessen their fear, or guide a group of teenagers with low self-esteem as they collaborate on a quilt or mural.

As the treatment unfolds, the art therapist observes behavior, analyzes the work, evaluates the progress being made, and prepares reports to share with other therapists or doctors. The therapist also maintains supplies and tools and makes purchases when necessary. Some therapists also do their own billing and other paperwork.

Duties and Responsibilities

- Providing art supplies to patients
- Helping patients express their feelings through art
- Counseling patients

WORK ENVIRONMENT

Physical Environment

Art therapists work in a variety of settings, including hospitals, mental health facilities, rehabilitation centers, prisons, senior citizen centers, and schools. Art therapists mostly use non-toxic materials that do not pose a health hazard, although they may work occasionally with a ventilation system. They also select tools and equipment with the safety of patients in mind.

Relevant Skills and Abilities

Creative/Artistic Skills
- Being skilled in art, music or dance

Interpersonal/Social Skills
- Being able to remain calm
- Being sensitive to others
- Cooperating with others
- Providing support to others
- Teaching others
- Working as a member of a team

Organization & Management Skills
- Coordinating tasks
- Demonstrating leadership
- Making decisions
- Managing people/groups
- Meeting goals and deadlines
- Paying attention to and handling details
- Performing duties that change frequently

Research & Planning Skills
- Creating ideas

Human Environment

Art therapy requires strong interpersonal and collaboration skills. A therapist must be able to work one-on-one and with a group of patients. If on a team of professionals, which is often the case, the therapist communicates regularly with doctors, psychologists, teachers, recreation leaders, or other staff. Most report directly to a supervisor and may be responsible for assistants or part-time employees.

Technological Environment

Art therapists use computer technology for many different applications, including projects with their patients. Art tools and media are dependent on projects, but could include a sewing machine, pottery wheel, woodworking tools, or a dry mounting press and printer for photography. Standard office equipment is also used.

EDUCATION, TRAINING, AND ADVANCEMENT

High School/Secondary

A college preparatory program supplemented with art courses and psychology will provide the best foundation for postsecondary studies. Other courses that develop the imagination, such as music, theatre, or creative writing, can be useful as well. Also important are extracurricular activities and volunteer work in the arts or with people with special needs.

Suggested High School Subjects
- Arts
- Child Care
- Child Growth & Development
- Crafts
- English
- Graphic Communications
- Health Science Technology
- Humanities
- Photography
- Pottery
- Psychology
- Sociology

Famous First

The first art therapist to receive a Fulbright Award for her work in the field was Frances E. Anderson. One of the founders of the American Art Therapy Association in 1969, Anderson is a researcher, professor, and practitioner who has influenced a number of key areas, including work with victims of trauma. One organization she has worked with is Communities Healing through Art, or CHART, which assists persons living in areas affected by natural disasters and other crises.

College/Postsecondary

A bachelor's degree in therapeutic recreation is the minimum requirement for state licensing. Coursework may include the arts, psychology, research methods, human development, theories of therapy, assessment and evaluation, therapeutic techniques, and ethics. An undergraduate internship or practicum provides the necessary clinical experience for licensure.

Graduate degrees in art therapy can be helpful for career development. A master's degree in art therapy or a similar program is required for certification as a Registered Art Therapist (ATR). Most professional positions require the certification. In most cases, a doctorate or several years of experience is necessary for advancement. Often, advancement can result in more creative freedom and teaching opportunities, or the ability to move into a supervisory position or private practice.

Related College Majors
• Art Therapy

Adult Job Seekers

Counselors, social workers, and others in related occupations with a master's degree or higher can obtain certification after completion of a one-year postgraduate art therapy program. Many artists also find that art therapy is the next logical step in their careers. Scholarships and night classes can make the transition easier for those with jobs or other responsibilities. Membership in a professional art therapy association can provide additional networking and job finding opportunities for adult job seekers.

Professional Certification and Licensure

Of the states that license art therapists, designations include Licensed Professional Art Therapist (LPAT) and Licensed Creative Arts Therapist (LCAT), while others classify them as recreational therapists, mental health counselors, or other related occupations. Requirements vary widely. Prospective art therapists should check the licensure requirements of their home state.

Certifications are available from professional art therapy organizations, such as the American Art Therapy Association and National Council for Therapeutic Recreation Certification. The American Art Therapy Association offers three levels of credentials.

Registered Art Therapist (ATR), for those who have met educational requirements and postgraduate clinical experience; Registered Art Therapist-Board Certified (ATR-BC), for those with the ATR who have passed the national exam; and Art Therapy Certified Supervisor (ATCS), for those who are certified and also have received specific training and skills in supervision. The National Council for Therapeutic Recreation Certification (NCTRC) offers certification for Certified Therapeutic Recreation Specialist (CTRS), for those with a related bachelor's degree and internship experience. Certification renewal usually requires continuing education.

Additional Requirements

Art therapists must maintain patient confidentiality. Certified art therapists must adhere to a code of ethics set forth by the credentialing organization.

Fun Fact

The client may determine the media used in art therapy. For instance, since it takes longer to cover a large surface using oil pastels than paint, clients have more time to discuss their feelings as they create.

Source: http://www.allpsychologycareers.com

EARNINGS AND ADVANCEMENT

Opportunities for advancement are limited. In larger institutions, an art therapist might be promoted to supervise other art therapists or a therapy team, but such positions are difficult to find. Median annual earnings of art therapists were $41,775 in 2012. The lowest ten percent earned less than $26,118, and the highest ten percent earned more than $66,430. Those who work in large institutions or who have more experience are likely to earn more. Art therapists in private practice earn amounts that vary according to the number of people they see.

Art therapists may receive paid vacations, holidays, and sick days; life and health insurance; and retirement benefits. These are usually paid by the employer.

Metropolitan Areas with the Highest Employment Level in this Occupation

Metropolitan area	Employment [1]	Employment per thousand jobs	Hourly mean wage
New York-White Plains-Wayne, NY-NJ	980	0.19	$25.67
Philadelphia, PA	580	0.32	$21.61
Chicago-Joliet-Naperville, IL	560	0.15	$21.94
Boston-Cambridge-Quincy, MA	510	0.29	$18.60
Nassau-Suffolk, NY	380	0.31	$23.94
Los Angeles-Long Beach-Glendale, CA	340	0.09	$30.24
Atlanta-Sandy Springs-Marietta, GA	320	0.14	$19.87
Washington-Arlington-Alexandria, DC-VA-MD-WV	300	0.13	$23.55
Warren-Troy-Farmington Hills, MI	260	0.23	$24.54
St. Louis, MO-IL	230	0.18	$20.05

[1]Does not include self-employed. Source: Bureau of Labor Statistics

EMPLOYMENT AND OUTLOOK

Recreational therapists, of which art therapists are a part, held about 20,000 jobs nationally in 2012. Most worked in nursing care facilities, hospitals, residential care facilities, community mental health centers, adult day care programs, correctional facilities, community programs for people with disabilities, substance abuse centers and state and local government agencies.

Employment of art therapists is expected to grow about as fast as the average for all occupations through the year 2022, which means employment is projected to increase 10 percent to 15 percent. This is mostly the result of a growing elderly population having more recreational therapy needs. Art therapy is a relatively new and growing field and there are an increasing number of positions available, especially for graduates who can creatively develop new opportunities for this specialty.

Employment Trend, Projected 2010–20

Health Diagnosing and Treating Practitioners: 20%

Art Therapists: 13%

Total, All Occupations: 11%

Note: "All Occupations" includes all occupations in the U.S. Economy. Source: U.S. Bureau of Labor Statistics, Employment Projections Program

Related Occupations
- Music Therapist
- Occupational Therapist

Conversation With . . .
DONNA BETTS

Professor of Art Therapy
George Washington University, Washington, DC
President of the American Art Therapy Association
Art Therapist, 20 years

1. What was your individual career path in terms of education/training, entry-level job, or other significant opportunity?

I did a lot of art in high school and it helped my growth and development. I got my Bachelor of Fine Arts from the Nova Scotia College of Art and Design University.

I found out about art therapy after I graduated and became really excited because I could combine all of my interests: helping other people; psychology; and art. I thought, "This is it!" I went back to school to complete my prerequisites in psychology so I could go on and get my master's, which is required to enter our field. I earned the degree at The George Washington University, then worked at a school for children and adults with multiple disabilities for four years. However, I wanted to conduct research so I went to Florida State University for my doctorate. There, I established myself as a scholar, more or less the go-to person for art therapy assessments. It took two years to complete my doctorate. I remained in Tallahassee for seven years because I also worked at an eating disorders clinic. I loved working with that population and appreciated the challenge. It inspired me to work harder.

I then returned to GWU where I am a research faculty member and also teach two classes each semester. Right now I am working with a company to help veterans with PTSD (post-traumatic stress disorder). We are in the preliminary stages of a research study that will employ a graphic novel authoring tool — a software program — that will enable clients to re-tell their trauma through narrative and visual format on a computer.

2. What are the most important skills and/or qualities for someone in your profession?

Compassion, good interpersonal skills, solid understanding of psychological theory and practice, and an ability to create artwork and to understand the way different art materials work. Also, an appreciation for the effects of art-making on neurobiological functions. For example, when you express yourself through art materials, you use a nonverbal part of your brain. That's where traumatic memories are stored, and that's why art therapy can be really successful. For instance, when people with PTSD make art, it's easier to deal with traumatic memories, which brings them to a point where they can start to talk about what happened to them.

3. What do you wish you had known going into this profession?

Between my timing — which, like so many things, is often luck — and my contacts, I've been very fortunate. Each career step forward has built upon the last one. I can't say there is anything I wish I'd known in advance.

4. Are there many job opportunities in your profession? In what specific areas?

Job opportunities tend to be in metro areas where there's an awareness of the benefits of art therapy, particularly cities where universities offer art therapy programs. The jobs can be anywhere you'd find mental health practitioners: Veteran's Administration services, psychiatric facilities, hospitals, schools, or private practices. Some therapists go back to their rural hometowns and start their own programs, and those people are pioneers who are creating jobs.

5. How do you see your profession changing in the next five years, what role will technology play in those changes, and what skills will be required?

The American Art Therapy Association is working hard to establish state licenses for art therapists to protect the public through enforcement of standards that restrict practice to qualified professionals. So far, eight states license art therapists, and 27 are taking steps in this direction.

In addition, telehealth is also a hot topic now. Say a patient has psychiatric issues and lives in a remote place with no access to a therapist. Under the telehealth movement, some therapists will Skype, or government entities may back the creation of internet-based tools that enable doing therapy from home. This raises ethical concerns for all mental health practitioners. In art therapy, we face a tech-related dilemma – if you create a drawing on an iPad, is it art therapy? Making art with paint or clay is a different experience than drawing on an iPad. I believe art therapists can successfully offer their clients a choice of traditional media as well as digital options.

6. What do you enjoy most about your job? What do you enjoy least about your job?

It was rewarding to see how art therapy contributed to the recovery of my clients with anorexia. When you see how your work and dedication is helping someone — that is why I went to work every day. The paperwork is the least enjoyable part, but that's true for any job.

7. **Can you suggest a valuable "try this" for students considering a career in your profession?**

When I evaluate master's program applicants now, a strong candidate is someone who has volunteered in some capacity helping others. Ideally, they would volunteer in a setting where they are able to facilitate the use of art, under the guidance of an art therapy supervisor.

SELECTED SCHOOLS

Many colleges and universities have bachelor's degree programs in recreational therapy or related subjects; some offer a focus on art therapy. The student may also gain an initial grounding at a technical or community college. Consult with your school guidance counselor or research post-secondary programs in your area. The online Therapeutic Recreation Directory (see below) contains a listing of accredited schools and programs; and the web site of the American Art Therapy Association (see below) has a list of approved graduate schools.

MORE INFORMATION

American Art Therapy Association
225 North Fairfax Street
Alexandria, VA 22314
888.290.0878
www.arttherapy.org

International Art Therapy Organization (IATO)
info@theiato.org
www.internationalarttherapy.org

National Council for Therapeutic Recreation Certification (NCTRC)
7 Elmwood Drive
New City, NY 10956
845.639.1439
www.nctrc.org

Sally Driscoll/Editor

Brickmason/ Stonemason

Snapshot

Career Cluster(s): Building & Construction, Architecture & Construction

Interests: Construction, architecture, design, working with your hands

Earnings (Yearly Average): $47,650

Employment & Outlook: Much Faster Than Average Growth Expected

OVERVIEW

Sphere of Work

Brickmasons and stonemasons use brick, natural stone, concrete blocks, mortar, and other materials to build structures such as fireplaces, chimneys, walls, and walkways. They may work on small projects such as stone paths, or on large office buildings. Masons cut the necessary stones or bricks, lay out the planned designs, prepare the site for construction, and assemble a structure that is visually appealing and meets the needs of the client. They may also perform repairs or reconstruction on preexisting brickwork.

Work Environment

Stonemasons and brickmasons typically work at project sites with strict safety protocols, including mandatory hard hats and equipment checks. They spend the majority of their day outdoors in all types of weather conditions. The work of stonemasons and brickmasons is physically demanding, requiring them to be on their feet for extended periods of time and lift heavy materials such as brick and stone. There is also a danger of physical injury due to this heavy lifting, cuts from sharp tools and stone fragments, and falls from scaffolding. Stonemasons typically work a forty-hour week, although those hours may vary based on the type of job performed, the weather, and other factors.

Profile

Working Conditions: Work both Indoors and Outdoors
Physical Strength: Medium Work
Education Needs: On-The-Job Training, High School Diploma with Technical Education, Apprenticeship
Licensure/Certification: Usually Not Required
Opportunities For Experience: Apprenticeship, Part-Time Work
Holland Interest Score*: ERS, REI, RES, RIE, RSE

* See Appendix A

Occupation Interest

Brickmasons and stonemasons should be detail oriented, have a strong sense of spatial awareness, and enjoy working with their hands. Jobs for both stonemasons and brickmasons are plentiful, with demand for these craftsmen expected to increase over the next few years at a rate higher than that of other professions. A large number of masons are self-employed or own their own businesses, which means that they set their own schedules, and should therefore be highly organized and motivated.

A Day in the Life—Duties and Responsibilities

Brickmasons and stonemasons consult with clients and general contractors to understand customers' aesthetic preferences and structural needs. These consultations include reviewing project blueprints and drawings and taking into account the client's budget for stonework. Based on this information, masons determine the type of equipment that will be needed and order the stones and other materials.

When the initial consultation is complete, brickmasons and stonemasons prepare the project site, a process which varies depending on the type of work being done. For example, a brickmason must decide whether to use poles or corner leads (complex pyramids of bricks) to mark the corners of the structure. Brickmasons and stonemasons also cut and prepare the bricks or stones that will be used, polishing or shaping them as necessary. Once the site is ready, they lay the foundation for the project with a binding material such as mortar, which is generally a combination of sand, water, and cement. The masons then stack or arrange the bricks or stones in place, using mortar to hold them together, until the project is complete. Upon completion, masons cut away excess mortar and clean up the structure for final presentation to the customer.

Duties and Responsibilities

- **Measuring distances**
- **Determining the alignment of brick or stones**
- **Cutting bricks and chopping stones to size**
- **Spreading mortar to serve as a base and binder**
- **Tapping bricks to align, level and place them in mortar**
- **Finishing mortar joints between bricks or stones**

OCCUPATION SPECIALTIES

Firebrick and Refractory Tile Bricklayers

Firebrick and Refractory Tile Bricklayers build, rebuild, reline or patch steam boilers, furnaces, cupolas or ovens using fire resistant (refractory) brick or tile and mortar.

Sewer Bricklayers

Sewer Bricklayers lay brick, concrete blocks or shaped tile to construct sewers and manholes.

Brick Chimney Builders

Brick Chimney Builders lay brick or tile to construct or repair industrial smokestacks or chimneys.

Marble Setters

Marble Setters cut and set marble slabs in walls or floors of buildings and repair or polish previously set slabs.

WORK ENVIRONMENT

Physical Environment

Brickmasons and stonemasons work primarily on project sites, most of which are located outdoors. They must lift heavy objects, use a variety of sharp tools, and be on their feet or knees in all types of weather during the course of their work.

Relevant Skills and Abilities

Organization & Management Skills
- Coordinating tasks
- Following instructions
- Managing people/groups
- Paying attention to and handling details

Technical Skills
- Working with machines, tools or other objects

Unclassified Skills
- Performing work that produces tangible results

Human Environment

In addition to their clients, brickmasons and stonemasons regularly interact with architects, construction personnel, interior designers, apprentices, construction supply company representatives, and other masons.

Technological Environment

Brickmasons and stonemasons use tools such as claw hammers and sledgehammers, hydraulic jacks, mortar mixers, power saws, and arc welders. Self-employed masons must also be familiar with trade-related software, such as project management systems, and basic word processing suites and programs.

EDUCATION, TRAINING, AND ADVANCEMENT

High School/Secondary

High school students should study industrial arts, including carpentry and construction trades, wood shop, masonry, and similar classes. They should also study math, including geometry and algebra, for help in calculating measurements and proportions. Additionally, subjects that build communication skills are very useful, as are courses in blueprint drafting and mechanical drawing.

Suggested High School Subjects
- Applied Math
- Blueprint Reading
- Building Trades & Carpentry
- Drafting
- English
- Masonry
- Mechanical Drawing
- Shop Math
- Woodshop

Famous First

The first brick building was constructed in 1633, the bricks being imported from Holland. The location of the building was a Dutch fort in New Amsterdam, or New York City, and was used as a residence for the fifth Dutch governor, Wouter Van Twiller. This was only the first of several brick buildings to be built within the fort.

Postsecondary

After graduation from high school, most brickmasons and stonemasons obtain jobs as apprentices, helpers, or laborers, where they can become familiar with the type of work that goes into masonry. An apprenticeship is the best and most recognized path to becoming a mason, combining practical instruction with classroom education, and many unions and contractors sponsor three-year programs. Some technical colleges and community colleges offer courses in masonry, which can improve a candidate's job prospects.

Related College Majors
* Masonry & Tile Setting

Adult Job Seekers

Individuals who are interested in becoming stonemasons and brickmasons should apply to local contractors or unions for apprenticeships. They may also join and network through trade associations such as the Associated General Contractors of America (AGC) or the Brick Industry Association (BIA).

Professional Certification and Licensure

There are no licensing requirements for brickmasons or stonemasons, but many construction unions require masons to pass a test in order to become members.

Additional Requirements

Brickmasons and stonemasons must be at least seventeen years old. They should be able to lift heavy objects and withstand long hours working on their feet or their knees. Masons must have strong math skills and an excellent grasp of construction and mechanical concepts. Those who aim to be self-employed should demonstrate competency in business management.

Fun Fact

Biblical scholars believe it's more likely that Jesus was a stonemason than a carpenter because most things in the region were made from rocks, not wood.

Source: http://christianity.stackexchange.com

EARNINGS AND ADVANCEMENT

Earnings depend on the geographic location of the employer. Nationally, in 2014, brickmasons and stonemasons earned median annual salaries of $47,650. The lowest ten percent earned less than $29,700, while the highest ten percent earned more than $80,350.

Earnings in these trades may be less because poor weather and downturns in construction activity limit the time brickmasons and stonemasons can work. Union apprentice brickmasons and stonemasons start at fifty percent of a journeyman's rate which increases as experience is gained. Brickmasons and stonemasons are required to purchase their own hand tools.

Brickmasons and stonemasons may receive paid vacations, holidays, and sick days; life and health insurance and retirement benefits. These are usually paid by the employer.

Metropolitan Areas with the Highest Employment Level in this Occupation

Metropolitan area	Employment	Employment per thousand jobs	Hourly mean wage
New York-White Plains-Wayne, NY-NJ	2,670	0.49	$32.47
Chicago-Joliet-Naperville, IL	2,020	0.54	$36.83
Houston-Sugar Land-Baytown, TX	1,480	0.52	$18.67
Washington-Arlington-Alexandria, DC-VA-MD-WV	1,420	0.60	$23.23
Nassau-Suffolk, NY	1,010	0.80	$37.93
Boston-Cambridge-Quincy, MA	930	0.52	$40.83
Baltimore-Towson, MD	920	0.71	$18.81
St. Louis, MO-IL	910	0.70	$31.17
Minneapolis-St. Paul-Bloomington, MN-WI	860	0.47	$30.91
Pittsburgh, PA	770	0.68	$24.16

Source: Bureau of Labor Statistics

EMPLOYMENT AND OUTLOOK

There were approximately 85,000 brickmasons and stonemasons employed nationally in 2012. About one-fourth were self-employed. Employment is expected to grow much faster than the average for all occupations through the year 2022, which means employment is projected to increase 30 percent or more. This is a result of a growing population and more homes, factories, offices, and other buildings being built using brick, which is energy-efficient. Also stimulating the demand will be the restoration of a large number of old brick buildings.

Employment Trend, Projected 2012–22

Brickmasons and blockmasons: 36%

Stonemasons: 29%

Construction trades workers: 22%

Total, all occupations: 11%

Note: "All Occupations" includes all occupations in the U.S. Economy. Source: U.S. Bureau of Labor Statistics, Employment Projections Program

Related Occupations
- Cement Mason
- Construction Laborer
- Plasterer
- Tile & Marble Setter

Conversation With . . .
TIMOTHY SMITH

Owner, T.D. Smith Stonemasonry
Philmont, New York
Stonemason, 40 years

1. What was your individual career path in terms of education/training, entry-level job, or other significant opportunity?

I was a schoolteacher and got a draft deferral to teach social studies in Bellows Falls, Vermont, so that I didn't have to go to Vietnam. When I moved to Vermont, I noticed all this stonework—and I also noticed poverty for the first time. I had grown up in an upper middle class environment in California. These kids had no money at all. So, I started an after-school program teaching kids to rebuild stone walls. I didn't know what I was doing, but these wonderful old Italian stonemasons in Barre, Vermont, taught me. People were paying us to repair these old stone walls, which were everywhere, and I was making so much money that I quit teaching school.

I stayed 10 years in Vermont and then I heard about a project constructing a new south tower at the Cathedral of St. John the Divine in New York City. I went down and applied to work under British master builders. They hired me because of my teaching background. We trained 150 kids from Harlem to do hand-cut Gothic stonework. I was very lucky because I worked on the cathedral for 10 years. There are no cathedrals being built anymore. After that, I settled in the culturally rich Hudson Valley, working for New York State Office of Parks, Recreation and Historic Preservation, and later started my own business. I still hire students as part of a work-based learning program for kids who aren't responding to regular school and teach them to build things like stone waterfalls and fireplaces.

2. What are the most important skills and/or qualities for someone in your profession?

Stonemasonry is a trade that requires a five-year apprenticeship. You don't get it from going to school or reading a book. For middle class kids, they'll need to take five years of their life during which they will actually do physical labor, which can be a whole new experience for many of them. So you have to have a good attitude about new experiences.

3. What do you wish you had known going into this profession?

The first thing a really good stonemason will tell you is forget everything you know. We're taught in school to know things, but in stonemasonry, especially when you're working in different climates, you need to do it and experience it and learn what works. And you learn by your mistakes. A lot of kids today want to hide their mistakes because they're taught to be perfect. I tell the kids working for me, "Be happy you made a mistake because you can learn from it and never make that mistake again."

4. Are there many job opportunities in your profession? In what specific areas?

In the United States, the trades are really flourishing. There's a lot of work in hardscape—in other words, a patio or a stone wall in the backyard. Almost every house has a brick chimney, so you should learn how to work with bricks as well as stone. You can very quickly teach young people to rebuild chimneys. It's a pretty easy skill to learn. There's a big demand for that.

Historic restoration is a fine trade. Most people won't let you do historic restoration until you can prove you have a good command of your trade. There's a tremendous amount of money to be made there.

5. How do you see your profession changing in the next five years? What role will technology play in those changes, and what skills will be required?

In five years, there's going to be more demand. Because of the digital age, there's no such thing as weekenders anymore. People are buying big old houses in the country and restoring them to live in year-round. They don't have to live in New York City or Boston.

Also, cell phone technology really helps a lot. If a young worker on a job has a question, he can text me a picture and say, "What should I do next?"

6. What do you enjoy most about your job? What do you enjoy least about your job?

The thing I like most is teaching young people the trade. I feel like I'm somehow making a contribution to the future. I teach them to teach themselves—I get a thrill out of that. When you build something, at the end of the day, you feel like you're accomplishing something. And you're outside.

I like it least when I have to fire a kid. Some kids are only interested in a job, but they don't want to truly learn the trade.

7. Can you suggest a valuable "try this" for students considering a career in your profession?

Summer jobs are great. Here's my best advice: Go out to building sites and tell them you'll work the first day for free, and then work your butt off. Really rip it up. Show the contractor you're a hard worker. That's a great way to get a job. Also, the National Park Service's Historic Preservation Training Center in Frederick, Maryland, has a masonry section.

MORE INFORMATION

Associated General Contractors of America
Director, Construction Education
Services
2300 Wilson Boulevard, Suite 400
Arlington, VA 22201
703.548.3118
www.agc.org

Brick Industry Association
1850 Centennial Park Drive
Suite 301
Reston, VA 20191-1525
703.620.0010
www.gobrick.com/default.aspx

Building Trades Association
16th Street, NW
Washington, DC 20006
800.326.7800
www.buildingtrades.com

International Masonry Institute
The James Brice House
42 East Street
Annapolis, MD 21401
410.280.1305
www.imiweb.org

International Union of Bricklayers and Allied Craftworkers
620 F Street NW
Washington, DC 20004
202.783.3788
www.bacweb.org

Mason Contractors Association of America
1481 Merchant Drive
Algonquin, IL 60102
224.678.9709
www.masoncontractors.org

Masonry Advisory Council
1400 Renaissance Drive, Suite 340
Park Ridge, IL 60068
847.297.6704
www.maconline.org

Masonry Institute of America
22815 Frampton Avenue
Torrance, CA 90501
800.221.4000
www.masonryinstitute.org

Masonry Society
3970 Broadway, Suite 201-D
Boulder, CO 80304
303.939.9700
www.masonrysociety.org

National Association of Home Builders
1201 15th Street, NW
Washington, DC 20005
800.368.5242
www.nahb.com

National Center for Construction Education and Research
13614 Progress Boulevard
Alachua, FL 32615
888.622.3720
www.nccer.org

National Concrete Masonry Association
13750 Sunrise Valley Drive
Herndon, VA 20171-4662
703.713.1900
www.ncma.org

Michael Auerbach/Editor

Camera/ Videographer

Snapshot

Career Cluster: Arts, A/V Technology & Communications
Interests: Photography, Broadcasting, Film Production
Earnings (Yearly Average): $42,813
Employment & Outlook: Slower Than Average Growth Expected

OVERVIEW

Sphere of Work

Camera operators record video footage for use in television and film and on the Internet. Camera operators work across all realms of visual media recording, including videography and cinematography. Professional camera operators are traditionally employed by companies specializing in visual media, including news media corporations, television networks, film production companies, and cable television stations. Camera operators are responsible for capturing events across a broad spectrum of subject matter, from live events such

as news and sports competitions to interviews, concerts, wildlife, and documentary and feature films.

Camera-operation professionals work closely with production teams in order to successfully capture the overall visual scope and narrative focus of an event or project. Camera operators must be able to accomplish a variety of filming techniques as specified by project directors, writers, producers, and other creative and technical staff. The numerous interactions and extensive cooperation involved in camera operations requires keen interpersonal communication savvy in concert with extensive technical skills.

Professional camera operators are traditionally broken down into two distinct disciplines: studio operators and field operators.

Work Environment

While the traditional work environment for camera operators is an enclosed studio or set, many work in a variety of external locations and weather conditions. Many camera operators change locations from project to project, meaning that much of their time is spent on the road. Camera-operator crews who specialize in recording live sporting events travel from stadium to stadium to cover events. News camera operators travel to places throughout the world to cover breaking news stories. Similarly, documentary and wildlife camera operators may travel great distances depending on whether their focus is on a particular climate, animal, or natural habitat.

A sense of adaptability and willingness to try new projects is paramount for camera operators, particularly those who are just starting out in the field. Acquiring experience through participation in a variety of different projects can help build the creative and technical skill sets necessary for camera operation.

Occupation Interest

Camera operators enter the field from a variety of creative and dramatic-arts arenas. Many have a foundation of study in traditional arts, including photography, perspective, colorfield exploration, and three-dimensional design. Some enter videography through an interest in drama or narrative arts, including English, theater, and music performance, while others may be drawn to camera work through exposure to reportage, broadcasting, or news journalism. A wide variety of universities offer associate, undergraduate, and postgraduate study in video production, camera operation, and cinematography.

A Day in the Life—Duties and Responsibilities

The day-to-day duties of a camera operator begin with preproduction planning with other technical and creative members of a project's production staff. The scope of production meetings can vary from project to project.

Studio telecasts often entail obtaining footage from fixed camera locations and established camera settings. Other projects, such as live event coverage, feature-film shoots, and documentary filmmaking, can require extensive preparation and a variety of input from several different team members. In concert with production managers and other set technicians, camera operators must also make sure their equipment is in proper working order and secured prior to filming.

The shooting process itself also varies from project to project. While studio operators normally set shooting schedules with more traditional working hours, field camera operators can work during all times of the day, depending on what parameters a particular project entails. If a particular shot or visual component is not captured during initial shooting, camera operators are called upon to reshoot footage.

Duties and Responsibilities

- **Operating various types and sizes of cameras**
- **Overseeing the handling and operation of cameras to be used**
- **Making sure that a scene through the camera lens appears the way it is intended to appear**
- **Evaluating the location to see what type of equipment is necessary**
- **Working with the director, sound engineer and lighting director to make sure everyone has the same idea for a shoot**

OCCUPATION SPECIALTIES

Cinematographers

Cinematographers film motion pictures. They usually have a team of camera operators and assistants working under them. They determine the best angles and types of cameras to capture a shot. They may use stationary cameras that shoot whatever passes in front of them or use a camera mounted on a track and move around the action. Some operators sit on cranes and follow the action. Others carry the camera on their shoulder while they move around the action. Some cinematographers specialize in filming cartoons or special effects.

Studio Camera Operators

Studio Camera Operators work in a broadcast studio and videotape their subjects from a fixed position. There may be one or several cameras in use at a time. Operators normally follow directions that give the order of the shots. They often have time to practice camera movements before shooting begins. If they are shooting a live event, they must be able to make adjustments at a moment's notice and follow the instructions of the show's director.

Videographers

Videographers film or videotape private ceremonies or special events, such as weddings. They also may work with companies and make corporate documentaries on a variety of topics. Some videographers post short videos on websites for businesses. Most videographers edit their own material. Many videographers run their own business or do freelance work. They may submit bids, write contracts, and get permission to shoot on locations that may not be open to the public. They also get copyright protection for their work and keep financial records.

WORK ENVIRONMENT

Physical Environment

Immediate work environments of camera operators vary greatly by discipline. Studio operators work primarily in closed studio locations, while field operators work in a diverse array of locations, from neighborhood street corners to crowded arenas and natural wildlife habitats.

Skills and Abilities

Creative/Artistic Skills
- Being skilled in photography or film

Interpersonal/Social Skills
- Being able to work both independently and as part of a team

Organization & Management Skills
- Paying attention to and handling details

Technical Skills
- Familiarity with cameras
- Knowing ways to achieve various lighting effects

Other Skills
- Working under different weather conditions

Human Environment

Strong collaborative skills are important for any camera operator, as he or she acts as the eyes for a particular creative or informative vision. Camera operators work in concert with production staff to deliver the most pertinent video that will advance a narrative outline and inform the viewing audience.

Technological Environment

Camera operators must possess a complex set of media-technology skills, ranging from extensive knowledge of video cameras and image-recording technology to basic knowledge of audio and lighting systems. Many camera operators are also versed in video-editing and special-effects software.

EDUCATION, TRAINING, AND ADVANCEMENT

High School/Secondary

Students can prepare for a career in camera operation at the high-school level with courses in geometry, visual arts, introductory computer programming, dramatic arts, and broadcast media. In addition to a survey of major dramatic works and theatrical history, participation in the technical aspects of scholastic theatrical productions is also highly encouraged. Many camera operators attain a basic grasp of lighting, audio rigging, and visual display through participation in school plays or on student television networks. Summer study, volunteer work, and internship programs at local cable-access outlets or television news studios can also be a tremendous asset for high-school students eager to gain experience in videography.

Suggested High School Subjects
- Arts
- Audio-Visual
- English
- Graphic Communications
- Journalism
- Photography
- Theatre & Drama

Famous First

The first portable movie cameras came out in 1923, manufactured separately by Kodak and the Victor Animatograph Company of Davenport, IA. Each company claimed to be the first in the field. Such cameras were operated by means of a hand crank that the photographer had to turn twice per second to achieve the desired effect. Within a few years Bell & Howell offered the first "ladies' camera," a thin, lightweight, and handsomely embossed item called the Filmo 75.

College/Postsecondary

Individuals aspiring to a career as a camera operator have a wide variety of postsecondary education opportunity options available at the associate, bachelor, and graduate level. Introductory and certificate-level coursework in camera operation often entails a survey of the basics of the discipline, including routine equipment maintenance, tripod setup, and command of basic camera focus settings.

Undergraduate programs in cinematography cover not only the basics of camera operation but also the historical development of visual arts and the theoretical foundations of contemporary media. Undergraduates also study location recording and computer animation.

Graduate-level study of cinematography includes an in-depth survey of the history of television and film as well as advanced coursework on film theory. Individual conception and production of one or more films is required for students at the graduate level.

Related College Majors
- Commercial Photography
- Film-Video Making/Cinema & Production
- Photography

Adult Job Seekers

Depending on the nature of the programs they are involved in, studio camera operators may often have schedules that involve working in the early morning or late into the evening. Field camera operators are always on the move, either covering events throughout specific regions in tandem with other traveling journalists or traveling to locations far and wide for more specialized projects.

Professional Certification and Licensure

While no specific certification is required to work as a camera operator, affiliation with professional groups or associations, such as the Society of Camera Operators, can boost credentials and present opportunities for networking. Continuing coursework on emerging technologies also helps camera operators stay abreast of contemporary trends in visual media. Cinematographers in the motion-picture industry often obtain professional certification.

Additional Requirements

Patience, cooperation, and attention to detail are qualities that tremendously benefit camera operators across all realms of work. The physical capacity to manipulate large camera equipment is also desirable. Camera operators must possess a sound technical aptitude as well as the ability to adapt to new technologies quickly.

Fun Fact

Over six billion hours of video are watched each month on YouTube, almost an hour for every person on earth.
Source: youtube.com.

EARNINGS AND ADVANCEMENT

Salaries of camera operators depend largely on the type and duration of the project, and the experience, education, and union affiliation of the employee. Median annual earnings for camera operators were $42,813 in 2012. The lowest ten percent earned less than $21,518, and the highest ten percent earned more than $86,146.

Camera operators may receive paid vacations, holidays, and sick days; life and health insurance; and retirement benefits. These are usually paid by the employer.

Metropolitan Areas with the Highest Employment Level in This Occupation

Metropolitan area	Employment[1]	Employment per thousand jobs	Hourly mean wage
New York-White Plains-Wayne, NY-NJ	1,680	0.33	$26.46
Chicago-Joliet-Naperville, IL	630	0.17	$33.17
Seattle-Bellevue-Everett, WA	410	0.29	$24.31
Houston-Sugar Land-Baytown, TX	330	0.12	$15.04
Miami-Miami Beach-Kendall, FL	320	0.32	$16.86
Washington-Arlington-Alexandria, DC-VA-MD-WV	300	0.13	$31.67
Boston-Cambridge-Quincy, MA	290	0.17	$22.71

[1] Does not include self-employed. Source: Bureau of Labor Statistics, 2012

EMPLOYMENT AND OUTLOOK

Camera operators held about 17,000 jobs nationally in 2012. Employment of camera operators is expected to grow slower than the average for all occupations through the year 2020, which means employment is projected to increase about 2 percent. The use of automatic camera systems is reducing the need for camera operators. However, the growing popularity of made-for-the-Internet broadcasts such as live music videos, digital movies, sports features and other entertainment programming could create some job growth.

Employment Trend, Projected 2010–20

Total, All Occupations: 14%

Film and Video Editors: 5%

Film and Video Editors and Camera Operators: 4%

Camera Operators, Television, Video, and Motion

Picture: 13%

Note: "All Occupations" includes all occupations in the U.S. Economy. Source: U.S. Bureau of Labor Statistics, Employment Projections Program

Related Occupations

- Cinematographer
- Photographer

Conversation With . . .
PAUL CHIN JR.
Videographer, 3 years

1. What was your individual career path in terms of education, entry-level job, or other significant opportunity?

I received a degree in business and economics and, coming out of school, worked in corporate finance for five years. I wanted to do something more creative with my business degree so I looked into being a commercial photographer and videographer who works with businesses. I loved the idea of making commercials.

I started off freelancing and came up with a business plan to generate work right away. I was looking to continue working and helping businesses so I went in more as a business consultant than a creative. My background in finance helped separate me from other videographers and photographers.

I'm self-taught and don't have any formal training. I took photography in high school and photographed some concerts in college.

2. Are there many job opportunities in your profession? In what specific areas?

The opportunities are amazing now for videographers. Once you develop a niche in your market, you can specifically address that need. It just depends on what you want to create.

3. What do you wish you had known going into this profession?

How to close deals better. I knew about marketing and a little bit about sales. But I was mostly an analyst and hadn't been out in the field, which is going out, meeting people, selling them on an idea you've brought to them. I wish I had known I needed stronger selling skills.

4. How do you see your profession changing in the next five years?

For commercial videography, the next five years are going to get more fast-paced. To get people's attention, you can't be a laggard. You're going to have to look at a client's situation, develop an idea, finish it, and get it out as fast as humanly possible. The first person that gets there with the idea wins. You'll have to understand how to create the most relevant content possible so that it will be seen.

5. What role will technology play in those changes, and what skills will be required?

Technology is everything. It allows me to do what I do, but it's always a source of competition. I always believe in the "blue ocean vs. red ocean" strategy, discussed in *Blue Ocean Strategy: How to Create Uncontested Market Space and Make Competition Irrelevant*, by W. Chan Kim and Renee Mauborgne. There are two ways you can look at things: you can look at the competition as a red ocean – fierce and bloody and everybody trying to get one over on another – or as a blue ocean, with technology being the blue ocean that opens up infinite opportunity and infinite competition. That's the way I see it.

6. Do you have any general advice or additional professional insights to share with someone interested in your profession?

Never get hung up on gear or equipment. What you need are customers.

As a creative you have to learn to balance the work you do for clients and the work you do for yourself. I still do the "48 Hour Film Projects", where you're given random elements to put into a three-to-eight minute film, then work in your region to go to the national or international level. I'm always trying to work with other script writers to do little short films so I can learn and build on my skill set.

If you are interested in being a news gatherer, find feature stories and try to pitch them to the wire services. A lot of local news stations pick up stories that are already put together. There are agencies out there that just produce that stuff. Or go out with very modest gear, shoot the story, and put them on a blog. Depending on the quality of work, it's possible a station will see it.

7. Can you suggest a valuable "try this" for students considering a career in your profession?

Shoot, edit, then edit some more. You're only going to make it professionally if you follow your vision. Think about why you like something and try it. Before freelancing, I was making cooking videos and really elaborate home videos, putting it on YouTube, and getting feedback from anybody. This industry is all about learning by doing.

SELECTED SCHOOLS

Many large universities offer programs in film and video production. The student can also gain initial training through enrollment in an arts program at a liberal arts college or in a film/video production program at a community college. Below are listed some of the more prominent institutions in this field.

Boston University
640 Commonwealth Avenue
Boston, MA 02215
617.353.3450
www.bu.edu

California Institute of the Arts
24700 McBean Parkway
Valencia, CA 91355
661.255.1050
calarts.edu

City College of New York
160 Convent Avenue
New York, NY 10031
212.650.7000
www.ccny.cuny.edu

Florida State University
600 West College Avenue
Tallahassee, FL 32 306
850.644.2525
www.fsu.edu

Loyola Marymount University
1 Loyola Marymount University Drive
Los Angeles, CA 90045
310.338.2700
www.lmu.edu

Syracuse University
900 S. Crouse Avenue
Syracuse, NY 13210
315.443.1870
syr.edu

University of California, Los Angeles
504 Hilgard Avenue
Los Angeles, CA 90095
310.825.4321
www.ucla.edu

University of North Carolina, Winston-Salem
1533 S. Main Street
Winston-Salem, NC 27127
336-770-3399
www.uncsa.edu

University of Southern California
Los Angeles, CA 90089
323.442.1130
www.usc.edu

University of Texas, Austin
100 Inner Campus Drive
Austin, TX 78712
512.475.7387
www.utexas.edu

MORE INFORMATION

American Society of Cinematographers
P.O. Box 2230
Hollywood, CA 90078
800.448.0145
www.theasc.com

International Cinematographers Guild
7755 Sunset Boulevard
Hollywood, CA 90046
323.876.0160
www.cameraguild.com/

National Association of Broadcast Employees and Technicians
501 3rd Street, NW
Washington, DC 20001
202.434.1254
www.nabetcwa.org

Society of Camera Operators
P.O. Box 2006
Toluca Lake, CA 91610
818.382.7070
www.soc.org

John Pritchard/Editor

Choreographer

Snapshot

Career Cluster(s): Arts, Performing Arts
Interests: Art, social activities, performance, dance, management
Earnings (Yearly Average): $51,560
Employment & Outlook: Average growth expected

OVERVIEW

Sphere of Work

A choreographer is an artist who designs and directs dance or other types of coordinated movement routines for various types of performances. Choreographers are often asked to create new dance steps and also help dancers to practice and perfect steps as part of a dance routine. While some choreographers work as independent agents or may direct and manage their own choreography companies, other work for dance studios or in educational institutions, such as

high schools, colleges, or universities. Other choreographers work for production companies, helping to craft dance routines for film and television. In addition to working with dancers, choreographers can choreograph routines for athletes and other professionals who engage in any kind of coordinated physical performance. Choreographers need to have detailed knowledge and experience with dance as well as the ability to teach, train, and manage individuals and groups.

Work Environment

Choreographers typically work in dance studios or other indoor environments, though some jobs may require choreographers to perform some of their work in outdoor environments. About half of all professional choreographers work in educational environments or in performing arts companies. Others work for athletics organizations, film and television production companies, or as independent agents. While dancers and athletes are prone to injuries, choreographers often spend less time performing difficult physical activities and so are less susceptible to work-related injury.

Profile

Working Conditions: Work Indoors
Physical Strength: Strenuous work
Education Needs: Not required
Licensure/Certification: Not required
Opportunities For Experience:
  On-Job Training, Part-Time Work,
  Internship, Teaching Assistant Positions
Holland Interest Score*: ASE

* See Appendix A

Occupation Interest

Most choreographers are former dancers who have either retired from professional dancing or have decided to transition from professional dancing to management roles, like choreography or stage management. Choreographers should have a strong passion for dance as well as interest in management, interpersonal communication, and artistic expression. Choreographers are typically also responsible for arranging dance and athletic routines to match musical accompaniment and so should also have an interest in music.

A Day in the Life—Duties and Responsibilities

The duties for a choreographer differ according to the details of their current production. Prior to beginning a production, a choreographer may meet with a director or producer to discuss an upcoming performance. Then, the choreographer may work independently, or with assistants, to create new ideas for a dance or other routine. Then, choreographers may use one or more dancers to practice and visualize the movements, helping to refine the routine. In some cases, choreographers compose routines for a single performer, or they may work with groups of dancers or performers to arrange group routines. Choreographers also work with costume department professionals to ensure that the costumes will work with a routine or to design a routine around the costumes used by a performer. Choreographers may also spend time working in a managerial or administrative capacity, such as hiring and working with assistants in the choreography department. Choreography is part artistic creation, part teaching, and part management and individuals may spend time on all or any of these activities during a given day.

Duties and Responsibilities

- **Create new movement routines or interpretations of existing routines**
- **Work with musicians or choose music for a routine**
- **Audition dancers for roles in a dance production.**
- **Teach dance or movement routines and work with dancers.**
- **Work with directors, costume and other production professionals.**
- **Study dance and other types of movement for future productions.**
- **Manage dancers and other employees in a production company.**
- **Rehearse with performers for upcoming performances.**

OCCUPATION SPECIALTIES

Fight Choreographer

Fight choreographers compose movements for fight sequences used in television, film, and live performances. Fight choreographers might need knowledge of martial arts and other combat disciplines in addition to dance, gymnastics, and other related athletic disciplines.

Skating Choreographer

Skating choreographers choreograph routines for figure skaters and other professionals performing using ice skates or roller skates. Skating choreographers typically need to have intimate knowledge of the various movements that are possible while skating as well as knowledge of various types of dance.

Fashion Choreographer

Fashion choreographers choreograph the movements of models performing in a fashion show. Fashion choreographers typically work with designers to choose music and movements that will help to display and highlight aspects of a designer's ensemble and often need detailed knowledge of fashion and fashion industry trends.

Aquatic Choreographer

Aquatic choreographers design routines for aquatic dancing and synchronized swimming performances. Professionals in this field typically use a combination of dance, gymnastics, and swimming skills to create artistic routines set to various types of music.

Animation Choreographer

Animation choreographers work on animate film and television sequences, creating routines of movement for animated characters that synch to music or other cues. Animation choreographers also help to direct the movements of non-animated characters, to help them synch to the movement of animated characters added in later stages of production.

WORK ENVIRONMENT

Relevant Skills and Abilities

Communication Skills
- Communicating with performers, directors, and other performance professionals
- Creating detailed written notes on routines.

Interpersonal/Social Skills
- Working with individuals and groups.
- Collaborating with directors, musicians, and performers.

Organization & Management Skills
- Teaching and mentoring performers
- Creating routines with exact timing to match with music and other cues.
- Creating and maintaining a practice and teaching schedule.

Research & Planning Skills
- Creating original routines and teaching routines to performers.

Technical Skills
- Utilizing computer film and playback technology.

Physical Environment

Choreographers spend much of their time working in studios, on stages, or in offices where they carefully compose and arrange dance steps or other movements into complex routines. Depending on the type of choreography, choreographers might also be asked to work in a variety of different environments. For instance, skating choreographers usually work in skating rinks or stadiums, while film and television choreographers might spend time working in film studios and sound stages.

Human Environment

Choreography is a social discipline and while choreographers may spend time working alone when developing new routines, much of a choreographer's time is spent working with performers, musicians, and directors. Choreographers often employ assistants or manage interns, and need to be skillful with managing individuals or groups of performers as well as to train performers on the skills needed to perform certain routines. In many cases, choreographers also participate in casting and hiring activities.

Technological Environment

Choreographers working in television and film may work with complex animation and film technology and, increasingly, choreographers have found ways to incorporate animation and other types of advanced technology into their work. In addition, modern production companies often make use of tablets and computers for handling scripts and other data and to facilitate communication between professionals working on the production. Digital technology has increasingly become an important tool in live performance as well and choreographers familiar with a variety of computer technology may therefore have an advantage in the field.

EDUCATION, TRAINING, AND ADVANCEMENT

High School/Secondary

While there are no specific educational requirements for choreographers, many choreographers enter the field after working as professional dancers. Many dancers begin training before school age or while in elementary school and may continue training throughout high school/secondary school and beyond. Individuals interested in careers in choreography can prepare at the secondary level by studying dance, theater, drama, and music.

Suggested High School Subjects

- English
- Public Speaking
- Drama I, Drama II, etc.
- Theatre
- Music Theory/Composition
- Dance
- Ballet
- Modern Dance

Famous First

Before the 1950s, individuals who arranged dances or other routines for performances weren't known by any specific title. Former dancer and later choreographer George Balanchine, who was one of the founders of the New York City Ballet and artistic director of the organization for more than 30 years, was the first to insist on the term "choreographer," a translation of the Greek terms for "dance writer," for himself and individuals who arranged dance routines for his productions. Balanchine, who's "neoclassical style" became characteristic of American ballet, was so famous and influential that soon the term "choreographer" became standard in the U.S. lexicon for individuals creating dance and other routines for performers.

College/Postsecondary

There are a number of colleges and universities that offer degrees in dance and related disciplines and those looking to become choreographers may have an advantage with a degree in performance art. The National Association of Schools of Dance estimated in 2015 that there were 85 dance programs at accredited colleges and universities in the United States. Many choreographers also study education and work as dance teachers/instructors while pursuing work in choreography. There are also advanced, post-graduate programs in dance, dance instruction, and specifically in choreography offered at some institutions.

Related College Majors
- Dance and Performance
- Dance Education
- Dance History
- Performance
- Choreography

Adult Job Seekers

Individuals with experience in dance or related fields may be able to transition into working as choreographers by applying for internships or assistant positions with performance production companies. Joining a professional association, like Dance/USA, can help individuals with experience in the field to locate positions in dance instruction or choreography.

Professional Certification and Licensure

There are no certifications or licenses requires for choreographers but those involved in childhood or high school education may need to adhere to state licensing requirements for teachers. Individuals working as private choreographers may also need to adhere to state guidelines for licensing independent businesses.

Additional Requirements

Choreographers need to adjust to new developments in their field and, as such, may continue learning about various types of dance or other athletic disciplines used in performance routines. In addition, choreographers need to have excellent communication skills in order be effective teachers and to facilitate working closely with performers, directors, and other professionals in the industry.

Fun Fact

Dance has historically been tied to religion ever since the ancient Egyptians celebrated their gods and Hindus danced as one of sixteen offerings during *puja*, a worship ritual. By seventeenth century, with the introduction of ballet, dance became a profession.

Source: http://www.historyworld.net/wrldhis/

EARNINGS AND ADVANCEMENT

The Bureau of Labor Statistics (BLS) estimated the median annual wage for choreographers at $51,560 in 2015. Those at the lowest 10 percent of the field earn around $9.00 per hour, while those in the highest 10 percent earn over $45.00 per hour. Average salaries in the field are skewed by the existence of star choreographers working in film and television and those running independent, high profile performance companies. To advance in the field, professionals need to build their professional reputation and those with skills in marketing and promotion may be more successful in finding positions that advance their careers to the next level.

Metropolitan Areas with the Highest Employment Level in this Occupation

Metropolitan area	Employment	Employment per thousand jobs	Hourly mean wage
New York-Jersey City-White Plains, NY-NJ Metropolitan Division	230	0.04	$36.23
Los Angeles-Long Beach-Glendale, CA Metropolitan Division	200	0.05	$20.81
New Orleans-Metairie, LA	200	0.35	N/A
Portland-Vancouver-Hillsboro, OR-WA	100	0.09	$26.27
Newark, NJ-PA Metropolitan Division	80	0.07	$36.18
Hartford-West Hartford-East Hartford, CT	70	0.12	$26.97
Las Vegas-Henderson-Paradise, NV	60	0.07	$33.61
San Francisco-Redwood City-South San Francisco, CA Metropolitan Division	50	0.05	$44.91
Casper, WY	50	1.07	$13.36

Source: Bureau of Labor Statistics

EMPLOYMENT AND OUTLOOK

The Bureau of Labor Statistics estimates that the choreography field will grow by 5-6 percent, which is similar or slightly less than the expected average growth of all industries in the United States. Large dance companies are not expected to grow significantly between 2014 and 2024, though there is expected to be significant growth in alternative performance venues, such as film and television, casinos, theme parks, and private dance instruction companies. Those willing to work in alternative venues may therefore be better able to cement their reputation in the field and may therefore have an advantage when seeking higher profile positions as they become available.

Employment Trend, Projected 2014–24

Total, All Occupations: 7%

Choreographers: 6%

Entertainers and Performers, Sports and Related Workers: 6%

Dancers and Choreographers: 5%

Dancers: 5%

Note: "All Occupations" includes all occupations in the U.S. Economy. Source: U.S. Bureau of Labor Statistics, Employment Projections Program

Related Occupations
- Actors
- Art Directors
- Musicians and Singers
- Producers and Directors
- Music Directors and Composers
- Postsecondary Teachers
- Athletes

Conversation With . . .
ROBERT MOSES

Artistic Director, Robert Moses' Kin
San Francisco, California
Choreographer/dancer, 30+ years

1. What was your individual career path in terms of education/training, entry-level job, or other significant opportunity?

I entered college with the thought that I might go into business—my family had a small store in the Philadelphia neighborhood I grew up in—and though I had begun dancing before enrolling and loved it greatly, I wasn't quite sure how to make a career of it. I had taken a gym class in dance and performed in high school.

I was lucky to have great teachers who were also mentors. They insisted I do my homework and learn as much about the profession as I could. With their help, I was able to decide to become a concert choreographer and dancer. During my first two years at Orange Coast College, I studied everything available, danced in my first professional company, and began a lifelong love of all-things-called-dance.

I went on to California State University, Long Beach, home to one of the West Coast's best dance programs, and found a fair amount of work in Los Angeles—commercial work, this play, that video. I danced with a lot of little companies that, though small, were significant. After graduation, I came to San Francisco and worked with ODC/Dance, then went on to dance with Twyla Tharp, then the American Ballet Theatre in New York. Then I started my own company, Robert Moses' Kin. I have choreographed pieces for companies ranging from Alvin Ailey American Dance Theater to the Cincinnati Ballet, and taught in numerous residencies and master classes both in the U.S. and abroad, including a post as Choreographer in Residence at Stanford University from 2005 to 2016.

When you work for someone else, you work for someone else. It becomes clear that what you really want to do as an artist, you have to do yourself. When I choreograph a work, it's based on what's in the room as an idea unfolds. You have to be deliberate, but you can't turn off the spigot.

2. What are the most important skills and/or qualities for someone in your profession?

Dancers need strength of will as well as body, a heart and mind to hold their self-respect and love of self, and a few good friends for when that audition doesn't go the way it should.

3. **What do you wish you had known going into this profession?**

I knew this was a choice for a profession but I did not quite understand it was a life choice as well—that people I met at 18 would still be friends in my 50s—or that the world can be both enormous and incredibly personal at the same time.

Say you're a senior and a junior kind of looks up to you. Twenty years later, you run into them, they say they've been following you and are going to bring their class to see you. You realize your roots mean something. Or, sometimes people's fortunes are up and down and you can give someone a hand up by giving them a word about a job. And then there are the people who are just there for your entire life.

4. **Are there many job opportunities in your profession? In what specific areas?**

Yes, there are opportunities but, in dance, creating the next new thing is part of the art. Artists are creatives and willfully create their careers. There is no waiting here.

Figure out where you can live, then look for the work. Your life is going to be more important than the job that may or may not work out. Do your homework. Look at the size of a company's budget and see if you can make a decent living. Are there other opportunities if for some reason this isn't what you thought it might be? Talk with the dancers in a company: Are you happy working with these people? They'll tell you.

Audition. I recently met with 100 kids and only two of them emailed or called to say, "Hey, we talked." Those are the two that are going to stick in my head. In fact, we have a tour to Mexico coming up and one of the two is a very good dancer and I think she'll fit in. I'm going to give her a call.

Get over your shyness or insecurity. You don't have to have a lot of ego, but you do have to put yourself out there because otherwise people won't know you're there.

5. **How do you see your profession changing in the next five years, what role will technology play in those changes, and what skills will be required?**

Technology has already changed the field so much. We no longer add it to performance as an afterthought. Artists use it to broaden their options and abilities. Today I create my own music, sketch costumes, write text, stage, choreograph and more using technology. Where it goes from here is anyone's guess.

6. **What do you enjoy most about your job? What do you enjoy least about your job?**

Getting to work with amazing individuals full of life, each of whom has different points of view on every moment we share, is very exciting. Regarding the least favorite part, I hold the idea that there is so much that is positive and available that the tough times are only bumps. But, being practical: continually raising funds is a bummer.

7. Can you suggest a valuable "try this" for students considering a career in your profession?

If you are a dancer or a choreographer, go to a different teacher one out of every four classes, or watch and learn about dance making from a form you know nothing about. If you're a ballet dancer, watch an expert tap dancer and deal with rhythm in the way they do. Or if you are a choreographer, watch theater and try to convey meaning without word and with words. The point is to always stretch.

When you learn from different people, one teacher will tell you have a fantastic line; another will say your approach to style is good, and someone else will tell you your rhythmic sense is strong or lacking. The best teachers give you information about yourself to help you grow.

MORE INFORMATION

National Association of Schools of Dance
11250 Roger Bacon Drive, Suite 21
Reston, VA, 20190-5248
703-437-0700
www.nasd.arts-accredit.org

SHAPE America
1900 Association drive
Reston, VA 20191
800-213-7193
www.shapeamerica.org

Dance/USA
1029 Vermont Ave NW, Suite 400
Washington, DC 20005
202-833-1717
www.danceusa.org

National Dance Education Organization (NDEO)
8609 Second Ave, Suite #203B
Silver Spring, MD 20910
www.ndeo.org

Stage Directors and Choreographers Association (SDC)
321 W. 44th Street, Suite 804
New York, NY 10036
212-391-1070
www.sdcweb.org

Society of American Fight Directors (SAFD)
1333 W. Devon Ave. #274
Chicago, IL 60660
www.safd.org

Micah Issitt/Editor

Cinematographer

Snapshot

Career Cluster: Arts, A/V Technology & Communications
Interests: Art, Filmmaking, Photography, Design, Media & Communications
Earnings (Yearly Average): $63,166
Employment & Outlook: Slower Than Average Growth Expected

OVERVIEW

Sphere of Work

Cinematographers, also known as directors of photography, define and help guide the photographic style or look of a motion picture. Cinematographers ensure that the director's vision for the film, such as its mood and appearance, is achieved. They receive guidance from directors on how photographic shots should be created, and work with other set personnel to design and frame shots appropriately.

Cinematographers have a strong knowledge of lighting, special effects, and other important pieces of filmmaking technology that are being used on the set. Many cinematographers are also specialized, and only focus on areas such as special effects or location shots.

Work Environment

Cinematographers work on the movie set, directing the cameras in such a way that the best shot is framed and taken. Such sets are busy and complex, with different groups working together to render a scene. This work environment is often tense, particularly in light of budget concerns and production deadlines. Cinematographers also work in studio offices and production studios, where they coordinate with writers, directors, producers, and other key artistic and technical professionals in the filmmaking process. Cinematographers generally work long and erratic hours. Their work hours may vary based on the production deadlines and the amount of film direction with which they are charged. The work itself can be draining both physically and psychologically, particularly as it may call for multiple shots, angles, and camera mountings in order to achieve the best take.

Profile

Working Conditions: Both Indoors And Outdoors
Physical Strength: Light Work
Education Needs: Bachelor's Degree
Licensure/Certification: Not Required But Sometimes Preferred
Physical Abilities Not Required: No Heavy Physical Work
Opportunities For Experience: Internship, Apprenticeship, Military Service
Holland Interest Score*: AES

* See Appendix A

Occupation Interest

Cinematographers are critical components of the filmmaking field. Cinematographers work closely with film directors and producers to make their artistic dreams a reality. They are also senior-level managers on the set, and must be effective communicators as they direct camera operators and many other production personnel to create the ideal shot. Cinematographers are exceptional students of film, having studied a wide range of past and present techniques and even developing innovative new approaches to filmmaking.

A Day in the Life—Duties and Responsibilities

As the head of a film's camera department, the cinematographer coordinates with the director and producer to determine the best action and blocking (the placement of actors and scene material) for the film. Based on the director's "shot list," the cinematographer determines how the cameras should be positioned, the type of lenses and filters to be used, and how the scene should be lit. After the scene is shot, the cinematographer ensures that the film is processed in accordance with the director's wishes.

In addition, the cinematographer acts as a type of set manager. The cinematographer or director of photography must coordinate the activities of gaffers (set electricians), lighting and audio equipment handlers, and camera operators. This managerial work is critical for ensuring that all film crew members operate according to the director's and/or producer's desires. Furthermore, the cinematographer is frequently at the creative heart of the production. He or she works with scriptwriters, set and costume designers, and even actors to ensure that shots are made according to specifications.

Duties and Responsibilities

- **Setting up lighting**
- **Discussing the interpretation of shots with director**
- **Setting up shots**
- **Checking the scene before shooting**
- **Supervising a support staff**
- **Shooting scenes**
- **Overseeing film processing**

WORK ENVIRONMENT

Physical Environment

Cinematographers and directors of photography work primarily at movie studios and sets. These are complex locations with a wide range of working parts, departments, and individuals. Sets are often in large, enclosed, and ventilated studios and lots, or on location throughout the country and world. Depending on the set and the film needs, a cinematographer may work outdoors in a variety of weather conditions.

Skills and Abilities

Creative/Artistic Skills
- Being skilled in art, film, or photography

Interpersonal/Social Skills
- Cooperating with others
- Coordinating the work of others
- Working independently as well as as a member of a team

Technical Skills
- Making sound decisions
- Managing time and budget
- Meeting goals and deadlines
- Paying attention to and handling details
- Solving problems
- Supervising others as necessary

Other Skills
- Appreciating both the business and the creative sides

Human Environment

Cinematographers are senior-level managers, directing the actions of camera operators and equipment operators on a movie set. They also coordinate directly with other important figures on the set and in the studio, including directors, producers, set and costume designers, special effects crews, screenwriters, and actors.

Technological Environment

Cinematographers interact with many pieces of technical equipment while directing photography on the set. In addition to various cameras, lenses, and filters, they must work with lighting equipment and other set technologies. Off the set, they work with graphics software and related programs and systems. Cinematographers also must keep up with the changing filmmaking technology available on the market.

EDUCATION, TRAINING, AND ADVANCEMENT

High School/Secondary

High school students are encouraged to take classes in photography, film, drama, and art. They must also study communications, computer science, and graphics. Interested high school students should also get involved in school audio-visual departments and clubs.

Suggested High School Subjects
- Applied Communication

- Arts
- Audio-Visual
- English
- Literature
- Mathematics
- Photography
- Theatre & Drama

College/Postsecondary

Famous First

The first full-length documentary film about cinematographers and their work was 1992's *Visions of Light: The Art of Cinematography*. The film garnered several major awards. Other documentaries followed in later decades, including *Cinematographer Style* (2006), *No Subtitles Necessary* (2008), *Cameraman* (2010), and *Side by Side* (2012). The last, hosted by Keanu Reeves, explores the differences between traditional film technology and digital technology—and presents the opinions of several major filmmakers.

Most cinematographers have postsecondary degrees from colleges or film schools. Many colleges offer bachelor's degrees in film studies and in fine arts, while a number of vocational and technical schools offer associate's degrees in specialized fields related to filmmaking. A large number of independent institutions, like the American Film Institute (AFI), offer similar specialized training in cinematography. The majority of the most popular programs are located in cities with thriving film and broadcast industries, such as Los Angeles and New York.

Related College Majors
- Film-Video Making/Cinema & Production
- Photography

Adult Job Seekers

Cinematographers attain their high-level jobs after gaining considerable experience in the film industry. Qualified adults who seek to become cinematographers should therefore be ready to work as a lighting specialist, camera operator, or similar role. This work experience helps build an aspiring cinematographer's qualifications and set-management skills. Cinematographers may also find opportunities by joining and networking through professional associations, such as the American Society of Cinematographers or the International Cinematographers Guild.

Professional Certification and Licensure

There is no licensure requirement for cinematographers. However, many individuals seek additional training and certification in cinematography from accredited universities, such as New York University's Certificate in Cinematography program. Such programs give job candidates highly valuable training that may enhance their job appeal.

Additional Requirements

 Cinematographers should have strong artistic vision and capabilities. They must also demonstrate attention to detail and composition. As shooting a scene often requires multiple takes, angles, and camera mounts, a cinematographer should have patience and persistence. As set managers, they should be comfortable working with and directing people on the set. Finally, they must be able to meet the demands of producers and directors.

Cinematographers may start out as camera operators or set designers. Individuals can advance to cinematographers with experience and

Fun Fact

Cinematography comes from the Greek *kinema*, which actually means revolution. The correct Greek word is *kinesis*, which means movement, since the intent was for the word to mean "to record movement." Cinesiography, anyone?

Source: allwords.com

EARNINGS AND ADVANCEMENT

talent in utilizing the camera in the most effective ways. Median annual earnings of cinematographers were $63,166 in 2012. Well-known cinematographers in the entertainment industry can earn much more.

Cinematographers may receive paid vacations, holidays, and sick days; life and health insurance; and retirement benefits. These benefits are usually paid by the employer.
Cinematographers are a specialized category within the group of camera operators and film and video editors. For the latter

EMPLOYMENT AND OUTLOOK

group, there were about 38,000 jobs held in 2012. Employment of cinematographers is expected to grow slower than the average for all occupations through the year 2020, which means employment is projected to increase 2 percent to 3 percent. While overall job growth in the entertainment industry is expected to be slow, an increase in special effects in motion picture industry may increase the need for these professionals.

Related Occupations
- Camera Operator
- Director/Producer
- Motion Picture Projectionist
- Motion Picture/Radio/TV Art Director
- Photographer

Related Military Occupations
- Audiovisual & Broadcast Director

Conversation With . . .
JEREMY TRAUB
Cinematographer, 24 years

1. What was your individual career path in terms of education, entry-level job, or other significant opportunity?

I got my first camera when I was quite young—a Kodak Instamatic X-15F. It took two weeks to get the pictures back from the drugstore, which felt like an eternity. I also shot a lot of Super 8 mm film, which I enjoyed immensely. We got one of the very first camcorders—a VHS model. In high school, I read every photography book and magazine I could and worked in a camera store. It was a huge help, just being around cameras and talking photography. I had a darkroom, and everything I talk about in a color grading session today goes back to the burning and dodging I did then. I was shooting stills for *Transworld Skateboarding Magazine*, the Associated Press, and the local paper, in addition to portraits, weddings, and events. I bought a few Hasselblads, which encouraged me to slow down and make each exposure count. But mainly I just shot a lot—there's no substitute for shooting—and studied light everywhere. When I saw beautiful light in a great painting, photograph, or just noticed it in real life, I would think about the light.

In college I studied computer science, which turned out to be useful when cameras turned into computers. I did visual effects for a while to learn what's possible. That's an essential part of the job today, because visual effects are used in all types of movies.

2. Are there many job opportunities in your profession? In what specific areas?

It's tough. There's a lot of competition. Focusing on the lighting department as a path makes sense, maybe working on the lighting crew for shorts or features. Get to know the lights and what's possible with them. Spend time in the grip department, too. If you're going to be in charge of these departments, it's important that you've done the jobs yourself. Try to get as much experience as possible as a camera operator. Being able to operate a camera with subtlety and purpose is crucial.

3. What do you wish you had known going into this profession?

Everybody's first movies are terrible. You'll have many, many years of this. The important thing is not to be discouraged. You've got to stick with it until the images you can create are as good as the ones you see in your head. Don't give up.

4. How do you see your profession changing in the next five years?

Cinematography is both an art and a science. The art changes very slowly, but the technology changes every few years. The last five to 10 years have been positively explosive in terms of camera technology. Understanding color spaces, how image sensors see the world, new types of lighting, and new and different ways to move the camera are all important.

5. What role will technology play in those changes, and what skills will be required?

Whatever happens next, technology will play a huge part. Historically, the movie business has been relatively slow to adopt new technologies, but I think that's changing as new technologies prove themselves.

6. Do you have any general advice or additional professional insights to share with someone interested in your profession?

Shoot as much as you can. Watch movies and think about how the camera moves, if at all, and why. In a good movie, there's a story-motivated reason for everything that happens. Notice how the best lighting and camera work underscore the story and characters, without calling attention to themselves. Learn all the technical stuff, then forget it and focus on the feeling.

Start by shooting shorts. You'll meet crew members, learn how a set works, what the jobs of the various departments are, and how they interact. When you shoot, stay close to the director. A good crew works together like a well-oiled machine, and this takes practice.

Experiment with new equipment or techniques on your own, never on an actual job. I learned that when I started in photography, and it has helped me avoid lots of problems.

Spend a lot of time reading, even if you think you already know something. There's always something more to learn.

7. Can you suggest a valuable "try this" for students considering a career in your profession?

Pick a movie scene that you like, and go through it shot by shot. Storyboard the whole scene. Figure out where the cameras were placed–their positions and approximate focal lengths. Try to figure out where every light in the scene is by looking at how it affects everything in the frame, and see why each shot was useful editorially. There's a lot of subtle stuff there that's only noticeable by slowing it down and drawing it out shot by shot yourself. Try to figure out how each camera move was done (Steadicam, dolly, jib, helicopter, etc.), and–more importantly–why. Good movies have a story-based motivation for everything you see and hear.

SELECTED SCHOOLS

Many large universities offer programs in film and video production. The student can also gain initial training through enrollment in an arts program at a liberal arts college or in a film/video production program at a community college. Below are listed some of the more prominent institutions in this field.

California Institute of the Arts
24700 McBean Parkway
Valencia, CA 91355
661.255.1050
calarts.edu

Columbia University
535 W. 116th Street
New York, NY 10027
212.854.1754
www.nyfa.edu

New York Film Academy
100 East 17th Street
New York, NY 10003
212.674.4300
www.nyfa.edu

Northwestern University
633 Clark Street
Evanston, IL 60208
847.491.3741
www.northwestern.edu

University of California, Los Angeles
504 Hilgard Avenue
Los Angeles, CA 90095
310.825.4321
www.ucla.edu

University of Miami
1320 S. Dixie Highway
Coral Gables, FL 33146
305.284.2211
www.miami.edu

University of North Carolina, Winston-Salem
1533 S. Main Street
Winston-Salem NC 27127
336-770-3399
www.uncsa.edu

University of Southern California
Los Angeles, CA 90089
323.442.1130
www.usc.edu

University of Texas, Austin
100 Inner Campus Drive
Austin, TX 78712
512.475.7387
www.utexas.edu

Wesleyan University
45 Willys Avenue
Middletown, CT 06459
860.685.2000
www.wesleyan.edu

MORE INFORMATION

American Society of Cinematographers
P.O. Box 2230
Hollywood, CA 90078
800.448.0145
www.theasc.com

International Cinematographers Guild
7755 Sunset Boulevard
Hollywood, CA 90046
323.876.0160
www.cameraguild.com
Offers the Emerging Cinematographer
Awards:
www.ecawards.net
Publishes the ICG Magazine:
www.icgmagazine.com

National Association of Broadcast Employees and Technicians
501 3rd Street NW, Suite 880
Washington, DC 20001
www.nabetcwa.org

Society of Camera Operators
P.O. Box 2006
Toluca Lake, CA 91610
818.382.7070
www.soc.org

Michael Auerbach/Editor

Curator

Snapshot

Career Cluster(s): Arts; Education & Training

Interests: History, culture, art, preserving documents, organizing information, research, communication

Earnings (Yearly Average): $50,250

Employment & Outlook: Average Growth Expected

OVERVIEW

Sphere of Work

Archivists and curators are preservationists of human culture and history and the natural world. They collect, appraise, organize, and preserve documents, artwork, specimens, ephemera, films, and many other objects for historical and educational purposes. Archivists usually handle documents and records that are of historical value. Curators are more likely to manage cultural or biological items, such as artwork or nature collections.

Work Environment

Archivists work in libraries, government depositories, universities, and historical museums, while curators are more often employed in art museums, zoos, nature centers, and other cultural or scientific institutions. Each typically divides the workweek between independent projects and interaction with other staff and outsiders, such as dealers, researchers, and the public.

Profile

Working Conditions: Work Indoors
Physical Strength: Light Work
Education Needs: Master's Degree, Doctoral Degree
Licensure/Certification: Usually Not Required
Opportunities For Experience: Internship, Apprenticeship, Volunteer Work, Part Time Work
Holland Interest Score*: AES, IRS

* See Appendix A

Occupation Interest

People interested in archivist or curator positions value the contributions of humans or the natural world and realize their importance in research. They are scholars who possess good organizational skills and a knack for handling irreplaceable items that are often fragile and extremely valuable. They need to be both detail-oriented and aware of larger cultural, scientific, and/or historical contexts. Other important traits include critical thinking, leadership ability, oral and written communication skills, and a high level of integrity.

A Day in the Life—Duties and Responsibilities

Archivists and curators build on their institution's collections by purchasing items or receiving them as gifts, often the result of bequests. A collection donated by a celebrated author might consist of boxes of unpublished manuscripts and drafts, personal correspondence, publishing contracts, and other printed matter. A collection obtained from a philatelist might include rare postal stamps, philatelic books and journals, microscopes, antique magnifying glasses, and other materials.

The archivist or curator is usually responsible for deciding what items to keep based on physical condition, financial, historical, and cultural value, and relevance to the institution's mission or purpose. While assessing each item, he or she authenticates its provenance (date and origin) and researches the item for any additional relevant information. The archivist or curator also determines how best to preserve and store items. For example, special cabinets may have to be ordered or an item may be given to a conservator for repairs.

Next, the archivist or curator catalogues or classifies items in a database so scholars can access the information. These databases also allow archivists or curators to keep track of their collections, provide reference service, and plan exhibits. Many different classification systems are used, although the most common one in the United States is the Library of Congress Classification System. Some items may be given a taxonomic classification as well as a call number.

Curators and archivists have other tasks in addition to their preservation work. Curators and archivists often write articles, grant proposals, and annual reports. Depending on their work environment, they may give tours and presentations to the public. Curators and archivists may also take care of other administrative duties or oversee assistants who handle some of these responsibilities, or they may do everything themselves.

Duties and Responsibilities

- Analyzing and appraising the value of documents, such as government records, minutes, meetings, letters and charters of institutions
- Selecting and editing documents for publication and display
- Preparing budgets, maintaining inventories, representing the institution at meetings and soliciting financial support
- Planning and designing exhibits
- Writing for technical publications
- Setting up educational displays at a museum

OCCUPATION SPECIALTIES

Museum Technicians

Museum Technicians prepare specimens for museum collections and exhibits. They preserve and restore specimens by reassembling fragmented pieces and creating substitute pieces.

Art Conservators

Art Conservators coordinate the examination, repair and conservation of art objects.

Historic-Site Administrators

Historic-Site Administrators manage the overall operations of an historic structure or site.

Museum Registrars

Museum Registrars maintain records of the condition and location of objects in museum collections and oversee the movement of objects to other locations.

WORK ENVIRONMENT

Physical Environment

Archivists and curators tend to work at least part of the time in climate-controlled storage facilities. They may have to wear white gloves or masks to protect items from human contamination. They sometimes deal with dust, mold, and insect infestations. Fieldwork may include visits to off-site locations such as auctions, schools, and private residences.

Relevant Skills and Abilities

Communication Skills
- Speaking effectively
- Writing concisely

Organization & Management Skills
- Coordinating tasks
- Making decisions
- Managing people/groups
- Paying attention to and handling details

Research & Planning Skills
- Analyzing information
- Creating ideas
- Developing evaluation strategies
- Using logical reasoning

Technical Skills
- Performing scientific, mathematical and technical work

Human Environment

Archivists and curators usually report to a director and may supervise assistants, volunteers, or interns. In some cases, the curator is the director and reports to a board of administrators. Archivists and curators also interact with clerical staff and fellow preservation professionals, such as librarians, conservators, or museum technicians. They also work with researchers and other members of the public who use their facilities.

Technological Environment

Archivists and curators rely heavily on computers for research, database management, file sharing, and communication. They also use a variety of digitization equipment for preservation purposes, including digital photography and video cameras. Microscopes are often used for detail work. In many cases, they must be familiar with radio-frequency identifications (RFIDs) and other inventory control and anti-theft systems.

EDUCATION, TRAINING, AND ADVANCEMENT

High School/Secondary

Archivist and curator positions require advanced education. A strong college preparatory program with electives in the areas of professional interest will provide the best foundation for postsecondary studies. History courses are especially important for aspiring archivists and curators. Students interested in becoming a curator of art should take art history and appreciation courses. Botany, zoology, and other natural sciences are important for curators of natural history. Students should also consider volunteering or working part-time in a library, museum, or other similar institution.

Suggested High School Subjects
- Algebra
- Arts
- Biology
- Chemistry
- College Preparatory
- Composition
- English
- Foreign Languages
- History
- Humanities
- Literature
- Social Studies

Famous First

The first museum devoted exclusively to American political memorabilia was the Museum of American Political Life, established in 1989 at the University of Hartford. The museum was designed to display political posters, buttons, banners, textiles, medals, and a host of other paraphernalia—nearly 70,000 items in all—amassed by insurance executive J. Doyle Dewitt. In 2003, however, the building in which the collection was housed was converted to other purposes. In 2016 there were plans afoot to auction off the collection, even as supporters sought to keep it together and possibly display it elsewhere.

College/Postsecondary

A bachelor's degree in history, art history, botany, political science, or other relevant discipline, with additional coursework in archival or museum studies, is the minimum requirement; however, most positions require a master's degree or doctorate in the specialized discipline or a master's degree in library science, archival studies, or museum studies. Business and public administration courses may also be useful. An internship or other work experience in a related institution is typically required for employment. Continuing education courses are expected as part of ongoing professional training.

Related College Majors
- American (U.S.) History
- Art History, Criticism & Conservation
- Art, General
- Historic Preservation/Conservation & Architectural History
- History
- Library Science/Librarianship
- Museology/Museum Studies
- Public History & Archival Administration

Adult Job Seekers

Adults who have experience working at a relevant institution, researching a particular type of collection, or writing grant proposals or fundraising have an advantage over inexperienced graduates, as maturity and experience are often desired in addition to education.

Advancement is highly dependent upon the size of the institution. In larger institutions, advancement usually takes the form of increasing responsibility, such as a supervisory or directorial position. In government positions, one can move into higher pay grades with proper experience and education. Consulting is also an option for experienced professionals.

Professional Certification and Licensure

Licensing is typically not necessary for archivists and curators, although some employers may require certification by a professional organization, such as the Academy of Certified Archivists (ACA). A master's degree and archival experience are necessary before one can take the ACA written exam for certification. Those interested in becoming certified should consult credible professional associations within the field and follow professional debate as to the relevancy and value of any certification program.

Additional Requirements

Physical strength is needed to lift heavy boxes or other items, and good eyesight is needed for detail work. Membership in professional archivist or curator associations may provide access to networking opportunities and professional development programs.

Fun Fact

The word "archivist" can conjure up images of a lonely desk in a dusty corner, but think again. Paramount Studios had an official archivist (Richard Arnold) for the show "Star Trek." According to Arnold, the words "Beam me up, Scotty," were never spoken on the TV show.

Source: http://articles.latimes.com

EARNINGS AND ADVANCEMENT

Earnings of archivists and curators vary greatly according to the individual's education and experience, the employer, geographic location and job specialty. The size and funds of a museum may also affect earnings. Salaries in the Federal government are generally higher than those in private organizations. Salaries of curators in large, well-funded museums may be several times higher than those in small ones.

Median annual earnings of archivists were $50,250 in 2015. The lowest ten percent earned less than $30,430, and the highest ten percent earned more than $86,040. Median annual earnings of curators were $51,520 in 2015. The lowest ten percent earned less than $28,440, and the highest ten percent earned more than $91,710.

Archivists and curators may receive paid vacations, holidays, and sick days; life and health insurance; and retirement benefits. These are usually paid by the employer.

Metropolitan Areas with the Highest Employment Level in this Occupation

Metropolitan area	Employment	Employment per thousand jobs	Annual mean wage
New York-Jersey City-White Plains, NY-NJ	540	0.08	$56,180
Los Angeles-Long Beach-Glendale, CA	320	0.08	$48,820
Washington-Arlington-Alexandria, DC-VA-MD-WV	320	0.13	$76,640
Boston-Cambridge-Newton, MA	180	0.10	$68,090
Seattle-Bellevue-Everett, WA	130	0.09	$62,840
Houston-The Woodlands-Sugar Land, TX	110	0.04	$63,840
Philadelphia, PA	100	0.11	$46,050
Baltimore-Columbia-Towson, MD	80	0.06	$47,440
Providence-Warwick, RI-MA	70	0.12	$61,480
Pittsburgh, PA	60	0.05	$37,960

Source: Bureau of Labor Statistics

EMPLOYMENT AND OUTLOOK

There were approximately 30,000 archivists and curators employed nationally in 2014. They were employed in museums and historical sites; federal, state, and local governments; and public and private educational institutions, mainly college and university libraries. Employment of archivists and curators is expected to grow as fast as the average for all occupations through the year 2024, which means employment is projected to increase 5 percent to 9 percent. Demand is expected to increase as public and private organizations emphasize establishing archives and organizing records, especially electronically. Museum and zoo attendance has been on the rise and is expected to continue increasing, which will generate demand for curators.

Employment Trend, Projected 2014–24

Archivists, curators, and museum workers: 7%

Total, all occupations: 7%

Librarians, curators, and archivists: 4%

Note: "All Occupations" includes all occupations in the U.S. Economy. Source: U.S. Bureau of Labor Statistics, Employment Projections Program

Related Occupations
- Anthropologist
- Librarian
- Media Specialist
- Research Assistant

Conversation With . . .
SAMANTHA NORLING

Archivist, Indianapolis Museum of Art
Indianapolis, Indiana
Archivist, 4 years

1. What was your individual career path in terms of education/training, entry-level job, or other significant opportunity?

My interest in archives took root while I was pursuing a bachelor's degree in American studies and interned at two museums in visitor services. After graduating, I cataloged artifacts part-time at the Scottish Rite of Freemasonry Museum and Library in Washington DC. While researching graduate programs in museum studies, my supervisor (a professional archivist) suggested that I keep library science in mind, which is a common academic path into archival work—many archivist job postings require a library science degree, often with an archives management concentration.

Ultimately, I selected a dual graduate program in public history and library science. Before moving to Indianapolis to begin grad school, I secured a part-time job as Project Archivist at the Indiana Historical Society, which I held throughout graduate school thanks to a work-study partnership between my school and the society. Each summer, I returned to DC for archival internships: first at the Library of Congress, and then at the Association of American Medical Colleges. This practical experience in a variety of settings, along with additional educational opportunities such as conferences, workshops, and webinars, made me a strong applicant for professional positions when I left school. I was offered my current job at the Indianapolis Museum of Art three months after graduating.

2. What are the most important skills and/or qualities for someone in your profession?

Attention to detail and strong organizational skills are necessary when arranging and describing sometimes overwhelmingly large collections of documents, photographs, or other materials. The ability to conduct research effectively is also important, as archivists are often asked to assist others in their research projects, which can reach outside the institution where you work. And strong communication and people skills are a must because, contrary to the popular image of the archivist sitting alone among stacks of books, collaboration with colleagues and interacting with the public are common.

3. What do you wish you had known going into this profession?

I cannot stress how important mentorship was in my career path, and that has been true for many early-career archivists that I know. Professors, supervisors, and connections made at conferences can really point students in the right direction and help you establish yourself in the profession before graduating and entering the job market.

4. Are there many job opportunities in your profession? In what specific areas?

There are many job opportunities in the archives profession, in a wide variety of organizations: museums, historical societies, public and university libraries, non-profits, city, state and national government, businesses, and more. However, there's a lot of competition for jobs among recent graduates, so it's important to enter the market with both practical experience and theoretical knowledge. It is common for recent graduates to work at least one temporary, grant-funded position (part- or full-time) for a year or longer before securing a permanent position. Taking courses in born-digital preservation and related topics could help give you an edge in the job market. (Born-digital records are those that were originally produced in a digital format, rather than converted from, for instance, print.)

5. How do you see your profession changing in the next five years? What role will technology play in those changes, and what skills will be required?

It's an exciting time as archivists face the challenges that born-digital records present and best practices evolve to meet those needs. Because of the digital nature of many records collected by archives today, technology in many forms is becoming more central to archival work. Knowledge of a wide variety of digital file formats, along with the systems and tools to help ingest and preserve those files long-term, will likely be a requirement for archivists in the not-so-distant future.

6. What do you enjoy most about your job? What do you enjoy least about your job?

I love when I get the chance to collaborate with colleagues in other departments of the museum. Creating exhibitions, selecting and implementing a new digital asset management system for the museum, and creating an online portal allowing the public to access our digitized collections are examples of cross-departmental projects I've worked on.

My least favorite part of the job is that I often work alone because I'm the only archivist in my institution. This is known as a "lone arranger" in the profession, and is somewhat common, though the majority of archivists work with other archivists on a daily basis.

7. **Can you suggest a valuable "try this" for students considering a career in your profession?**

Visit a local archives (believe me, there are many in every city!) and talk the archivists. If possible, go with a research need in mind, perhaps a collection that the archives hold that you would like to look through. Students should find an opportunity to conduct primary source research in an archives for an assignment—most colleges and universities have special collections and university archives right on campus.

MORE INFORMATION

Academy of Certified Archivists (ACA)
1450 Western Avenue, Suite 101
Albany, NY 12203
518.694.8471
ww.certifiedarchivists.org

American Association for State and Local History
1717 Church Street
Nashville, TN 37203-2991
615.320.3203
www.aaslh.org

American Association of Museums
Attn
Bookstore
1575 Eye Street NW, Suite 400
Washington, DC 20005
202.289.1818
www.aam-us.org

American Institute for Conservation of Historic & Artistic Works (AIC)
1156 15th Street NW, Suite 320
Washington, DC 20005
202.452.9545
www.conservation-us.org

Association for Art Museum Curators (AAMC)
174 East 80th Street
New York, NY 10075
646.405.8065
www.artcurators.org

Association of Moving Image Archivists (AMIA)
1313 North Vine Street
Hollywood, CA 90028
323.463.1500
www.amianet.org

National Association of Government Archives and Records Administrators (NAGARA)
1450 Western Avenue, Suite 101
Albany, NY 12203
518.694.8472
www.nagara.org

National Council on Public History
327 Cavanaugh Hall - IUPUI
425 University Boulevard
Indianapolis, IN 46202
317.274.2716
www.ncph.org

National Trust for Historic Preservation
1785 Massachusetts Avenue, NW
Washington, DC 20036-2117
202.588.6000
www.nthp.org

Organization of American Historians
112 N. Bryan Avenue, P.O. Box 5457
Bloomington, IN 47408-5457
812.855.7311
www.oah.org

Society for History in the Federal Government
P.O. Box 14139
Benjamin Franklin Station
Washington, DC 20044
www.shfg.org

Society of American Archivists (SAA)
17 North State Street, Suite 1425
Chicago, IL 60602-3315
866.722.7858
www2.archivists.org

Sally Driscoll/Editor

Director/Producer

Snapshot

Career Cluster: Arts, A/V Technology & Communications, Entertainment
Interests: Theater, Film, Event Planning, Business Management
Earnings (Yearly Average): $72,546
Employment & Outlook: Average Growth Expected

OVERVIEW

Sphere of Work

Directors and producers oversee all aspects of a film or theatrical production. Directors plan, coordinate, and manage the creative aspects of the production, including interpreting scripts, casting talent, approving artistic designs, and directing the work of actors, cinematographers, set designers, wardrobe designers, and other members of the cast and crew. Producers plan, coordinate, and manage the business side of a production, which includes raising money, approving and developing the script, and performing any related administrative tasks. In most cases, directors and producers must both report to the executive producer (usually the

person or entity who finances the project), who must approve all final decisions.

Work Environment

Like actors, directors and producers must be willing to work an irregular schedule with long hours and evening and weekend work, punctuated by frequent periods of unemployment. Productions may last from one day to several months, and during that time, directors and producers are expected to be on call and available to solve problems that arise before, during, and after a production has finished. They may also be away from home, or "on location," for extended periods. The irregular hours and intense competition in these occupations can result in stress, fatigue, and frustration. Most directors and producers must work day jobs or other employment unrelated to entertainment.

Profile

Working Conditions: Work Indoors (Primarily)
Physical Strength: Light Work
Education Needs: Prior Experience College And/Or Bachelor's Degree Apprenticeship
Licensure/Certification: Usually Not Required
Physical Abilities Not Required: No Heavy Work
Opportunities For Experience: Internship, Apprenticeship, Military Service, Part-Time Work
Holland Interest Score*: ESA, SEC, SEI

* See Appendix A

Occupation Interest

Prospective directors should be highly creative, confident, and possess a strong desire to tell stories. They must be extremely organized, be natural leaders, and understand all aspects of coordinating a theatrical or film production, including the role that each cast and crew member plays in the successful completion of a production. Prospective producers should be detail-oriented people who have a desire to take on both small and large tasks. Producers should enjoy planning, coordinating, and organizing an event from start to finish and should be willing to handle and resolve any issues that arise.

A Day in the Life—Duties and Responsibilities

There are many different styles of directing films and plays, just as there are many different styles of acting. Directors are ultimately responsible for the appearance, stylistic and emotional tone, and aesthetic organization of a dramatic production. A film studio or independent producer normally hires a director through the director's agent or manager. Before production begins, a director auditions and chooses actors, holds rehearsals, and prepares the cast for production. He or she also consults with set designers, choreographers, cinematographers, music supervisors, and other creative personnel to plan and develop a successful production. During production, a director guides and oversees the entire creative execution of a project, often with help from assistant directors and production assistants. Once production is finished, a director oversees any postproduction responsibilities, such as video and sound editing, graphic design, and music selection.

Producers are responsible for handling the business aspects of a production. They secure funds, set budget limitations, coordinate schedules, and ensure smooth management of the whole project. Producers also work with directors to approve their decisions regarding talent, locations, and other creative choices, as well as to ensure that deadlines are met and money is spent according to financier instructions. Larger productions usually require the services of associate or line producers to assist the producer with his or her duties.

Duties and Responsibilities

- Judging and motivating acting talent
- Making artistic interpretations of scripts
- Making optimum use of taping and production equipment
- Working with union representatives
- Managing contractual obligations
- Maintaining strict production time schedules

OCCUPATION SPECIALTIES

Stage Directors

Stage Directors interpret scripts, direct technicians, and conduct rehearsals to create stage presentations.

Motion Picture Directors

Motion Picture Directors read and interpret scripts, conduct rehearsals, and direct the activities of cast and technical crews for motion picture films.

Television Directors

Television Directors interpret scripts, conduct rehearsals, and direct television programs.

Radio Directors

Radio Directors direct radio rehearsals and broadcasts.

Casting Directors

Casting Directors audition and interview performers for specific parts.

Motion Picture Producers

Motion Picture Producers initiate and manage all the business needs of a motion picture production.

WORK ENVIRONMENT

Physical Environment

Most directors and producers work on set during the production of a theatrical project. Set locations vary greatly and may be indoors or outdoors in any weather conditions. Some productions are held in different locations across the country or around the world. Before production begins (during "preproduction") and after a production finishes (during "postproduction"), directors and producers may work from an office or home studio.

Human Environment

Directors and producers constantly interact with other cast and crew members. Their coworkers typically include executive producers, actors, production staff, set designers, costume and makeup personnel, and assistants. Producers regularly work with external vendors, such as caterers, insurance representatives, and establishment owners.

Skills and Abilities

Communication Skills
- Describing motivations and feelings (to actors)
- Expressing thoughts and ideas clearly
- Persuading others

Creative/Artistic Skills
- Creating ideas
- Understanding narrative and its power

Interpersonal/Social Skills
- Asserting oneself
- Being sensitive to others
- Cooperating with others
- Working as a member of a team

Organization & Management Skills
- Managing conflict
- Managing time
- Organizing information or materials
- Paying attention to and handling details
- Performing duties which change frequently

Technological Environment

Directors and producers employ a wide variety of tools and equipment to assist them in the completion of their daily tasks. Directors use video cameras, lighting and sound equipment, two-way radios, cell phones, audiovisual editing equipment and software, and the Internet. Producers use schedules, budgets, contracts, e-mail and the Internet, laptops, cell phones, and other devices.

EDUCATION, TRAINING, AND ADVANCEMENT

High School/Secondary

High school students who wish to become directors or producers should have an inherent interest in the dramatic arts and should foster that interest by pursuing academic study in English literature, theater, public speaking, communications, and cinema. They should also learn as much as they can about management, business, and event planning. Involvement in school groups or extracurricular activities, such as drama clubs, plays, musical productions, dance performances, film clubs, and photography clubs, can provide a solid background in the arts. They should also enroll in a basic acting class to become familiar with the fundamentals of acting, dramatic literature, and theater production.

Suggested High School Subjects
- Accounting
- Arts
- Audio-Visual
- Business
- College Preparatory
- English
- Literature
- Mathematics
- Speech
- Theatre & Drama

Famous First

The first blockbuster movie was D. W. Griffith's *Birth of a Nation*, which premiered in 1915. A silent epic, it told the story of the South in the aftermath of the Civil War. Although innovative in its cinematic techniques and strong in its emotional impact, it was protested by the NAACP for its stereotypical depiction of blacks. Three years later, the first African American director, Oscar Micheaux, released his *Within Our Gates* as a rejoinder to Griffith's film.

Postsecondary

Although an undergraduate degree is not necessarily required for one to become a director or producer, many people consider it essential to have received some formal training at the postsecondary level. Many universities and colleges offer bachelor's degree programs in the dramatic arts. Some directors find it beneficial to have studied directing, filmmaking, writing, acting, designing, radio broadcasting, film history, or public speech at the college level. Producers can benefit by taking undergraduate business courses in marketing, public relations, management, and finance.

After obtaining a bachelor's degree, some directors and producers earn a master of fine arts degree (MFA) in directing, producing, acting, or screenwriting. Some conservatories, like the American Film Institute (AFI) in Los Angeles, offer MFA programs that teach students the practical skills needed to start a career in filmmaking. Often, students are required to complete a thesis film as part of their coursework, designed to simulate a large-scale production. Producers and directors must raise money, find talent, and promote their thesis films.

Related College Majors
- Acting & Directing
- Business Management
- Drama/Theater Arts, General
- Film-Video Making/Cinema & Production
- Film/Cinema Studies
- Playwriting & Screenwriting
- Radio & Television Broadcasting

Adult Job Seekers

Prospective directors and producers possess varying levels of experience. Those who attend conservatories often make valuable connections with faculty and other students, which eventually lead to production work. Others become apprentices, interns, or assistants for established directors or producers. Some job seekers begin by taking other employment positions in the entertainment industry and working their way up to director or producer positions through networking and industry contacts.

Many directors and producers are members of professional organizations, such as the Producers Guild of America and the Directors Guild of America, which protect the rights of the producers and provide networking opportunities.

Professional Certification and Licensure

Directors and producers are not required to receive any kind of professional certification or licensure in dramatic production. There is no official training for producers, but many directors train or take classes in directing and cinematography.

Additional Requirements

Directing and producing are highly competitive fields, and few people are able to achieve financial stability through these occupations. Candidates must be able to handle criticism well, demonstrate emotional and physical stamina, and remain incredibly driven to succeed. Being talented is not enough to make one successful in these fields—directors and producers must not give up easily, especially after experiencing rejection. They should be self-promoters who are passionate about their work and use every opportunity to meet potential investors, employers, and talent. Long hours and demanding or difficult employers or work conditions are common in these occupations.

EARNINGS AND ADVANCEMENT

Due to the entrepreneurial nature of directing and producing, earnings vary according to the success of the productions in progress. Earnings of directors and producers also vary greatly due to the type of production they are producing or directing, location, project budget, and personal reputation. Median annual earnings of directors and producers were $72,546 in 2012. The lowest ten percent earned less than $34,068, and the highest ten percent earned more than $176,384. Median annual earnings were $98,389 in motion picture and video industries and $57,367 in radio and television broadcasting.

Fringe benefits for directors are typically provided according to union guidelines, but vary according to the size and financial scope of a given production. Producers, being entrepreneurs, are responsible for their own fringe benefits.

Metropolitan Areas with the Highest Concentration of Jobs in this Occupation

Metropolitan area	Employment	Employment per thousand jobs	Hourly mean wage
Los Angeles-Long Beach-Glendale, CA	19,570	5.06	$66.13
New York-White Plains-Wayne, NY-NJ	14,150	2.74	$55.71
Washington-Arlington-Alexandria, DC-VA-MD-WV	2,210	0.94	$42.93
Chicago-Joliet-Naperville, IL	1,780	0.49	$34.17
Atlanta-Sandy Springs-Marietta, GA	1,770	0.78	$33.51
Philadelphia, PA	1,580	0.86	$41.78
Boston-Cambridge-Quincy, MA	1,450	0.85	$34.98
Seattle-Bellevue-Everett, WA	1,400	1.00	$28.31

[1] Does not include self-employed. Source: Bureau of Labor Statistics, 2012

EMPLOYMENT AND OUTLOOK

Directors and producers held about 87,000 jobs in motion pictures, stage plays, television and radio in 2012. Employment of directors and producers is expected to grow about as fast as the average for all occupations through the year 2020, which means employment is projected to increase about 11 percent. Expanding cable and satellite television operations, increasing production and distribution of major studio and independent films, and continued growth and development of interactive media, online movies and mobile content for cell phones and other portable devices, should increase demand.

Employment Trend, Projected 2010–20

Total, All Occupations: 14%

Arts, Designing, Entertainment, Sports and Media Occupations: 13%

Art Directors: 9%

Note: "All Occupations" includes all occupations in the U.S. Economy. Source: U.S. Bureau of Labor Statistics, Employment Projections Program

Related Occupations
- Actor
- Cinematographer
- Dancer/Choreographer
- Motion Picture/TV/Radio Art Director

Related Occupations
- Audiovisual & Broadcast Director
- Audiovisual & Broadcast Technician

Conversation With . . .
CAROLINE BATH
Network News Producer

7 years in the profession

1. What was your individual career path in terms of education, entry-level job, or other significant opportunity?

In high school I was the subject of a story for a national broadcast news magazine. I learned during the shoot that I hated being on camera, but I loved watching what went on behind the scenes. I was already a news hound but that experience pointed me towards broadcast news.

I stayed in touch with the story's producer, then reached out to him my junior year of college, where I studied journalism and history, and was hired as an intern at his network's morning show. I used that internship to learn more about the industry and to lay the groundwork for a job out of college. I met with producers and studied the network's technical and editorial systems so when I applied for a production assistant job I was able to say, "I can hit the ground running."

If you are entering broadcast news at a national level, the entry-level position is typically a production assistant. It varies from show to show, but at my show I was running Teleprompter, delivering scripts, greeting on-air guests, and filling in on associate producer jobs.

After about a year as a production assistant, I was promoted to the graphics associate producer position, where I managed all the show's graphics to ensure they were editorially correct and looked good. After two years as graphics AP, I became a segment producer. Every day I was assigned a guest or two who would come on the show to discuss a current event ranging from elections to accidents. I would research the subject, talk to the guest on the phone, and then draft five questions I thought our anchor should ask during a live interview.

I'm still segment producing, now seven years out of college, and I just picked up tape producing. Tape producing, or field producing, means you come up with a story idea (say, a behind-the-scenes tour at a candy factory), film the story, and then write and edit the piece.

2. Are there many job opportunities in your profession? In what specific areas?

My industry looks for experience, ideally internships, for all jobs. This is not an industry you can casually enter because you are interested in being on-air. There are two routes you can take: technical and editorial. If editing, directing, filming, or graphics appeal to you, the technical path is a good option. If you love writing, investigating, and telling a good story, then the editorial side is a good fit.

You also need to decide whether you would like to go down the local news route, or the national news route. If you go the local route, you can start off as a producer at a small station and will write and produce entire half-hour shows. The entry-level jobs at the national level require a lot more busy work such as answering the phone or delivering scripts. You might not write a script until you hit the producer level, but then you can cover major stories that have implications for millions. Some local-producers may find the small-town stories tiresome after a few years. Others love it, especially the freedom to essentially pick where you want to work in the country. At the national level you are generally stuck with New York, Washington, and Los Angeles.

3. What do you wish you had known going into this profession?

It can take over your life! It's an addicting job and your work-life balance can get out of whack.

4. How do you see your profession changing in the next five years?

As cameras become smaller and more user-friendly, networks want their producers to be able to shoot and edit video themselves. There's also a push for online interactivity. Producers and reporters must be social-network savvy: that's where the feedback comes from, and that's how you can find some of the best stories.

5. What role will technology play in those changes, and what skills will be required?

Producers are now expected to shoot some footage themselves. Shooting and editing skills are must-haves for producer positions.

6. Do you have any general advice or additional professional insights to share with someone interested in your profession?

I have found that the people who succeed in my industry are the go-getters. Sure, delivering scripts isn't the most exciting job on the planet, but you better act like those scripts are the Magna Carta. You don't need to be a genius to succeed, but if you don't have a sense of urgency, if you don't exude passion for news, you are going to be found out quick, or just be miserable.

7. Can you suggest a valuable "try this" for students considering a career in your profession?

Watch your local TV broadcast with a watch and a timer. "Log" the show – write down the time each story started, and how long the story lasted. Example:
6:01: Apartment Fire – 2min
6:03: Pet Adoption Story – 1min 30secs
If you can, record a competing station's broadcast, then log how they handled their day's broadcast. Compare logs. What was their "lead" (first) story? How did they cover stories differently? Compare the logs to the local newspaper. Did the broadcasts miss any stories? It's a great way to familiarize yourself with a broadcast and get a sense as to how the producers prioritized the news coming into their station.

SELECTED SCHOOLS

Many colleges and universities offer bachelor's degree programs in the arts; some have programs in theater, film, and television production as well. The student may also gain initial training through enrollment at a community college. Below are listed some of the more prominent institutions in this field.

Columbia University
116th Street and Broadway
New York, NY 10027
212.854.1754
www.columbia.edu

New York University
70 Washington Square S.
New York, NY 10012
212.998.1212
www.nyu.edu

Emerson College
120 Boylston Street
Boston, MA 02116
617.824.8500
www.emerson.edu

Purdue University
610 Purdue Mall
West Lafayette, IN 47907
765.494.4600
www.purdue.edu

Loyola Marymount
1 Loyola Marymount University Drive
Los Angeles, CA 90045
310.338.2700
www.lmu.edu

University of Arizona
1401 E. University Boulevard
Tucson, AZ 85721
520.621.2211
www.arizona.edu

University of California, Los Angeles
405 Hilgard Avenue
Los Angeles, CA 90095
310.825.4321
www.ucla.edu

University of Colorado, Denver
Boulder, CO 80309
303.492.1411
www.colorado.edu

University of Southern California
Los Angeles, CA 90089
323.442.1130
www.usc.edu

University of Texas, Austin
110 Inner Campus Drive
Austin, TX 78712
512.471.3434
www.utexas.edu

MORE INFORMATION

American Film Institute
2021 North Western Avenue
Los Angeles, CA 90027-1657
323.856.7600
www.afi.com

Association of Independent Commercial Producers
3 West 18th Street, 5th Floor
New York, NY 10011
212.929.3000
www.aicp.com

Directors Guild of America
7920 Sunset Boulevard
Los Angeles, California 90046
310.289.2000
www.dga.org

National Association of Schools of Theatre
11250 Roger Bacon Drive, Suite 21
Reston, VA 20190-5248
703.437.0700
nast.arts-accredit.org

Producers Guild of America
8530 Wilshire Boulevard, Suite 450
Beverly Hills, CA 90211
310.358.9020
www.producersguild.org

Stage Directors and Choreographers Society
1501 Broadway, Suite 1701
New York, NY 10036
800.541.5204
www.sdcweb.org

Briana Nadeau/Editor

Fashion Designer

Snapshot

Career Cluster(s): Visual and Performing Arts
Interests: Design, arts, performance, industrial design
Earnings (Yearly Average): $63,670
Employment & Outlook: Slower than average growth expected

OVERVIEW

Sphere of Work

Fashion design is a field that blurs the lines between industrial product design and artistic expression. Fashion designers create and design original clothing, footwear, and accessories, translating sketches into patterns that can be used by manufacturers to create garments and other fashion items. Fashion design is an artistic field, but also appeals to individuals with interest in practical design, creating artistic items that also serve a function. At the upper levels, fashion design is a highly competitive and potentially lucrative field as the world's top clothing companies search for new designers to create the fashion trends for the next era.

Work Environment

Fashion designers typically work indoors, in either design studios or workshop environments and the typical equipment used in fashion design is similar to that used in other forms of artistic design. Many fashion designers are employed by apparel companies and by design firms, while others can work directly for wholesale manufacturers. Other designers find alternative employment by working with theatrical or film/television production companies to design costumes for performers. Most fashion designers work full-time schedules, while overtime work may be common when approaching key fashion or trade shows or to organize work around production deadlines.

Profile

Working Conditions: Work Indoors
Physical Strength: Light to strenuous work
Education Needs: Bachelor's Degree, Master's Degree
Licensure/Certification: N/A
Opportunities For Experience: On-Job Training, Part-Time Work, Internship
Holland Interest Score*: AER

* See Appendix A

Occupation Interest

Fashion design appeals to individuals who like working with their hands and also have an interest in aesthetics and artistic expression. Imagination and creativity are important when creating new designs, but fashion designers must also be practical in their effort to transform their creative ideas into wearable garments. Fashion designers should also have an interest in performance, as designs are often exhibited through choreographed fashion shows.

A Day in the Life—Duties and Responsibilities

Fashion designers spend much of their time studying both current fashion trends and fashion of past eras in their attempt to stimulate ideas that can lead to new fashion trends or innovative designs. When beginning a new design project, a designer will often spend time attempting to create a theme or concept for a new collection. Many designers begin designing specific garments by making basic sketches and fashion concept drawing is a subfield within the industry that can take years of practice to perfect. Some designers may also use Computer Aided Design (CAD) tools to create digital designs that can be altered on the screen.

When the designs have been finalized, designers spend time sourcing or investigating types of materials that could be used to create garments in a collection. Working with assistants and textile specialists, designers then create prototypes using different materials than will be used in the final design, which will be used to guide the creation of prototypes using the selected materials. From the prototype stage, designers may need to meet with executives or to market their designs to company representatives. If the design is approved for production, the templates and prototypes are used to begin manufacturing. Designers may also need to organize and produce fashion shows to display their designs to potential retailers or manufacturers. In some cases, a designer working in a large company may be one member under a team led by a creative designer, or may oversee groups of other designers in a managerial capacity.

Duties and Responsibilities

- Create original themes/styles for fashion collections
- Sketch or use CAD design tools to create design templates
- Market designs to production executives or companies.
- Source and purchase materials used to create garments
- Work with textile companies or team members to create prototypes
- Showcase designs in private or public fashion shows
- Research fashion trends and attend industry trade shows
- Attend professional meetings or continuing education sessions to learn about new techniques and materials in the field

OCCUPATION SPECIALTIES

Footwear Designer

Footwear designers are fashion designers who specialize in designing various types of footwear for consumers. Some footwear designers specialize in a specific type of footwear, such as in making boots or athletic shoes, while others may design footwear in a variety of categories.

Costume Designer

Costume designers are fashion designers who design garments for performers in television, film, and stage productions. Costume designers need to have detailed knowledge of existing and past fashion trends as well as the ability to creatively interpret concept drawing and other source material to create practical garments that combine fantasy and fashion.

Fashion Educator

A fashion educator teaches students seeking to become fashion designers and typically works for a college, university, or through a private design company. Design educators not only teach aspects of design production, but also teach design history and introduce students to the process of working in the design industry.

Clothing Designer

Clothing designers are fashion designers who specialize in creating wearable garments, and can also choose to further specialize in men's, women's, or children's apparel. Clothing designers can work for a variety of companies, from high end companies that make garments for special order, to those working for companies that mass produce clothing for the general market.

WORK ENVIRONMENT

Relevant Skills and Abilities

Communication Skills
- Writing clear instructions for manufacturers
- Communicating with staff, retailers, manufacturers, and executives

Interpersonal/Social Skills
- Being able to work in a group environment
- Participating in trade shows and fashion shows
- Marketing designs to company representatives and retailers

Organization & Management Skills
- Maintaining design records
- Creating portfolios and presentations of designs
- Managing staff and/or other designers

Research & Planning Skills
- Researching fashion history and trends
- Planning design projects to coincide with industry targets and trends

Technical Skills
- Utilizing computer programs for design and drawing
- Utilizing textile tools and measurement devices

Physical Environment

Fashion designers tend to work in design studios or office environments. Some designers participate in making physical prototypes of their designs, which may require working in environments with equipment for working with textiles. Fashion designers may also work in offices or spaces within factories, facilitating the process of translating their designs into products.

Human Environment

Fashion design is both an independent and a collaborative process. Designers may work alone when conceptualizing and preparing basic sketches of designs, but then need to work with others, including textile specialists, manufacturers, retailers, and a variety of other individuals, to transforming designs into completed products. In some cases, designers work as part of a design team which may include several designers working under a managing or creative design director.

Technological Environment

While many designers use pencils and pens to sketch designs, others use Computer Aided Design (CAD) software and digital design programs like Autodesk or AutoCAD Design Suite and programs designed specifically for the industry like C-DESIGN Fashion. In addition, designers typically use hand-tools that are also used in textile manufacturing and drafting including design and drawing desks, graphics tablets, digital scanners, and various types of measuring devices. Some designers involved in manufacturing their own prototypes might also work with ironing machines and presses and a variety of sewing and leatherworking tools.

EDUCATION, TRAINING, AND ADVANCEMENT

High School/Secondary

Most professional fashion designers have at least a bachelor's or other postsecondary degree in fashion design, merchandising, or a related field and so high school students should prepare for postsecondary education. High school students can also prepare for a career in design by studying art, mathematics, history, English, world languages, and any class that helps orient students to using computers and digital technology.

Suggested High School Subjects

- English
- History
- Geometry
- Drafting/Design
- Art History
- Drawing/Painting
- Graphic Design
- Modern History
- Physics
- Public Speaking
- Introduction to Computer Technology

Famous First

French designer Madeleine Chéruit was the first woman to run one of the major fashion houses in France, and a pioneer for women in fashion design around the world. Chéruit began her career as a dressmaker for the Haute Couture clothing maker Raudnitz & Cie House in the 1880s. Demonstrating her exceptional skill, by 1905, Chéruit was leading the designer's salon, renaming it Chéruit. Though the Chéruit house closed in 1935, she remained an important influence on feminine fashion and internationally famous designer Elsa Schiaparelli decided to establish her own headquarters in the then venerable buildings where Chéruit first established herself as one of fashion's most advanced designers.

College/Postsecondary

There are at least 320 postsecondary institutions with programs in art and design, many of which also offer programs and degrees specifically for fashion design and merchandising. There are also post-graduate degree programs in fashion merchandising, design, and other related fields. To prepare for one of these degrees, students will typically take classes in fashion history, marketing and PR, advertising, drawing and drafting, and computer or digital design.

Related College Majors

- Fashion Design
- Apparel Design
- ashion Marketing
- Fashion Merchandising

Adult Job Seekers

Those with degrees in fashion design or a related field can apply for work in a fashion design studio or for a retailer or manufacturing company. Internships are often available for aspiring fashion designers as well as assistant designer positions working under a designer or team of designers in a firm or wholesaler. In addition, thanks to the proliferation of digital marketing and production systems, designers can also choose to market their designs directly to the public through a private website or through online markets that cater to user-made goods and services. Designers can therefore supplement their experience by marketing their own designs or can attempt to build an independent career by designing, creating, and selling their own clothing and accessories.

Professional Certification and Licensure

There are no licenses of professional certificates needed to work in the fashion design industry.

Additional Requirements

Fashion designers need to be proficient with research, as designers typically need to stay abreast of current fashion trends around the world. In addition, fashion designers need to develop their ability to think creatively in order to generate innovative ideas for new collections. Designers should therefore look not only to other designers and to the history of fashion design, but also to other trends in culture and art that might inspire new designs and potential trends.

Fun Fact

Did you know men are more likely to approach a woman for a date if she is wearing red? Or that people walk faster when approaching someone wearing red compared to someone wearing blue? Or that an offender wearing black in court often receive a harsher sentence than they otherwise might?

Source: http://www.huffingtonpost.co.uk/karen-pine/

EARNINGS AND ADVANCEMENT

The median annual salary for fashion designers as of 2015 was estimated at $63,670, with those in the lowest-paid 10 percent of the industry earning less than $33,000 and those in the upper 10 percent earning over $125,000. Hourly wages in the industry ranged from $15.95 to over $60.00. In terms of advancement, designers may begin their careers working as assistant designers or through internships, and can advance to become managing designers or creative designers working for manufacturers or design firms. Experienced fashion designers and those who have gained a reputation working in design firms or for retailers/wholesalers can also consider starting their own design companies or can sell their products directly to retailers. A very small percentage of fashion designers can achieve fame in the industry, becoming one of the small number of elite designers whose works are highly sought for fashion shows and imitated by other designers.

Metropolitan Areas with the Highest Employment Level in this Occupation

Metropolitan area	Employment	Employment per thousand jobs	Hourly mean wage
New York-Jersey City-White Plains, NY-NJ Metropolitan Division	7,150	1.10	$38.16
Los Angeles-Long Beach-Glendale, CA Metropolitan Division	4,020	0.98	$36.63
Anaheim-Santa Ana-Irvine, CA Metropolitan Division	600	0.40	$31.76
Nassau County-Suffolk County, NY Metropolitan Division	330	0.26	$31.48
San Diego-Carlsbad, CA	330	0.25	$33.74
Boston-Cambridge-Newton, MA NECTA Division	240	0.14	$43.31
Kansas City, MO-KS	240	0.23	$27.05
Oakland-Hayward-Berkeley, CA Metropolitan Division	230	0.21	$38.01
Dallas-Plano-Irving, TX Metropolitan Division	190	0.08	$28.05
Riverside-San Bernardino-Ontario, CA	180	0.14	$23.34

Source: Bureau of Labor Statistics

EMPLOYMENT AND OUTLOOK

The Bureau of Labor Statistics (BLS) estimates that the fashion design industry will experience 3 percent growth between 2014 and 2024, which is about half as fast as the average for all U.S. industries and is therefore considered slower than average growth. The lack of growth in the industry is due to the long trend in outsourcing design and manufacturing internationally. The BLS therefore estimates that, if current trends continue, that there will be a 47 percent reduction in job availability over the 2014 to 2024 period in the apparel manufacturing field specifically. However, employment is expected to grow in the wholesale industry, in which designers are asked to mimic the trends in high end fashion for mass market consumers. Individuals with educational credentials and who display innovative portfolios and design projects are expected to fare the best in competition for industry jobs.

Employment Trend, Projected 2014–24

Total, All Occupations: 7%

Fashion Designers: 3%

Art and Design Workers: 2%

Note: "All Occupations" includes all occupations in the U.S. Economy. Source: U.S. Bureau of Labor Statistics, Employment Projections Program

Related Occupations
- Art Directors
- Buyers and Purchasing Agents
- Fashion Forecasters
- Fashion Journalists
- Floral Designers
- Graphic Designers
- Industrial Designers
- Jewelers and Precious Stone and Metal Workers
- Models
- Merchandisers
- Retail Sales Associates

Related Occupations
- Military Apparel Designer
- Military Fashion Consultant

Conversation With . . .
DANIELLE N. JONES

Associate Designer at Justice Headquarters
New Albany, Ohio
Fashion design, 6 years

1. What was your individual career path in terms of education/training, entry-level job, or other significant opportunity?

By the time I was 10, I was styling my younger siblings. In high school, I'd style my friends and family who would come to me and my closet—with its many accessories and hip clothes—instead of shopping for an outfit for a big party or event!

I took a practical route in college and studied graphic and web design at Columbus State Community College, then landed a job at a small multimedia company. Only 18 months later, I experienced my first layoff. Boo! I didn't let that stop me. I took my artistic talents to a private preschool and taught art. It paid the bills until I could land my next gig, doing graphic design and working as a production assistant at Office Max. But I reached a point where graphic design was no longer making me happy. My sister had taught me how to sew and we started a side business selling tote bags, like you might carry in the summer. I applied with a portfolio in hand to Columbus College of Art and Design (CCAD), received a scholarship, and decided to go back to what I loved: fashion.

A teacher there told us: "Fashion isn't just styling your friends or wearing the prettiest clothes – it's technical, creative, and will be hard." She told us half the class would not be there in three years; I said to myself, "I will!" I interned every summer, in tech design and as a sample room assistant; marketing; and CAD design, and at major brands including Abercrombie & Fitch, Chico's and Express. One month before graduating, I turned down an offer for a full-time job in tech design to wait for my final interview for the dream job I really wanted — assistant designer at Justice, where I currently am today!

Eventually, my sister and I want to expand our business, Nickel & Ash Home LLC. Right now, it's soft goods for home and kitchen. I could also see becoming a design director at a fashion company.

2. What are the most important skills and/or qualities for someone in your profession?

Change, flexibility and a good design eye. Beyond being creative, fashion is an ever-evolving industry. Your line may be completed and the next thing you know everything (or at least 80 percent) has to change based on what's selling, new trends, or new information telling you the girl you're designing for might like something better. For instance, she might not like a bag with hearts on it anymore, so you update to a different icon, like an emoji or a star. A good designer can scrap a line and come up with something better. And a good design eye means you can look at something and know what needs to be changed or tweaked. People in the industry say most designers are born with it. I believe so, too.

3. What do you wish you had known going into this profession?

Much of my job is to design the current, but also know the upcoming. CCAD made me use every part of my brain, stretching it to the very core. It prepared me to continually look to the next thing.

4. Are there many job opportunities in your profession? In what specific areas?

There are many avenues within fashion. You can be a designer (who creates the vision), a tech designer (who figures out construction details and how an item will be made) or a merchant; you can go into trends; sourcing, which means managing materials and timelines; or be a sample room assistant or stylist. Every company wants the best talent. Internships and training will set you apart as a growing professional versus just a student. I can't say enough about internships! I was fortunate to have four, which helped me decide what avenue was the best fit for me.

5. How do you see your profession changing in the next five years, what role will technology play in those changes, and what skills will be required?

We don't have much time to draw by hand anymore. Almost everything is digital, at least at my company. Digital is fast. Everyone wants the fastest and most efficient way to get the end result. New programs are being utilized. Continuously learning new design programs will be required.

6. What do you enjoy most about your job? What do you enjoy least about your job?

I enjoy our customers! I design for the tween girl between the ages of 8 and 12. She is fun, confident, loves life and loves to be herself. On top of that, she is trendy and likes the hottest fashion. That opens up an array of excitement when designing. In addition, Justice is a very fun environment. Everyone is so friendly.

I wish I got to travel as much as I'd like for work. Part of being a designer is bringing in inspiration from all over. Luckily, the internet is a valuable resource and can make you feel as though you've traveled to places you haven't.

7. Can you suggest a valuable "try this" for students considering a career in your profession?

Research your favorite brand to see what it's currently making and think about what trends it should bring out next. Make a mood board featuring colors and fabrics for your clothes and use that, as well as your trend information, to sketch croquis (a sketch of a person) and clothing that the "models" should wear. Color in your illustrations and you've got your first portfolio piece.

MORE INFORMATION

National Association of Schools of Art and Design (NASAD)
11250 Roger Bacon Drive, Suite 21
Reston, VA 20190-5248
703-437-0700
www.nasad.arts-accredit.org

Council of Fashion Designers of America (CFDA)
65 Bleecker St, 11th Floor
New York, NY 10012
212-302-1821
www.cfda.com

United States Fashion Industry Association (USFIA)
1717 Pennsylvania Ave. NW
Suite 430
Washington, D.C., 20006
202-419-0444
www.usfashionindustry.com

American Apparel and Footwear Association (AAFA)
740 6th Street, NW
3rd and 4th Floors
Washington, D.C. 20001
202-853-9080
www.wewear.org

Custom Society of America (CSA)
P.O. Box 852
Columbus, GA 31902
706-615-2851
www.costumesocietyamerica.com

Micah Issitt/Editor

Fine Artist

Snapshot

Career Cluster(s): Arts and Fine Arts
Interests: Art, interior design, hands-on work
Earnings (Yearly Average): $45,080
Employment & Outlook: Slower than average

OVERVIEW

Sphere of Work

Fine artists create a variety of original works of art for both exhibition and retail art markets. The field includes professionals working in fields like painting, sculpture, drawing, pottery, textiles, and illustration. Fine art can be an individual pursuit, with artists working independently on their artworks from beginning to completion, other artists work with other artists or with groups of assistants to complete artistic projects. Fine art is a discipline that combines both practical, physical skills and creative ability and fine artists may either work on art based on their own interests or may work on artistic products for commercial or industrial use.

Work Environment

Most artists work in studios located in either industrial, office, or residential buildings. Some fine artists, such as glass workers, glass blowers, and sculptors, require specialized equipment and may therefore need to do some or all of their work in studios or other facilities equipped with specialized equipment and tools. Some forms of artistic production are more physically strenuous than others, but most fine arts disciplines require physical coordination and endurance. Artists are also sometimes exposed to potentially hazardous conditions, including fumes produced by paints, glues, and inks, or the physical danger posed by heated materials and equipment. While half of all fine artists are self-employed, and many work independently, others work in collaborative teams, and other work as teachers or instructors in schools or private arts education institutions.

Profile

Working Conditions: Indoor or outdoor work

Physical Strength: Light to strenuous work

Education Needs: Bachelor's Degree, Master's Degree

Licensure/Certification: Not required

Opportunities For Experience: Adult education, Teaching assistant positions, Part-time work

Holland Interest Score*: AR

* See Appendix A

Occupation Interest

Those seeking a career in fine arts need to be highly motivated and creative. Fine artists often create their own ideas for art projects, while some artists work on commissioned works in which the customer provides input or guidance on the final product, and those seeking to become artists should ideally have an interest in both collaboration and self-expression. Most types of art require some physical, hands-on activities and artists should therefore also have a strong interest in practical, hands-on creative work.

A Day in the Life—Duties and Responsibilities

A typical day for a fine artist depends largely on the type of art and the type of medium that the artist is working with. Artists use and study techniques based on their particular media, which may include drawing and painting, knitting, weaving, glassblowing, sculpting, or any of a wide variety of potential techniques and skills. Artists often create plans, sketches or templates for artistic products before creating a final work and also must spend time selecting materials to use in their artworks, such as textiles, paints, and various drawing tools. Those marketing their own work might also spend time developing their artistic portfolio, which is a collection of images or artistic samples that an artist can use to demonstrate their work to potential clients, employers, and galleries. Artists with completed works or collections may spend time talking with gallery owners or managers to negotiate displaying their art in public spaces or selling their art. In some cases, artists may need to obtain funding for their work and so might apply for grants and other types of funding before starting a new project. Artists must also continually practice the skills required for their craft and might spend time researching the work of other artists, art history, or current trends in the effort to inspire new projects or collections of works.

Duties and Responsibilities

- Use specialized tools and techniques to create original artworks
- Negotiate with clients or customers for commissioned works
- Research, source, and obtain materials and equipment
- Market and display artworks at galleries, art shows, or other venues
- Apply for artistic fellowships, grants, and commercial projects
- Teach or train assistants, interns, or student artists
- Organize time to meet required deadlines for completing work
- Manage a studio or design team

OCCUPATION SPECIALTIES

Illustrators

Illustrators create pictures for books, commercial projects, magazines and other types of publications and may work with drawing, painting, and digital illustration techniques. There are many different types of illustration, from concept illustrators who create images for television or film productions to medical illustrators who create illustrations of biological or medical procedures and objects of instructional books and displays.

Glass Artists

Glass artist use a variety of techniques, including glass blowing, shaping, and joining, to create artistic works using glass as their medium. Glass workers can create commercial artworks, like lamps and stained glass windows/art pieces, and can also create jewelry, ornaments, and furniture using various techniques.

Furniture Makers

Furniture makers are artisans who sculpt, cut, join, and finish wood to create handcrafted furniture or artistic furnishings. Furniture makers can design for mass production or can create individual pieces on commission.

Ceramic Artists

Ceramic artists use clay to create works of art that can include sculpture, pottery, or a variety of other types of ceramic objects. Working with ceramics requires knowledge of specialized techniques including glazing, firing, and sculpting.

Video Artists

Video artists use digital or analog video recording and projection equipment to create visual art. Visual artists can display their work in galleries or in film and video productions and often use a blend of practical and digital technology in their work.

WORK ENVIRONMENT

Relevant Skills and Abilities

Communication Skills
- Writing grants and proposals
- Communicating with gallery owners and managers

Interpersonal/Social Skills
- Being able to work in a group environment
- Being able to work with clients on commission projects

Organization & Management Skills
- Managing time to meet deadlines
- Managing assistants, interns, or art students
- Being detail oriented when preparing and completing projects

Research & Planning Skills
- Researching development, equipment, and materials used in artistic fields
- Creating mock-ups, prototypes, and sketches of projects

Technical Skills
- Utilizing hand-held manual tools and equipment to create art works
- Utilizing digital tools for design and planning

Physical Environment

Fine artists work in a variety of environments, but tend to do most of their work in indoor studios or workshops. Some artists rent or share space in commercial studios, while others lease or purchase private studio space and others set up studios in their homes. Artists typically work on arts or craft tables which may be purchased commercially or built specially to accommodate the needs of the artist. Because some art techniques involve the use of potentially hazardous equipment, chemicals, and gasses, arts studios typically need safety equipment and need to be well ventilated and artists should keep and use safety equipment to prevent injury.

Human Environment

About half of all visual artists in the United States are self-employed and many who work for institutions or companies also spend time working independently. In some cases, artists may work with assistants, interns, or art students to complete a project. Though the level of interaction varies depending on the type of work, artists benefit from being able to discuss technical and creative aspects of their work with others and with being able to collaborate with customers on commission project. In addition, artists often need to market their own work and should be comfortable meeting with studio and gallery owners, customers, and retail managers and buyers.

Technological Environment

In a variety of fine arts fields, the equipment used in the 21st century is similar or identical to equipment that has been used by artists working on similar projects for decades or centuries. However, modern equipment can also be used to supplement or replace traditional equipment. In addition, the advent and spread of Computer Aided Design (CAD) programs and other forms digital design have dramatically altered some fields of fine arts, especially illustration and graphic arts. Many illustrators, sketch artists, and others working in drawing and painting now complete some of their work using digital tools like graphics tablets and drawing/painting/illustration programs.

EDUCATION, TRAINING, AND ADVANCEMENT

High School/Secondary

While there are no specific educational requirements to become a fine artist, there are a variety of classes offered in many high schools/secondary schools that can help artists learn and practice the tools of various artistic trades, such as drawing and painting classes, sculpture, metalworking, and design. In addition, professional artists benefit from a broad education in the arts, introducing them to cultural and artistic history that can serve as the inspiration for later artistic endeavors.

Suggested High School Subjects
- English
- Composition
- Literature
- Drawing/Painting
- Sculpture

- Graphic Design
- Textile Arts
- Marketing
- Introduction to Business
- Metalworking/Shop
- Industrial Design

Famous First

Henry Ossawa Tanner, an African American painter born in Pittsburgh, Pennsylvania in 1859, became internationally famous for his landscape paintings and was the first African American student to enroll in the Pennsylvania Academy of the Fine Arts in Philadelphia. Tanner moved to Paris in 1891 to study painting and, in 1896, was invited to showcase his work at the official exhibition of the Académie des Beaux-Arts in Paris, becoming the first African American artist to gain international acclaim.

College/Postsecondary

After completing secondary education, many artists go on to earn bachelor's and master's degrees in the fine arts. Some universities and colleges offer general degrees in the arts, while others, especially institutions specializing in arts education, offer more specific degree programs aimed at artists in a specific field, like ceramic arts or painting. Depending on one's intended field, other classes might also be helpful and/or needed. For instance, those who want to work as artists in film or television, should consider studying film history and filmmaking techniques. Those interested in technical illustration, should also study subjects that will help with the field. Medical illustrators, for instance, need experience in anatomy, biology, and medical techniques. Many colleges also help artists learn how to develop a portfolio and how to market their art to companies, galleries, and the public.

Related College Majors
- Marketing

- Business Management
- Art History
- Painting
- Illustration
- Sculpture
- Textile Arts
- Art Education

Adult Job Seekers

Adults looking to market their artistic talents or to transition to the fine arts as a career can attempt to create a portfolio to showcase their art and to market their work to studios, galleries, design companies, and other potential clients/employers. Individuals can also attempt to find internships or assistant positions with established artists. National and international arts organizations, like the National Endowment for the Arts (NEA), can help connect artists with institutions and employers or with internships, educational opportunities, and potential grants.

Professional Certification and Licensure

There are no professional licenses or certification requirements needed to work as an artist though individuals who plan to work as arts instructors/teachers, especially at the elementary, middle, and high school levels, will need to adhere to licensing requirements in their area.

Additional Requirements

Artists need to be highly self-motivated and aggressive about promoting and marketing their work. In addition, most types of fine art require certain physical skills or abilities. For instance, sculptors and ceramics artists need coordination and sufficient strength to work with clay and other materials, while graphic artists, illustrators, and other visual artists need to have highly developed visual acuity and perception.

Fun Fact

Leonardo da Vinci's fabled painting The Last Supper is actually a mural, painted on a wall at the Convent of Santa Maria delle Grazie in Milan, Italy. In 1652, while installing a door, workers cut out Jesus's feet!

Source: http://mentalfloss.com/article/64372/

EARNINGS AND ADVANCEMENT

According to the Bureau of Labor Statistics (BLS), the median salary for fine artists in the United States was $46,460 in 2015, with those at the lower 10 percent earning less than $19,000 and those at the highest 10 percent earning more than $99,000 annually. Advancing within the fine arts industry depends on the specific type of art and other factors. Individuals working for companies might be able to advance from entry-level positions to higher-level and management positions, while, for independent artists, advancement may mean developing new collections and better strategies for marketing work to galleries and customers. More than half of all working fine artists are self-employed and so need to be active in marketing their work to advance in their careers.

Metropolitan Areas with the Highest
Employment Level in this Occupation

Metropolitan area	Employment	Employment per thousand jobs	Hourly mean wage
Los Angeles-Long Beach-Glendale, CA Metropolitan Division	1,390	0.34	$37.31
New York-Jersey City-White Plains, NY-NJ Metropolitan Division	1,040	0.16	$31.09
Atlanta-Sandy Springs-Roswell, GA	350	0.14	$21.93
Cincinnati, OH-KY-IN	300	0.29	$10.48
Chicago-Naperville-Arlington Heights, IL Metropolitan Division	280	0.08	$25.06
Seattle-Bellevue-Everett, WA Metropolitan Division	260	0.17	$35.93
Houston-The Woodlands-Sugar Land, TX	220	0.07	$16.89
Portland-Vancouver-Hillsboro, OR-WA	210	0.19	$25.23
Dallas-Plano-Irving, TX Metropolitan Division	210	0.09	$34.40
Anaheim-Santa Ana-Irvine, CA Metropolitan Division	160	0.10	$30.69

Source: Bureau of Labor Statistics

EMPLOYMENT AND OUTLOOK

On the whole, the BLS estimates that careers in the fine arts will grow by only 2 percent between 2014 to 2024, which constitutes slower than average growth compared to the 6-7 percent growth estimated for all career fields during this same period. Growth in fine art sales depends on broader economic patterns as the sale of art increases as consumers have more income for investment in non-essential goods. Those with experience in graphic art and digital art are likely to fare better than many other categories of artists due to a rising demand for digital graphics and the potential for digital artists to capitalize on broader cultural/social trends. While the fine arts field grows slowly, in general, there are always opportunities for artists who demonstrate the ability to innovate within their field and there is always a market for artists who help to start new artistic trends.

Employment Trend, Projected 2014–24

Total, All Occupations: 7%

Art and Design Workers: 2%

Craft and Fine Artists: 2%

Note: "All Occupations" includes all occupations in the U.S. Economy. Source: U.S. Bureau of Labor Statistics, Employment Projections Program

Related Occupations

- Art Directors
- Fashion Designers
- Industrial Designers
- Graphic Designers
- Photographers
- Woodworkers
- Jewelers and Precious Stone and Metal Workers.
- Multimedia Artists and Animators
- Archivists, Curators, and Museum Workers

Conversation With . . .
ABIGAIL MCBRIDE

Painter, Abigail McBride Studio
Chesapeake City, Maryland
Artist, 24 years

1. **What was your individual career path in terms of education/training, entry-level job, or other significant opportunity?**

I've always been around artists and wanted to be an artist. My grandmother was a watercolorist who got married, moved to a dairy farm in rural Minnesota, and had six kids. She did illustrations and taught women in her area to paint. She taught me to paint at the farm in the summer. My mother has always had a gallery, primarily in Annapolis, MD. I thought of being an artist as just another career choice. Because I saw it as ordinary, I was less inclined to pity myself or give up when I went through the inevitable hard times early in my career.

When I was in high school in Annapolis, Maryland, I started studying with professional artists at our city's arts center in charcoal, oil and sculpture. Instead of parties, I went to open studio figure drawing groups. I earned a BFA from Westmont College in Santa Barbara, California, majoring in art and minoring in religious studies. I spent nearly a year in Europe, including studying painting in France.

After graduation, I returned to Annapolis and studied again at Maryland Hall. Through a well-known area family of painters, the Egelis, I also discovered the Cape Cod School of Art in Provincetown, MA. Five summers living and working there as an assistant—while painting and learning as much as possible—amounted to what I think of as my grad school.

As a painter, I'm a realist. I've always been interested in painting what things look like: portraits and landscapes and still lifes. Realism was not in vogue when I was studying. Only now is realism rising again; I credit the internet for that.

I opened my own studio the minute I graduated from college and had my first solo show in Maryland Hall's café. I also did web design in my initial years, including making my own web site, which helped to garner national exposure that gave me an invaluable boost early on.

Today I teach at two schools, am represented by four galleries, do portraits, and tend to paint in my yard or do still lifes. I actually met my husband because he collected my paintings through a gallery in Philadelphia. We have two young sons. I have done more shows in spaces that aren't a gallery—such as art centers, colleges, museums and town halls—since moving to a small town and having my children.

I have put my energy into being an artist full-time and, when I was single, always saved three months of expenses so I could make it. You can be a teacher who paints—and teaching is the steadiest money—but I was clear on my focus from the start.

2. What are the most important skills and/or qualities for someone in your profession?

You need persistence, drive, passion and integrity. You need to love what you do. Every career has a part that is fun and exciting and a part that is no fun at all because it's awkward, boring, and outside your natural skill set. I've had to learn the business and marketing part, from keeping a frame inventory to tracking miles driven for taxes.

Artists today must bring their own audience to a gallery. It used to be the other way around. So, I have joined with other artists to create a collective, called the Maryland Colorists, to create exhibit opportunities. In the beginning, I kept my prices low because your collectors will grow with you. Use Facebook because older people use it and they collect work. I use Instagram if I'm trying to market to students.

3. What do you wish you had known going into this profession?

That a lack of entrepreneurial and business acumen can hold you back no matter how skilled you are.

4. Are there many job opportunities in your profession? In what specific areas?

Many occupations utilize creative skills in the visual arts: graphic design, set design, animation for film or games, advertising, teaching. But I have found that those who thrive are those with their own businesses. Creative control is key in the fine arts.

5. How do you see your profession changing in the next five years, what role will technology play in those changes, and what skills will be required?

Artists reflect a culture as its chroniclers, healers and prophets, so I see two paths here. Digital painting and Virtual Reality will become as mainstream as photography. At the same time, I expect to see a resurgence of handmade, one of a kind objects because, as humans, we have always used art-making to understand the world.

6. What do you enjoy most about your job? What do you enjoy least about your job?

I enjoy discovering my work has meaning for someone, seeing a new skill manifest in my work, and the beginning of every new painting. I least enjoy marketing and slogging through tax time.

7. Can you suggest a valuable "try this" for students considering a career in your profession?

Create something, frame it and find a coffee shop to hang it in. Better, put a body of work together. The act of making the work, preparing it for presentation, and getting it on display will tell you a lot about the reality being an artist.

MORE INFORMATION

National Association of Schools of Art and Design (NASAD)
11250 Roger Bacon Drive, Suite 21
Reston, VA 20190
703-437-0700
www.nasad.arts-accredit.org

National Craft Council
1224 Marshall Street NE, Suite 200
Minneapolis, MN 55413
612-206-3100
www.craftcouncil.org

Society of Illustrators
128 East 63rd Street
New York, NY 10065
212-838-2560
www.societyillustrators.org

National Endowment for the Arts (NEA)
400 7th Street, SW
Washington, D.C. 20506
202-682-5400
www.arts.gov

New York Foundation for the Arts (NYFA)
20 Jay Street, Suite 740
Brooklyn, NY 11201
212-366-6900
www.nyfa.org

National Art Education Association (NAEA)
901 Prince Street
Alexandria, VA 22314
703-860-2960
www.arteducators.org

Micah Issitt/Editor

Florist

Snapshot

Career Cluster: Art & Design; Hospitality & Tourism; Sales & Service

Interests: Horticulture, flowers, plants, creative tasks

Earnings (Yearly Average): $25,550

Employment & Outlook: Decline Expected

OVERVIEW

Sphere of Work

Florists, also called floral designers, work with flowers, plants, and greenery to fashion and assemble arrangements and bouquets according to customer needs. Florists are responsible for the configuration of each arrangement, from conception to completion. They are creative individuals who use their talents to produce attractive arrangements for various occasions, including weddings and funerals, parties, holidays, corporate and school functions, and other special events. Some florists may have long-term agreements with hotels and restaurants or the owners of office buildings and private homes to replace old flowers with new

flower arrangements on a recurring schedule—usually daily, weekly, or monthly—to keep areas looking fresh and appealing. Some work with interior designers in creating these displays.

Work Environment

Most florists work out of retail florist shops under the supervision of a store manager or owner. Increasingly, however, many work in grocery stores with floral departments. Some florists own their own businesses and may work out of a small shop or within a home environment. Others are employed by wholesale floral companies and nurseries. Florists should expect to work in varying temperatures, as certain flowers are kept in refrigerated or humid storage areas, which florists must access regularly. They usually work a standard eight-hour day during the week and often work on weekends, especially during periods when flowers are in high demand.

Profile

Working Conditions: Work Indoors
Physical Strength: Light Work
Education Needs: On-The-Job Training, High School Diploma Or G.E.D.
Licensure/Certification: Recommended
Physical Abilities Not Required: No Heavy Labor
Opportunities For Experience: Part-Time Work
Holland Interest Score*: RAE

* See Appendix A

Occupation Interest

Those who are interested in pursuing a career in floral design must be passionate about horticulture and the history of plants and flowers. They should be able to create emotionally meaningful arrangements in various settings and with different plant materials. Florists must also interpret and translate the ideas of customers into unique floral arrangements. They must also have an interest in the concepts of business, as many florists are also shop managers or owners.

A Day in the Life—Duties and Responsibilities

Florists normally spend the majority of the workday in a flower shop or retail setting, cutting and clipping flowers, and designing various floral arrangements for private clients and large events. The frequency of customer orders may vary by season, and before or during popular holidays, a florist may be required to work overtime or longer hours to accommodate customer demands.

Florists are generally responsible for most daily back-end operations of a flower business. When a client requests an arrangement, the florist must evaluate the client's idea and choose the appropriate floral arrangement or bouquet for the occasion. A florist's clients may include private individuals, hotels, restaurants, museums and libraries, banks, retail stores, religious institutions, and corporations. A large part of the day is spent trimming and cutting flowers and materials, planning and preparing floral arrangements, and working with wreaths, terrariums, and related items. Some florists decorate store windows and travel to various locations to prepare large-scale floral arrangements or landscapes.

Florists commonly perform administrative duties in order to keep the business running smoothly. They track financial transactions and orders, take messages via phone and the Internet, and often purchase and maintain the inventory of flowers and plants. Depending on the type of floral business, they may also be responsible for the sale of items, including plant food, gardening equipment, storage containers, and decorative accessories. They may also spend a good deal of time interacting with customers and advising them on how to care for various kinds of plants and flowers.

Duties and Responsibilities

- Talking with customers regarding the price and type of arrangement desired
- Planning the arrangement according to the customer's requirements and costs, using knowledge of design and properties of materials or an appropriate standard design pattern
- Choosing the flora and foliage necessary for the arrangement
- Trimming material and arranging bouquets, sprays, wreaths, dish gardens, terrariums and other items
- Packing and wrapping completed arrangements
- Decorating buildings, churches, halls or other facilities where events are planned

WORK ENVIRONMENT

Physical Environment

Most florists work in clean, comfortable, and well-ventilated settings. In some cases, they may be required to gather and harvest flowers and plants in outdoor environments. Storage areas for collected flowers and plants are typically cool and humid. Some florists travel to various locations to deliver floral arrangements.

Human Environment

Florists generally work with a small number of other employees or administrative personnel. Some florists report to a shop manager or owner, while others hold supervisory positions themselves. Florists who have home-based businesses usually work alone. Most florists frequently interact with clients who place orders for bouquets and arrangements. Some florists also collaborate with interior designers and other design professionals for residential or corporate projects.

Relevant Skills and Abilities

Creative/Artistic Skills
- Being skilled in art and design

Interpersonal/Social Skills
- Cooperating with others
- Perceiving others' feelings
- Working as a member of a team

Organization & Management Skills
- Meeting goals and deadlines
- Selling ideas or products
- Working quickly when necessary
- Paying attention to and handling details

Research & Planning Skills
- Gathering information
- Creating ideas

Technological Environment

Florists work with various tools and materials to produce their floral creations. They regularly use pruners, wires and wire cutters, shears, pins, foams, spray paints, knives, and other sharp tools. They also work with many different kinds of flowers and plants. Florists must also be familiar with office equipment and cash registers.

EDUCATION, TRAINING, AND ADVANCEMENT

High School/Secondary

High school students who wish to become florists should concentrate on subjects related to the sciences, agriculture, and botany. In addition to these core subjects, students should also take courses that emphasize creative art design, communications, and business. Interested students should familiarize themselves with flower and plant growing, harvesting, and arranging by visiting public gardens or local farms or by experimenting with plants and flowers in their own private gardens. Students are also encouraged to participate in apprenticeships or summer internships that allow them to work with flowers and plants.

Suggested High School Subjects
- Agricultural Education
- Applied Math
- Arts
- Bookkeeping
- Crafts
- English
- Ornamental Horticulture

Famous First

The first flowers to be dispensed in a vending machine were placed in New York City's Grand Central Station in 1961 by the Automated Flowers Company of Greenwich, Conn. The machine was six feet high, by three feet wide, and two feet deep. It was a self-contained refrigerated unit that required no plumbing. Since that time floral vending machines have grown steadily in use in large public facilities and now offer everything from small lapel decorations to substantial floral arrangements.

Postsecondary

Though florists are not required to earn an undergraduate degree to begin working in their field, many choose to study floral design or basic design and color concepts at vocational schools, community colleges, or universities. Postsecondary programs in floral design teach students the fundamentals of preparing, designing, and packaging flowers and floral arrangements. They also cover sales and business approaches, customer service, garden construction, and horticulture and greenhouse management. Students work with fresh, dry, and artificial flowers. In addition to practical approaches to floral design, students gain an understanding of the philosophical ideas behind designing flowers. They also learn about current trends in the industry. Training in general horticulture or botany is also useful.

Adult Job Seekers

Many florists start out by gaining experience in the floral industry as cashiers, delivery people, or assistants in retail floral shops. These jobs provide opportunities to develop skills related to floral design like drawing and sketching, molding clay, and creating displays and exhibits.

Job seekers commonly apply directly to floral shops or private employers. Those who complete a formal floral design program often have learned how to manage a floral shop or start their own business. Some floral design programs also provide job placement services. Membership in professional floral design associations may provide networking opportunities and job listings for adults seeking employment as florists.

Professional Certification and Licensure

Certification in floral design is not generally required. However, some florists find it helpful to become accredited by a professional association, such as The American Institute of Floral Designers (AIFD), as a demonstration of their expertise in the field. For the AIFD examination, test-takers should expect to complete a written portion that covers basic principles and terminology of floral design and pass a practical section that demonstrates their proficiency in creating displays and arrangements. Continuing education is often a requirement for certification renewal. As with any voluntary certification program, it is useful to consult credible professional associations within the field, and follow professional debate as to the relevancy and value of the certification program.

Additional Requirements

Because floral design is a highly creative and interpretive line of work, prospective florists should be able to process and translate the customer's artistic concepts and general feelings into an evocative floral product. Florists rely on their senses to make informed decisions; therefore, potential florists should be able to recognize differences in color, scents, and textures. As customers often need arrangements at the last minute, florists should be organized, possess a sense of urgency, and have great time-management skills.

EARNINGS AND ADVANCEMENT

Earnings of florists depend on the geographic location of the employer and the individual's level of skill and years of experience. Mean annual earnings of florists were $25,550 in 2012. The lowest ten percent earned less than $17,956, and the highest ten percent earned more than $37,990.

Florists may receive paid vacations, holidays, and sick days. Because most floral shops are small, other fringe benefits are limited. Some employers pay part of the cost of life and health insurance, but few contribute to retirement plans other than Social Security.

Metropolitan Areas with the Highest Employment Level in this Occupation

Metropolitan area	Employment[1]	Employment per thousand jobs	Hourly mean wage[1]
New York-White Plains-Wayne, NY-NJ	1,540	0.30	$16.00
Chicago-Joliet-Naperville, IL	1,330	0.37	$13.12
Philadelphia, PA	950	0.52	$12.47
Houston-Sugar Land-Baytown, TX	650	0.25	$12.22
Los Angeles-Long Beach-Glendale, CA	650	0.17	$14.14
Dallas-Plano-Irving, TX	650	0.31	$12.36
Boston-Cambridge-Quincy, MA	650	0.38	$13.26
Miami-Miami Beach-Kendall, FL	600	0.60	$12.23

[1]Does not include self-employed. Source: Bureau of Labor Statistics

Fun Fact

It took 20 florists and a small contingent of engineers and builders to create the world's tallest floral arrangement: a tower of pompon flowers reaching more than 89 feet (about seven stories) skyward. According to Guinness World Records, the arrangement of 65,000 yellow, blue, green and white flowers was organized by the Mexican beer maker Cerveza Modelo Especial in Mexico City on May 10, 2013 in honor of Mother's Day.

EMPLOYMENT AND OUTLOOK

Florists held about 62,400 jobs nationally in 2012. About one-half worked in florist shops, and many others worked in the floral departments of grocery stores. Employment is expected to decline through the year 2022.

Opportunities should be available in grocery store and Internet floral shops as sales of floral arrangements from these outlets grow. The prearranged displays and gifts available in these stores appeal to consumers because of the convenience and because of prices that are lower than can be found in independent floral shops.

Employment Trend, Projected 2012–22

Total, All Occupations: 11%

Arts, Design, Entertainment, Sports, and Media Occupations: 7%

Florists: -8%

Note: "All Occupations" includes all occupations in the U.S. Economy. Source: U.S. Bureau of Labor Statistics, Employment Projections Program

Related Occupations
- Gardener & Groundskeeper
- Interior Designer

Conversation With . . .
TIMI HUSKINSON
Florist, 19 years

1. What was your individual career path in terms of education/training, entry-level job, or other significant opportunity?

While volunteering as a Master Gardener as part of the Cooperative Extension in Las Vegas, I became aware of an Ornamental Horticulture Program at College of Southern Nevada. I began taking classes in Floral Design and in Urban Horticulture, thinking the two areas would benefit me in floral design. Armed with beginning classes and training from the Master Gardener program, I stepped out in faith and opened my business offering xeriscape maintenance, horticulture management and floral design, as I continued with my education.

Right now corporate events and convention events are probably 40 percent of my business. I'll get a call from, let's just say IBM, saying "We need 220 centerpieces because we'll be in town for a convention." Generally for a corporate event, they don't want as many flowers; they want something with a more modern, streamlined look to it.

2. What are the most important skills and/or qualities for someone in your profession?

I'd say hands-on training through a college that offers specific instruction in floral design is invaluable. An art, interior design, or horticulture background are natural for the skills and creativity required to be a top-rated floral designer. Qualities should include a passion for nature in order to work with fresh-cut flowers and plants and unusual textures from the horticultural world. You must be self-motivated to keep up with ever-changing design styles and continue your education.

3. What do you wish you had known going into this profession?

I felt lucky to have a background in management. I would encourage anyone entering the profession to continue with a balance of design and management classes. An internship in a flower shop, event company or floral design studio will help you learn about the profession before getting into it.

4. Are there many job opportunities in your profession? In what specific areas?

The opportunities in floral design are endless. Every city, county and state has flower shops. You can take the skills you acquire from classes in floral design anywhere. Resorts and hotels have their own floral departments, as do cruise ships. Upscale couture floral design studios are in great demand, as are opportunities in the Event Design end of the industry. If you have a passion for teaching, there's also a need for trained, qualified educators and instructors.

5. How do you see your profession changing in the next five years? What role will technology play in those changes, and what skills will be required?

Floral designers are leaving cookie cutter membership services that dictate the exact style of floral design offered to consumers. With mobile technology and Internet mapping, consumers are searching the zip code of the person receiving flowers, then selecting a florist from an actual small business to custom design their order. Consumers want to send flowers that convey their emotions and prefer to have an original design. Owners of florist shops are quickly adapting to these changes. In the next five years, we will need to continue to acquire social media skills, including joining conversations and circles. The Internet will continue to be the best source for consumers to find reliable service companies, florists included. Social networking skills, such as posting images of your most current designs instantly and spontaneously, are technology skills we will be need to perfect.

6. What do you enjoy most about your job? What do you enjoy least?

I love flowers! I enjoy using my flower shop and the original designs we feature as a ministry to connect the good word of the Gospel to our clients, especially on occasions when they are at a loss for words. Flowers speak a language of comfort at times of grief and loss. I have a passion for designing with unusual and original elements found in nature. I like to be inspired by other professionals who also keep up with the newest design styles. Attending national symposiums, like those offered by the American Institute of Floral Designers (AIFD), is an exciting way to see what's happening around the world.

My least favorite thing about this industry? Easy: clients trying to place last minute orders at the end of the workday and weekend, and on major holidays when we are closed.

7. Can you suggest a valuable "try this" for students considering a career in your profession?

Get to know your local florist. They are the eyes and ears of the industry, and are in the know about classes and opportunities. Ask your local florist to put together a mixed bunch of flowers for you to take home and arrange, to see if this is a skill that comes naturally to you and makes you happy. Volunteer organizations frequently have events where all hands are needed, with instructors there to oversee and give some hands-on training.

SELECTED SCHOOLS

Training beyond high school is not necessarily expected of beginning florists. However, such training can prove beneficial. Interested parties may find relevant programs at selected technical/community colleges or at privately run vocational schools with floral design programs or programs in horticulture.

MORE INFORMATION

American Floral Endowment
1601 Duke Street
Alexandria, VA 22314
703.838.5211
www.endowment.org

American Institute of Floral Designers
720 Light Street
Baltimore, MD 21230
410.752.3318
www.aifd.org

Association of Specialty Cut Flower Growers
PO Box 268
17½ West College Street
Oberlin, OH, 44074
440.774.2887
www.ascfg.org

Master Florists Association
1171 Broadway Street
San Francisco, CA 94109
415.298.1943
www.masterfloristsassn.org

National Garden Clubs, Inc.
4401 Magnolia Avenue
St. Louis, MO 63110
314.776.7574
www.gardenclub.org

Society of American Florists
1601 Duke Street
Alexandria, VA 22314
800.336.4743
www.safnow.org

Briana Nadeau/Editor

Graphic Designer & Illustrator

Snapshot

Career Cluster: Arts, A/V Technology & Communications, Business, Management & Administration, Information Technology

Interests: Visual Arts, Advertising, Communications, Media

Earnings (Yearly Average): $46,110

Employment & Outlook: Average Growth Expected

OVERVIEW

Sphere of Work

Graphic designers and illustrators create visually appealing products and illustrative materials that range from simple logos or business cards to picture books and entire corporate branding campaigns. Their work is intended to convey a commercial or educational message or otherwise draw attention to an idea, which they accomplish mostly with sophisticated graphic design and illustration techniques. Traditional artistic mediums, such as printmaking or painting, continue to be used, but sporadically. A designer interested

in a long-term career must also learn skills in animation, digital video production, and web design, or collaborate frequently with people who possess these skill sets or perform these job functions.

Work Environment

Graphic designers and illustrators work mostly in the publishing, advertising, and marketing industries, but some work for graphic design firms or government agencies. Many are self-employed. They spend much of their time working on computers, but may also have access to a full art studio. If self-employed, they interact heavily with clients. If employed in a design firm or design department, they interact with a team of professionals and staff and have less direct contact with clients; however, some customer service is necessary when choosing the final design—a process that can take anywhere from a couple of days to several weeks.

Profile

Working Conditions: Office/Studio Environment
Physical Strength: Light Work
Education Needs: Bachelor's Degree
Licensure/Certification: Usually Not Required
Physical Abilities Not Required: No Heavy Work
Opportunities For Experience: Apprenticeship, Part-Time Work
Holland Interest Score*: AES

* See Appendix A

Occupation Interest

People who are attracted to graphic design and illustration tend to be creative thinkers who are interested in solving problems with images or in making the world more visually interesting. They are artistic and have a good eye for detail, but are also capable of seeing the big picture and being flexible in their presentation of multiple design or pictorial ideas for a single project. They must have excellent interpersonal and communication skills since they almost always work closely with members of a team. They must be able to handle criticism and work under pressure to meet deadlines.

A Day in the Life—Duties and Responsibilities

Graphic designers and illustrators are responsible for planning and carrying out projects that fulfill their clients' needs. A major specialty today, for example, is branding, in which the designer works with a team of writers, artists, market researchers, and others to create a company's image, including a recognizable logo, stylized advertisements, catchy slogans, and high-tech trade show displays. The designer will suggest colors, images, fonts, and other artistic elements, then create several sample designs for each element of the branding campaign.

Graphic designers and illustrators create the covers and interior layouts for magazines, books, brochures, newspapers, and other print materials. Typically, they work with editors to acquire the articles and advertisements, and then fit them into the allotted space in the most appealing manner. Graphic designers select fonts, graphics, and other design elements (in collaboration with the client or author if the project is a book) and also design internal advertisements that are presented with the final product.

Study of graphic design and illustration includes the option to learn website design skills, so some designers/illustrators specialize in web design and are able to earn a living without working on any print design projects. Some graphic designers/illustrators collaborate with programmers to create video games, with authors to create graphic novels, and even with interior decorators and architects to design building spaces.

Self-employed graphic designers/illustrators must also spend some of their time marketing their services, billing customers, preparing contracts, and handling other administrative and business management tasks.

Duties and Responsibilities

- Designing images that convey a message or identify a product or organization
- Creating designs or illustrations by hand or using computer software
- Meeting with clients to determine their needs
- Deciding on the message that a design or illustration should portray
- Giving advice to clients on ways to reach an audience through visual means

OCCUPATION SPECIALTIES

Cartoonists

Cartoonists draw political cartoons, newspaper comics, or comic books. Their work is used in commercial applications, as well. They may work with animators in creating digital productions.

Drafters

Drafters use software to convert the designs of engineers and architects into technical drawings and plans.

Fashion Artists

Fashion Artists draw stylish illustrations of new clothing fashions for newspapers or related advertisements.

Illustrators

Illustrators create pictures for books, magazines, billboards, posters, and CD/DVD packages. They may work with multimedia artists in creating digital productions.

Medical and Scientific Illustrators

Medical and Scientific Illustrators draw precise illustrations of machines, plants, animals or parts of the human body or animal bodies for business and educational purposes.

Typographers

Typographers create type fonts for use in print and online publications. One major use is in signage, including "wayfinding" signs for drivers and other travelers.

WORK ENVIRONMENT

Physical Environment

Graphic designers and illustrators usually work in studios or offices surrounded by art samples and design reference materials. If a project has a tight deadline, the designer/illustrator can expect to work some evening hours or work on the design from their home computer until the project is done.

Human Environment

In larger design firms and departments, a graphic designer or illustrator is often one member of a creative team comprised of photographers, multimedia artists, web developers, and others who collaborate on projects under the supervision of a creative director. Designers/illustrators may also work with market researchers, architects, interior designers, content editors, clients, authors, and other professionals outside the firm.

Technological Environment

Graphic designers most often use Adobe Creative Suite software (Photoshop, Illustrator, and InDesign) for cover design, manipulating and creating illustrations, page layout design, editing and placing digital photographs, and other purposes. They also use digital photography and video cameras, scanners, printmaking equipment, printing and publishing equipment, and other tools. Each design project

Skills and Abilities

Communication Skills
- Expressing thoughts and ideas clearly
- Speaking and writing effectively

Creative/Artistic Skills
- Being able to create new ideas
- Being skilled in art and design

Interpersonal/Social Skills
- Being able to work independently and as part of a team
- Understanding others' wishes

Organization & Management Skills
- Managing time
- Meeting goals and deadlines

Technical Skills
- Applying technology to a task
- Performing technical work
- Working with different tools and media

is different and may require different resources, so graphic designers should enjoy learning new skills. Illustrators make use of computer software and traditional art materials in creating their works.

EDUCATION, TRAINING, AND ADVANCEMENT

High School/Secondary

Students should pursue a comprehensive college-preparatory program that includes courses in art, graphic design, computer science, and the social sciences. Other relevant courses include film, new media, photography, and industrial arts. Awareness of contemporary graphic design, web design, and animation software programs is extremely important. Most college admissions programs require a portfolio of artistic work, which might include digital designs, as well as hand-drawn sketches or paintings, sculpture, and other sample work.

Suggested High School Subjects
- Applied Communication
- Applied Math
- Arts
- Composition
- Computer Science
- Drawing & Painting
- English
- Graphic Communications
- Industrial Arts

Famous First

The first graphic design to receive a patent was a typeface designed by George Bruce of New York in 1842. The typeface was used in printed school primers. The first company logo to receive a trademark was that of the Bass brewery of England, which still uses its distinctive red triangle on its label.

College/Postsecondary

Most entry-level positions require a bachelor's degree from an art school or program. Graphic design programs include courses in studio art, design, computer graphics, printing, and other graphic design specialties. Programs should include the option to work an internship. A general awareness of contemporary design is also helpful. Illustration programs focus more on drawing, painting, and other manual methods while not excluding digital technologies. In either case, the development of a portfolio for use in future job searches is essential, so many graphic design and illustration students make an effort to obtain freelance work.

Related College Majors
- Design & Visual Communications
- Drawing & Painting
- Commercial Art & Illustration
- Graphic Design
- Industrial Design

Adult Job Seekers

Adults with a background in fine art, illustration, photography, typography, or another creative discipline can learn the fundamentals of graphic design and illustration and update their skills by taking graphic arts courses, which some schools offer in the evenings and on weekends to accommodate adult professionals. A portfolio can be assembled independently and/or in conjunction with classes.

Advancement for graphic designers and illustrators comes with experience or taking classes in new software or techniques to supplement current skills. Some designers/illustrators choose to establish their own firms. Advanced degrees can help experienced artists begin to obtain work in a different specialty, such as web animation.

Professional Certification and Licensure

There are no state licenses or nationally recognized certificates required for graphic designers or illustrators; however, the idea of professional certification has gained popularity, so it is advisable to follow the issue as it progresses. Getting certified on the use of a particular software program or type of equipment, for example, may be in order as one's career advances.

Additional Requirements

Graphic artists and illustrators must have a good eye for aesthetics, be extremely creative, enjoy art and design, and find satisfaction in continuing professional development. They should be willing to follow trends in advertising, web media, design, and illustration and should enjoy brainstorming for a single project. Although creativity is a plus, graphic designers/illustrators must be able to distance themselves from their work enough to accept a client's criticism and revisions of their ideas. Excellent people skills are a must in this collaborative field, which can be highly competitive and requires the ability to make and maintain good contacts with clients and colleagues.

Fun Fact

The typical client/graphic designer relationship lasts, on average, three years. In addition, it takes six months to a year (or more) from first contact to closing the deal.
Source: www.graphicdesign.com.

EARNINGS AND ADVANCEMENT

Earnings for self-employed graphic designers and illustrators vary widely. Those struggling to gain experience and a reputation may be forced to charge less for their work. Well-established freelancers may earn much more than salaried artists. Median annual earnings of graphic designers/illustrators were $46,110 in 2012. The lowest ten percent earned less than $27,772, and the highest ten percent earned more than $81,525.

Graphic designers and illustrators on salary may receive paid vacations, holidays, and sick days; life and health insurance; and retirement benefits. These are paid by the employer. Self-employed graphic designers must arrange for their own ways of meeting these costs.

Metropolitan Areas with the Highest Concentration of Jobs in this Occupation

Metropolitan area	Employment	Employment per thousand jobs	Hourly mean wage
New York-White Plains-Wayne, NY-NJ	14,260	2.77	$30.37
Los Angeles-Long Beach-Glendale, CA	9,260	2.39	$27.80
Chicago-Joliet-Naperville, IL	8,100	2.23	$24.63
Minneapolis-St. Paul-Bloomington, MN-WI	4,460	2.55	$23.84
Washington-Arlington-Alexandria, DC-VA-MD-WV	4,390	1.87	$30.85
Atlanta-Sandy Springs-Marietta, GA	3,750	1.66	$23.67
Philadelphia, PA	3,630	1.99	$24.60
Boston-Cambridge-Quincy, MA	3,190	1.87	$26.79

[1] Does not include self-employed. Source: Bureau of Labor Statistics, 2012

EMPLOYMENT AND OUTLOOK

Graphic designers and illustrators held about 191,000 jobs nationally in 2012. Some designers/illustrators do freelance work on the side while holding down a salaried position in the field or in another occupation. Employment of graphic designers/illustrators is expected to grow about as fast as the average for all occupations through the year 2020, which means employment is projected to increase about 13 percent. Demand for graphic designers and illustrators should increase because of the rapidly expanding demand for interactive media for mobile devices, websites, electronic publications and video entertainment. Advertising firms will also need designers and illustrators to create Web-based and print materials to promote the growing number of products and services available to consumers.

Employment Trend, Projected 2010–20

Total, All Occupations: 14%

Graphic Designers and Illustrators: 13%

Arts, Design, Entertainment, Sports, and Media Occupations: 13%

Note: "All Occupations" includes all occupations in the U.S. Economy. Source: U.S. Bureau of Labor Statistics, Employment Projections Program

Related Occupations
- Art Director
- Designer
- Desktop Publisher
- Drafter
- Industrial Designer
- Medical & Scientific Illustrator
- Multimedia Artist & Animator
- Web Developer

Related Occupations
- Graphic Designer & Illustrator

> # *Conversation With . . .*
> # NICK COMPARONE
> ### Graphic Designer, 7 years

1. What was your individual career path in terms of education, entry-level job, or other significant opportunity?

I went to school for graphic design; I got a bachelor's degree from Central Connecticut State University. I'd always done a lot of art and for me, design seemed a more feasible career path than fine art. Our design department had an in-house design firm, portfolio-reviewed, where four people per semester worked. I did that one semester, and I also designed for the college, for on-campus events and promotions, a paid, part-time position. Design firms recruited entry-level people and I interviewed at a local firm and was working there part-time by my last semester. After I graduated, they hired me full-time. When the firm dissolved, I took the majority of clients I was already working with and started freelancing.

2. Are there many job opportunities in your profession? In what specific areas?

As with anything, if you're good at what you do and work hard, you're going to be able to find a job. Always being on top of whatever the new thing is — that is always going to be helpful.

3. What do you wish you had known going into this profession?

We had a tough program in college and a lot of people felt like it was a lot of work and a lot of pressure. One of the biggest things I realized getting out of school is that the actual industry is more intensive. It's fast-paced with a quick turnaround. If you don't have a passion to do it, graphic design might not be the best direction to go in.

4. How do you see your profession changing in the next five years?

You're always going to have different trends, aesthetically. It depends on your demographic audience. But if you are gearing your work toward the up-and-coming generation, these are people who are used to constant, multiple messages. If you don't grab people's attention with a couple of seconds, you're done.

5. What role will technology play in those changes, and what skills will be required?

The whole in-your-hands-device technology in our culture is definitely big, and how we manufacture apps and devices in the future will continue to be big. It's information on the go, and being able to develop and design things to get into people's hands. All your bigger companies and industries need a mobile version of what they're doing.

A lot of people who may be versed in web design are going into app development. It's not as static; you are designing things that are more interactive. A lot of people think print's going to disappear; it's not. People are always going to need catalogs and brochures, and any of your higher-end companies are still going to use a lot of print stuff. You get a really nice piece in your hand, you feel the paper and see the ink. You can't do that on a computer screen. But there are always new technologies with print; digital presses let small businesses start up and have lower costs. A lot of designers are talking about 3D printing. That's going to be huge. You can print out mechanical things.

6. Do you have any general advice or additional professional insights to share with someone interested in your profession?

You're going to be working long hours, so it's really got to be something you know you can spend the time with and enjoy. It's also one of those fun professions where you can play around with things and get your hands dirty and see if you like it.

7. Can you suggest a valuable "try this" for students considering a career in your profession?

Redesign something – your favorite book cover or movie poster – and see how you feel about it.

SELECTED SCHOOLS

Many colleges and universities offer programs in graphic design and illustration. The student may also gain initial training at a technical/community college. Below are listed some of the more prominent institutions in this field.

Art Center College of Design
1700 Lida Street
Pasadena, CA 91103
626.396.2200
www.artcenter.edu

California Institute of the Arts
24700 McBean Parkway
Valencia, CA 91355
661.255.1050
www.calarts.edu

Carnegie Mellon University
5000 Forbes Avenue
Pittsburgh, PA 15213
412.268.2000
www.cmu.edu

Cranbrook Academy of Art
39221 Woodward Avenue
Bloomfield Hills, MI 48303
248.645.3300
www.cranbrookart.edu

Maryland Institute College of Art
1300 W. Mount Royale Avenue
Baltimore, MD 21217
410.669.9200
www.mica.edu

Pratt Institute
200 Willoughby Avenue
Brooklyn, NY 11205
718.636.3600
www.pratt.edu

Rhode Island School of Design
2 College Street
Providence, RI 02903
401.454.6100
www.risd.edu

School of Visual Arts
209 E. 23rd Street
New York, NY 10010
212.592.2100
www.sva.edu

Virginia Commonwealth University
821 W. Franklin Street
Richmond, VA 23284
804.828.0100
www.vcu.edu

Yale University
New Haven, CT 06520
203.432.4771
www.yale.edu

MORE INFORMATION

American Institute of Graphic Arts
164 Fifth Avenue
New York, NY 10010
212.807.1990
www.aiga.org

Association of Independent Colleges of Art and Design
236 Hope Street
Providence, RI 02906
401.270.5991
www.aicad.org

Graphic Artists Guild
32 Broadway, Suite 1114
New York, NY 10004-1612
212.791.3400
www.graphicartistsguild.org

National Art Education Association
1806 Robert Fulton Drive, Suite 300
Reston, VA 20191-1590
703.860.8000
www.naea-reston.org

National Association of Schools of Art & Design
11250 Roger Bacon Drive, Suite 21
Reston, VA 20190-5248
703.437.0700
nasad.arts-accredit.org/index.jsp

Society for Environmental Graphic Design
1000 Vermont Avenue NW, Suite 400
Washington, DC 20005
202.638.5555
www.segd.org

Society of Illustrators
128 E. 63rd Street
New York, NY 10065
212.838.2560
www.societyillustrators.org

Society of Publication Designers
27 Union Square W., Suite 207
New York, NY 10003
212.223.3332
www.spd.org/

Briana Nadeau/Editor

High School Teacher

Snapshot

Career Cluster(s): Education & Training

Interests: Teaching, lesson planning, leading instructional activities, adolescent development, student safety, peer mentoring

Earnings (Yearly Average): $57,200 (high school); $55,860 (middle school)

Employment & Outlook: Average Growth Expected

OVERVIEW

Sphere of Work

Secondary and Middle school teachers, also called middle and high school teachers, are teaching professionals that focus on the educational needs of adolescents. Secondary and Middle school teachers may be generalists with knowledge and talents in a wide range of subjects, or they may have an academic specialization, such as history, language arts, mathematics,

physical science, art, or music. Secondary and Middle school teachers work in both public and private school settings. They may be assigned student and peer mentoring and administrative tasks in addition to their teaching responsibilities.

Work Environment

Secondary and Middle school teachers work in high schools and middle schools designed to meet the social and educational needs of adolescents. The amounts and types of resources in middle and high schools and middle and high school classrooms such as art supplies, music lessons, physical education facilities, fieldtrips, and assistant teachers, differ depending on the school's financial resources and the educational philosophy directing the curriculum. Middle and high schools may be private or public. They may be an independent entity or part of a larger school that encompasses more grade levels.

Profile

Working Conditions: Work Indoors
Physical Strength: Light Work
Education Needs: Bachelor's Degree, Master's Degree
Licensure/Certification: Required
Opportunities For Experience: Internship, Volunteer Work, Part Time Work
Holland Interest Score*: SAE

* See Appendix A

Occupation Interest

Individuals drawn to the profession of Secondary and Middle school teacher tend to be intelligent, creative, patient, and caring. Secondary and Middle school teachers, who instruct and nurture secondary and middle school students, should find satisfaction in spending long hours instructing and mentoring adolescents. Successful Secondary and Middle school teachers excel at long-term scheduling, lesson planning, communication, and problem solving.

A Day in the Life—Duties and Responsibilities

A Secondary and Middle school teacher's daily duties and responsibilities include planning, teaching, classroom preparation, student care, family outreach, school duties, and professional development.

Secondary and Middle school teachers plan and execute specific teaching plans and lessons. They may also be responsible for buying or securing donations for classroom or project supplies. They assign homework and projects, teach good study habits, grade student work, maintain accurate academic records for all students, and lead and administer activities such as lab sessions, reviews, exams, student clubs, and small group learning.

Classroom preparation and cleaning duties may include labeling materials, organizing desk and work areas, displaying student work on bulletin boards and display boards, and, depending on janitorial support, cleaning up and sanitizing spaces at the end of the school day.

Secondary and Middle school teachers greet students as they arrive in the classroom, promote a supportive learning environment, maintain student safety and health, provide appropriate levels of discipline in the classroom and school environment, build student cooperation and listening skills, and work to present lessons in multiple ways to accommodate diverse learning styles.

Some teachers may provide family outreach by greeting student families at school drop off and dismissal times and using a student school-family communication notebook when required. All teachers must communicate regularly with families regarding student academic performance.

Secondary and Middle school teachers must attend staff meetings, participate in peer mentoring, enforce school policies, and lead open houses for prospective families. Teachers may also be responsible for overseeing students in the school hallways and for supervising school fieldtrips. Their professional development duties include attendance at professional meetings, continued training, and recertification as needed.

Secondary and Middle school teachers must work on a daily basis to meet the needs of all students, families, fellow teachers, and school administrators.

Duties and Responsibilities

- Preparing lesson plans
- Guiding the learning activities of students
- Instructing students through demonstrations or lectures
- Evaluating students through daily work, tests and reports, or through a portfolio of the students' artwork or writing
- Computing and recording grades
- Maintaining discipline
- Counseling and referring students when academic or other problems arise
- Conferring with parents and staff
- Assisting with student clubs, teams, plays and other student activities
- Supplementing lecturing with audio-visual teaching aides

OCCUPATION SPECIALTIES

Resource Teachers

Resource Teachers teach basic academic subjects to students requiring remedial work using special help programs to improve scholastic levels.

WORK ENVIRONMENT

Physical Environment

A Secondary and Middle school teacher's physical environment is the middle and high school classroom. Secondary and Middle school teachers tend to have a fair bit of autonomy in deciding classroom layout and curriculum. Secondary and Middle school teachers generally work forty-hour weeks and follow an annual academic schedule with ample winter, spring, and summer vacations. Summer teaching opportunities in summer school and summer camps are common.

Relevant Skills and Abilities

Communication Skills
- Expressing thoughts and ideas
- Persuading others
- Speaking effectively
- Writing concisely

Interpersonal/Social Skills
- Being patient
- Cooperating with others
- Working as a member of a team

Organization & Management Skills
- Coordinating tasks
- Making decisions
- Managing people/groups

Research & Planning Skills
- Creating ideas
- Using logical reasoning

Human Environment

Secondary and Middle school teachers are in constant contact with adolescents, student families, school administrators, and fellow teachers. Secondary and Middle school teachers may have students with physical and mental disabilities as well as students who are English language learners (ELL). Secondary and Middle school teachers must be comfortable working with people from a wide range of backgrounds and able to incorporate lessons on diversity into their teaching.

Technological Environment

Secondary and Middle school classrooms increasingly include computers for student use. Teachers should be comfortable using Internet communication tools and teaching adolescent students to use educational software. Teachers may also use computers to perform administrative tasks and record student progress. Secondary and Middle school teachers should be comfortable with standard office and audiovisual equipment.

EDUCATION, TRAINING, AND ADVANCEMENT

Middle and high school/Secondary and Middle

Middle and high school students interested in becoming Secondary and Middle school teachers should develop good study habits. Interested middle and high school students should take a broad range of courses in education, child development, science, mathematics, history, language arts, physical education, and the arts. Those interested in the field of education may benefit from seeking internships or volunteer/part-time work with children and teachers at camps and afterschool programs.

Suggested High School Subjects
- Algebra
- Arts
- Audio-Visual
- Biology
- Child Growth & Development
- College Preparatory
- Composition
- Computer Science
- English
- Foreign Languages
- Government
- Graphic Communications
- History
- Humanities
- Literature
- Mathematics
- Political Science
- Psychology
- Science
- Social Studies

- Sociology
- Speech
- Theatre & Drama

Famous First

The first junior high school, or middle school, was the Indianola Junior High School in Columbus, OH, which opened in September 1909. The school served 7th, 8th, and 9th grade students along with "such of the first six grades as might be necessary to relieve neighboring districts."

College/Postsecondary

College students interested in working towards a degree or career in Secondary and Middle school education should consider majoring in education and earning initial teaching certification as part of their undergraduate education program. Aspiring teachers should complete coursework in education, child development, and psychology. Those interested in pursuing a career in secondary education often major in the subject area they wish to teach. Prior to graduation, college students intent on becoming Secondary and Middle school teachers should gain teaching experience through an internship or volunteer/part-time work; prospective teachers should also research master's of education programs and state teaching certification requirements.

Related College Majors
- Agricultural Teacher Education
- Art Teacher Education
- Bilingual/Bicultural Education
- Business Teacher Education (Vocational)
- Computer Teacher Education
- Education Admin & Supervision, General
- Education of the Blind & Visually Handicapped
- Education of the Deaf & Hearing Impaired
- Education of the Specific Learning Disabled
- Education of the Speech Impaired

- Elementary/Pre-Elem/Early Childhood/Kindergarten Teacher Education
- English Teacher Education
- Family & Consumer Science Education
- Foreign Languages Teacher Education
- Health & Physical Education, General
- Health Teacher Education
- Marketing Operations Teacher Education (Vocational)
- Mathematics Teacher Education
- Music Teacher Education
- Physical Education Teaching & Coaching
- Science Teacher Education, General
- Secondary and Middle/Jr. High/Middle School Teacher Education
- Special Education, General
- Speech Teacher Education
- Technology Teacher Education/Industrial Arts Teacher Education
- Trade & Industrial Teacher Education (Vocational)
- Vocational Teacher Education

Adult Job Seekers

Adults seeking jobs as Secondary and Middle school teachers should research the education and certification requirements of their home states as well of the schools where they might seek employment. Adult job seekers in the education field may benefit from the employment workshops and job lists maintained by professional teaching associations, such as the American Federation of Teachers (AFT).

Professional Certification and Licensure

Professional certification and licensure requirements for Secondary and Middle school teachers vary between states and between schools. Secondary and Middle school teachers generally earn a master's in education, with a single-subject teaching concentration in language arts, history, science, political science, music, physical education, or art, and obtain a state teaching license for grades eight through twelve. Single-subject teaching licenses for Secondary and Middle school teachers require academic coursework, supervised student teaching, and successful completion of a general teaching exam. Background checks are also typically required. State departments of education offer state teaching licenses and require continuing education and recertification on a regular basis. Savvy and successful job seekers will find out the requirements that apply to them and satisfy the requirements prior to seeking employment.

Additional Requirements

Individuals who find satisfaction, success, and job security as Secondary and Middle school teachers will be knowledgeable about the profession's requirements, responsibilities, and opportunities. Successful Secondary and Middle school teachers engage in ongoing professional development. Secondary and Middle school teachers must have high levels of integrity and ethics as they work with adolescents and have access to the personal information of student families. Membership in professional teaching associations is encouraged among beginning and tenured Secondary and Middle school teachers as a means of building status in a professional community and networking.

Fun Facts

Teachers earn 14 percent less than people in other professions that require similar levels of education. They work 52 hours per week.
Source: http://www.theteachersalaryproject.org

Neuroscientists from the Brain and Creativity Institute at the University of Southern California conducted a five-year study showing that music instruction appears to accelerate brain development in young children, especially areas responsible for processing sound, language development, speech perception, and reading skills.
Source: https://news.usc.edu/102681/

EARNINGS AND ADVANCEMENT

Earnings of Secondary and Middle school teachers depend on their education and experience, and the size and location of the school district. Pay is usually higher in large, metropolitan areas. Secondary and Middle school teachers in private schools generally earn less than public Secondary and Middle school teachers.

Median annual earnings of secondary school teachers was $57,200 in 2014; the comparable figure for middle school teachers was $55,860. Secondary and Middle school teachers receive extra pay for coaching sports and working with students in extracurricular activities. Some Secondary and Middle school teachers earn extra income during the summer working in the school system or in other jobs.

Secondary and Middle school teachers have vacation days when their school is closed, as in during the summer and over holidays. They may also receive life and health insurance and retirement benefits. These are usually paid by the employer.

Metropolitan Areas with the Highest Employment Level in this Occupation

Metropolitan area	Employment	Employment per thousand jobs	Annual mean wage
New York-Jersey City-White Plains, NY-NJ	40,590	6.26	$82,260
Los Angeles-Long Beach-Glendale, CA	29,170	7.11	$76,710
Chicago-Naperville-Arlington Heights, IL	24,010	6.72	$74,960
Houston-The Woodlands-Sugar Land, TX	22,930	7.83	$57,520
Dallas-Plano-Irving, TX	17,080	7.33	$55,330
Washington-Arlington-Alexandria, DC-VA-MD-WV	13,910	5.75	$73,330
Atlanta-Sandy Springs-Roswell, GA	13,300	5.36	$56,620
Minneapolis-St. Paul-Bloomington, MN-WI	12,650	6.73	$67,200
Nassau County-Suffolk County, NY	12,020	9.42	$101,950
Baltimore-Columbia-Towson, MD	11,570	8.80	$64,400

Does not include self-employed.

EMPLOYMENT AND OUTLOOK

There were approximately 1.6 million Secondary and Middle school teachers employed nationally in 2014. Employment is expected to grow about as fast as the average for all occupations through the year 2024, which means employment is projected to increase 4 percent to 8 percent. Most job openings will occur as a result of the expected retirement of a large number of teachers.

The supply of Secondary and Middle school teachers is likely to increase in response to growing student enrollment, improved job opportunities, more teacher involvement in school policy, greater public interest in education and higher salaries. Job prospects are greater in central cities and rural areas. However, job growth could be limited by state and local government budget deficits.

Employment Trend, Projected 2014–24

Total, all occupations: 7%

Preschool, primary, secondary, and special education school teachers: 6%

Secondary and Middle school teachers: 6%

Note: "All Occupations" includes all occupations in the U.S. Economy. Source: U.S. Bureau of Labor Statistics, Employment Projections Program

Related Occupations
- Career/Technology Education Teacher
- College Faculty Member
- Education Administrator
- Elementary School Teacher
- Principal
- Special Education Teacher
- Teacher Assistant

Conversation With . . .
PHILLIP RIGGS

Music Instructor band and choir
North Carolina School of Science and Mathematics
Durham, North Carolina
Music teacher, 29 years

1. What was your individual career path in terms of education/training, entry-level job, or other significant opportunity?

Early on, I knew I wanted to be a music teacher. I started playing trumpet in junior high school and went on to euphonium and snare drum in my high school concert and marching bands. During high school, I also played in several honor band events. One stands out. Composer Dr. Jack Stamp was conducting, and I remember thinking, "I would really like to do what he does."

I graduated with a B.A in Music Education from Appalachian State University. My first teaching job was in a small 8-12 grade school. As a new teacher, I needed to learn to understand my community's expectations. For instance, the school wanted the traditional "Pomp and Circumstance" for graduation, while I wanted something more ambitious. I moved on to teach middle school band in a larger rural system where the veteran music teachers took time to nurture my growth as a teacher.

Ten years after graduating, I earned my Master in Education from the University of North Carolina Greensboro—with a concentration in technology and supervision—while continuing to teach. Waiting to go back to school gave me a greater appreciation for the new material I was learning and helped me focus on the areas I needed for growth.

After team-teaching middle and high school for many years, I became the Fine Arts Chair of a new high school in the Winston-Salem/Forsyth County School System. It was an exciting time, and I assumed I would retire from such a challenging and prestigious job.

However, after three years, an opportunity presented itself that I couldn't pass up: becoming the band director at the country's first state-sponsored residential school. NCSSM is consistently recognized as a top 20 school. Teaching here allows me to make music with some of our state's best and brightest juniors and seniors. Part of the school's mission is outreach, so I also visit music teacher's classrooms across the state and conduct workshops for various students and their directors.

I'm active in a number of professional organizations that support music education. In 2016, I was named the GRAMMY Music Educator of the Year after being nominated by a former student. It's been a wonderful experience but it all comes back to relationships. I've had the opportunity cast a wider net professionally, and to be a spokesman for music education.

2. What are the most important skills and/or qualities for someone in your profession?

Relationship building with students, their parents, colleagues and the community; and establishing a support network by seeking out mentors.

3. What do you wish you had known going into this profession?

Teaching music is not a job that you go to in the morning and leave in the afternoon. You are always thinking about the next event, new teaching methods, and certain students that you can help.

4. Are there many job opportunities in your profession? In what specific areas?

If willing to go to another state and willing to teach various age levels, new teachers can usually find a job. However, I am concerned when new teachers take a job that may not be ideal – say the school has a tiny band budget, or a tough band schedule. Since the average new teacher leaves the profession after three years, and since many music teachers are the only music teacher in the school, they may leave based on limited experience. If the teaching position is a revolving door, students will never benefit. To counteract that, quality mentor programs are offered by state associations of the National Association for Music Educators and organizations like the National Band Association. They also help young teachers discover solutions in their current jobs and help them determine if their current job is the best fit.

5. How do you see your profession changing in the next five years, what role will technology play in those changes, and what skills will be required?

Research using fMRI (functional MRI) shows objectively how brain neurons are firing when students are participating in musical ensembles. This activity is likely the only thing that students do during the school day that uses both hemispheres of the brain simultaneously. In short, music makes better brains.

Music teachers often are the first teachers in a school to embrace new technology and search for ways to incorporate it in their classrooms, even if they are teaching traditional concepts and content.

6. What do you enjoy most about your job? What do you enjoy least about your job?

Conducting a successful student concert following many hours of rehearsal is exciting. However, enjoying the journey of making music daily is important. Even more gratifying is the look of success after an individual masters a concept that they have struggled with.

Unfortunately, the emphasis on standardized testing limits teachers' opportunities to take advantage of "teachable moments," or explore an individual class's interests.

7. Can you suggest a valuable "try this" for students considering a career in your profession?

Most prospective music education students had a music teacher who made a difference in their lives. I encourage these students to visit as many music classrooms as possible. You can't start too early.

MORE INFORMATION

American Association for Employment in Education
3040 Riverside Drive, Suite 125
Columbus, OH 43221
614.485.1111
www.aaee.org

American Association for Health Education
1900 Association Drive
Reston, VA 20191-1598
800.213.7193
www.aahperd.org/aahe

American Association of Colleges for Teacher Education
1307 New York Avenue, NW
Suite 300
Washington, DC 20005-4701
202.293.2450
www.aacte.org

American Federation of Teachers
Public Affairs Department
555 New Jersey Avenue, NW
Washington, DC 20001
202.879.4400
www.aft.org

National Association for Sport and Physical Education
1900 Association Drive
Reston, VA 20191
800.213.7193
www.aahperd.org/naspe

National Board for Professional Teaching Standards
1525 Wilson Boulevard, Suite 500
Arlington, VA 22209
800.228.3224
www.nbpts.org

National Council for Accreditation of Teacher Education
2010 Massachusetts Avenue, NW
Suite 500
Washington, DC 20036-1023
202.466.7496
www.ncate.org

National Council of Teachers of English
1111 W. Kenyon Road
Urbana, Illinois 61801-1096
877.369.6283
www.ncte.org/second

National Council of Teachers of Mathematics
1906 Association Drive
Reston, VA 20191-1502
703.620.9840
www.nctm.org

National Education Association
1201 16th Street, NW
Washington, DC 20036-3290
202.833.4000
www.nea.org

National Science Teachers Association
1840 Wilson Boulevard
Arlington, VA 22201
703.243.7100
www.nsta.org

Simone Isadora Flynn/Editor

Industrial Designer

Snapshot

Career Cluster: Art & Design; Manufacturing

Interests: Design, consumer culture, technological trends, solving problems, being creative

Earnings (Yearly Average): $64,620

Employment & Outlook: Slower than Average Growth Expected

OVERVIEW

Sphere of Work

Industrial designers, also known as commercial designers or product designers, plan and create new products that are both functional and stylish. They improve older products by enhancing certain features or by making them safer or more user-friendly. They usually specialize in certain consumer goods, such as cars, toys, housewares, or personal grooming accessories. In addition to designing products, some industrial designers also design packaging for the products or displays for trade shows and may even put their creative skills to work on corporate branding campaigns.

Work Environment

Industrial designers are employed by specialized design firms as well as larger companies and manufacturers. Some are self-employed. They spend much of their time in offices or studios where they design products and in conference rooms with members of product development teams, typically comprised of engineers, strategic planners, financial managers, advertising and marketing specialists, and other creative consultants. They may need to spend some time working in factories and/or testing facilities. Most work a forty-hour week, with additional evening and weekend hours as needed to meet deadlines.

Profile

Working Conditions: Work Indoors
Physical Strength: Light Work
Education Needs: Bachelor's Degree, Master's Degree
Licensure/Certification: Usually Not Required
Opportunities For Experience: Internship
Holland Interest Score*: AES

* See Appendix A

Occupation Interest

Industrial design attracts artistic people who look upon consumer products as potential canvases for their creativity. They take satisfaction in products that look good while also being functional and user-friendly. Industrial designers keep up with the latest trends and stay engaged with contemporary consumer culture, design, and technological trends. They must be technically savvy, with strong spatial, communication, and problem-solving skills. The ability to work under deadlines is important.

A Day in the Life—Duties and Responsibilities

The work performed by an industrial designer depends on the size and type of his or her employer and the particular types of products that employer manufactures or builds. Although many industrial designers work for product manufacturers, others work for specialized businesses like architectural firms and medical companies, and still others are self-employed. The work done by industrial designers is increasingly more commercial as companies focus more closely on consumer trends and market research.

Industrial designers are included early on in the corporate product development phase. They may be asked to sketch products that have already been identified or specific details or components for products that need to be upgraded. In some cases, an industrial designer sees a need for a product and recommends the idea to a research and development team for consideration. During the early stages, the designer may research other products, sometimes attending a trade show to view the competition, or survey potential users for desired features.

Once a product has been conceptualized, the industrial designer sketches out designs, either by hand or with design software. The designs might show a smaller model, a product that is easier to hold or more ergonomic, or some other type of innovation. The designer might also create a model from clay or foam board, often first rendering it in 3-D software. The designer suggests specific colors, materials, and manufacturing processes that are within the limitations of the budget. Those who work for manufacturers might render drawings in computer-aided industrial design (CAID) programs that can direct machines to build the products automatically. Industrial designers also communicate their designs and ideas in writing and give presentations to clients or managers.

Before a product is released for the market, the industrial designer might oversee or participate in its testing, at which time he or she may need to make refinements to the design to correct unforeseen issues or improve the quality of the product.

Duties and Responsibilities

- Studying the potential need for new products
- Studying other similar products on the market
- Consulting with sales and marketing personnel to obtain design ideas and to estimate public reaction to new designs
- Sketching designs
- Making comprehensive drawings of the product

OCCUPATION SPECIALTIES

Package Designers

Package Designers design containers for products, such as foods, beverages, toiletries, cigarettes and medicines.

WORK ENVIRONMENT

Transferable Skills and Abilities

Communication Skills
- Expressing thoughts and ideas
- Speaking effectively

Creative/Artistic Skills
- Being skilled in art, music or dance

Interpersonal/Social Skillss
- Cooperating with others
- Working as a member of a team

Organization & Management Skills
- Making decisions
- Paying attention to and handling details
- Performing routine work

Research & Planning Skills
- Creating ideas
- Setting goals and deadlines
- Using logical reasoning

Technical Skills
- Performing scientific, mathematical and technical work
- Working with data or numbers

Physical Environment

Industrial designers usually work in comfortable offices or studios. Those who regularly oversee product manufacturing might be at some risk for health issues related to their factory environments.

Human Environment

Industrial designers usually report to the creative director of the design firm or manager of a department, and they may oversee an intern or assistant as he or she gains experience. Interaction with clients and other members of a product development team may include lively brainstorming sessions as well as harsh criticism about ideas and designs. Self-employed industrial designers interact with others less often as they usually work from home offices.

Technological Environment

Industrial designers use a variety of art tools and supplies to build models and sketch designs, but much of their work is also performed using computer-aided design (CAD) software, computer-aided industrial design (CAID) software, and modeling, animation, and design software.

EDUCATION, TRAINING, AND ADVANCEMENT

High School/Secondary

Students should take a college-preparatory program that includes courses in English, math, and science, including physics and trigonometry. Electives should include drafting, drawing, and other art courses (sculpture, painting, ceramics, and photography) and/or industrial arts (woodworking and metalworking). Other useful courses include psychology, engineering, and business. Students need to prepare a portfolio for admission to postsecondary art and design programs. Because this is a hands-on field, students should put together models, visit art museums, and engage in other cultural and educational activities that encourage critical and creative thinking skills.

Suggested High School Subjects

- Algebra
- Applied Communication
- Applied Math
- Applied Physics
- Arts
- Blueprint Reading
- College Preparatory
- Drafting
- English

- Geometry
- Industrial Arts
- Mechanical Drawing
- Photography
- Pottery
- Trigonometry
- Woodshop

Famous First

The first patent for a design was issued in 1844 to George Bruce of New York City for a printing typeface.

College/Postsecondary

A bachelor's degree in industrial design or engineering, ideally with a minor in art or design, is the standard minimum requirement for most entry-level jobs in this field; some employers prefer to hire those with a master's degree. Students must acquire skills in drawing, CAD and design software, and building 3-D models by hand, as well as knowledge about industrial materials and manufacturing processes. Courses that build understanding of humans and society, such as psychology, anthropology, human ecology, and philosophy, are also important. Business skills are required for some jobs. Students should plan to apply for an internship and prepare a portfolio of their best work.

Related College Majors
- Industrial Design
- Industrial/Manufacturing Technology

Adult Job Seekers

Industrial design draws on many different abilities, skills, and knowledge. Adults with a close familiarity with industry-specific products, such as medical equipment or sporting goods, could build upon that experience by taking industrial design classes. Adults with a background in art might simply need to add engineering and/or CAD training to their current skill set. Interested adults should discuss options with college admissions counselors.

Most industrial designers begin their careers as interns. They are given assignments of increasing responsibility and prestige as they become more experienced and prove their abilities. In time, an industrial designer may be able to advance to a supervisory position or establish his or her own design firm. Teaching at the college level, writing books, and consulting are other options for those with adequate experience and education.

Professional Certification and Licensure

No professional license or certification is required. Certificates are sometimes awarded upon completion of associate's degree programs.

Additional Requirements

Designers must have good eyesight, including the ability to see different colors. Problem-solving skills, creativity, self-discipline, awareness of cultural trends, and open-mindedness are all desirable. Industrial designers should develop a strong portfolio of their work, as this is often the deciding factor in the hiring process.

Fun Fact

Red Dot Design Awards are like the Oscars of the industrial design world. A few products that won in 2015 include plastic Birkenstock sandals, the Triumph Magic Wire bra, and the BackBeatFIT sports headset.
Source: http://www.dexigner.com

EARNINGS AND ADVANCEMENT

Earnings of industrial designers depend on the individual's education and experience and the type, size, and geographic location of the employer. Industrial designers who have their own consulting firms may have fluctuating incomes, depending on their business for the year. Some industrial designers may work on retainers, which means they may receive flat fees for given periods of time. During any given period, industrial designers can work on retainers for many different companies.

Median annual earnings of industrial designers were $64,620 in 2014. The lowest ten percent earned less than $37,030, and the highest ten percent earned more than $100,070.

Industrial designers may receive paid vacations, holidays, and sick days; life and health insurance; and retirement benefits. These are usually paid by the employer.

Metropolitan Areas with the Highest Employment Level in this Occupation

Metropolitan area	Employment	Employment per thousand jobs	Annual mean wage
New York-White Plains-Wayne, NY-NJ	1,920	0.36	$75,240
Warren-Troy-Farmington Hills, MI	1,900	1.66	$78,240
Detroit-Livonia-Dearborn, MI	1,590	2.21	$81,150
Los Angeles-Long Beach-Glendale, CA	1,510	0.37	$64,120
Chicago-Joliet-Naperville, IL	710	0.19	$67,220
Santa Ana-Anaheim-Irvine, CA	560	0.38	$73,180
Atlanta-Sandy Springs-Marietta, GA	540	0.23	$68,490
Columbus, OH	420	0.43	$63,920
Cincinnati-Middletown, OH-KY-IN	420	0.41	$70,890
Minneapolis-St. Paul-Bloomington, MN-WI	390	0.21	$61,700

Source: Bureau of Labor Statistics

EMPLOYMENT AND OUTLOOK

Industrial designers held about 40,000 jobs in 2014. Employment is expected to grow somewhat slower than the average for all occupations through the year 2024, which means employment is projected to increase 0 percent to 4 percent. Demand for industrial designers will stem from continued emphasis on product quality and safety, design of new products that are easy and comfortable to use and high technology products in medicine, transportation and other fields.

Employment Trend, Projected 2014–24

Total, all occupations: 7%

Art and design workers: 2%

Commercial and industrial designers: 2%

Note: "All Occupations" includes all occupations in the U.S. Economy. Source: U.S. Bureau of Labor Statistics, Employment Projections Program

Related Occupations

- Designer
- Graphic Designer
- Merchandise Displayer
- Multimedia Artist & Animator

Conversation With . . .
JONATHAN DALTON, IDSA

CEO and Co-Founder, thrive
Atlanta, Georgia
Industrial design, 20 years

1. What was your individual career path in terms of education/training, entry-level job, or other significant opportunity?

Originally, I wanted to be an aerospace engineer, but I quickly found I wasn't good enough at math. Growing up I was always very creative, always building and drawing things. My grandfather built me my first drawing board when I was nine. With my engineering ambitions shelved, I started thinking about architecture school. One of my mum's cousins, who is an architect, said, "It sounds great, but the reality is you're going to be working on homes and additions and it's all code and very dry." He suggested industrial design. I found the book, Presentation Techniques: A Guide to Drawing and Presenting Design Ideas by English designer Dick Powell. It's basically how to do great product renderings. I thought, "Wow—you get paid to do that?" I'm from England, and I was doing my A Levels—the three big subjects you do at the end of high school. I was doing chemistry, physics, and math at first, but I dropped math and took design instead. That's where it all began.

Out of college, I worked for Electrolux for three years. A lot of my friends had interned in the States and there were great agencies doing great work that turned all our heads. So after three years, I joined Ziba Design in Portland, Oregon—one of the world's best industrial design agencies. It was an incredible experience. In five years, I went from junior designer to creative director. I then joined Altitude Inc. in Boston and from there, I joined Philips Design, the world's largest design group, in Atlanta. I headed up their industrial design group and outside consulting for four years. It helped me understand how to launch my business—thrive—which I did in 2010. Most of my design work has been appliances and medical products, but I've done lots of other stuff over the years.

2. What are the most important skills and/or qualities for someone in your profession?

The biggest one is problem-solving. You have to be a good analytical thinker. Obviously, you've got to be creative. You have to be empathetic and able to walk in someone else's shoes. Design sits between two worlds in many ways. Designers can be consumer advocates in terms of designing products that people love, but also have to consider engineering and marketing needs. "Design thinking" is a big buzzword in the corporate world.

3. What do you wish you had known going into this profession?

To be successful, you have to put a business lens on design. It can't be creativity for creativity's sake.

4. Are there many job opportunities in your profession? In what specific areas?

It's exploding right now. Chief Design Officer is a title that has become more prevalent in the last five years as organizations start to realize that they can't differentiate their products just on technology and features alone; they have to differentiate on experience.

5. How do you see your profession changing in the next five years? What role will technology play in those changes, and what skills will be required?

We're seeing big shifts. There will always be physical products but physical products now are more often a portal to a digital experience. Industrial design principles are being transferred to the services around a product, the product ecosystem, and a lot of that will obviously be more virtual than tangible. It's a real golden age of design right now. Design is being seen as a strategic business tool and that was never the case before. It was always the lipstick on the product at the end of the day.

6. What do you enjoy most about your job? What do you enjoy least about your job?

You never do the same thing twice. I get easily bored and I have never been bored in this profession. There's always a challenge or a problem to solve.

I'm not very good at helping steer design through bureaucracy. I got good at explaining the value of design, because I had to, but in an ideal world it's something you wouldn't have to do because everyone understood it already.

7. Can you suggest a valuable "try this" for students considering a career in your profession?

The Industrial Designers Society of America (idsa.org) has chapters across the country and many run outreach programs for schools, taking a problem and working as a team to solve it, typically over two weekends. It's sponsored by design agencies and corporations that value design. It's all about teaching kids how to think like a designer. My company, thrive, is an ISDA Ambassador of Excellence. Also, many cities hold a "Design Week" event with various activities like open houses at agencies. It's a great way to peek inside and speak to people who work there and get a sense of what the profession's about.

SELECTED SCHOOLS

Many colleges and universities offer programs in design and illustration. The student may also gain initial training at a technical/community college. Below are listed some of the more prominent institutions in this field.

Art Center College of Design
1700 Lida Street
Pasadena, CA 91103
626.396.2200
www.artcenter.edu

California College of the Arts
1111 Eighth Street
San Francisco, CA 94107
415.703.9523
www.cca.edu

Carnegie Mellon University
5000 Forbes Avenue
Pittsburgh, PA 15213
412.268.2000
www.cmu.edu

Cranbrook Academy of Art
39221 Woodward Avenue
Bloomfield Hills, MI 48303
248.645.3300
www.cranbrookart.edu

Ohio State University
258 Hopkins Hall
Columbus, OH 43210
614.292.5072
art.osu.edu

Pratt Institute
200 Willoughby Avenue
Brooklyn, NY 11205
718.636.3600
www.pratt.edu

Rhode Island School of Design
2 College Street
Providence, RI 02903
401.454.6100
www.risd.edu

Rochester Institute of Technology
73 Lomb Memorial Drive
Rochester, NY 14623
585.475.2239
www.rit.edu

School of the Art Institute of Chicago
37 South Wabash Avenue
Chicago, IL 60603
800.232.7242
www.saic.edu

School of Visual Arts
209 E. 23rd Street
New York, NY 10010
212.592.2100
www.sva.edu

MORE INFORMATION

Association of Women Industrial Designers
P.O. Box 468, Old Chelsea Station
New York, NY 10011
www.awidweb.com

Core77
561 Broadway, 6th Floor
New York, NY 10012
212.965.1998
www.core77.com

Industrial Designers Society of America
45195 Business Court, Suite 250
Dulles, VA 20166-6717
703.707.6000
www.idsa.org

Organization of Black Designers
300 M Street, SW, Suite N110
Washington, DC 20024-4019
202.659.3918
www.core77.com/OBD/welcome.html

University & College Designers Association
199 W. Enon Springs Road, Suite 300
Smyrna, TN 37167
615.459.4559
www.ucda.com

Sally Driscoll/Editor

Interior Designer

Snapshot

Career Cluster(S): Art & Design; Hospitality & Tourism
Interests: Art; business, helping others, communicating with others
Earnings (Yearly Average): $52,970
Employment & Outlook: Average Growth Expected

OVERVIEW

Sphere of Work

Interior designers are responsible for the aesthetic aspects of the interior of a building or specific space, whether it is commercial or residential. They deal with how colors, textures, light, furniture, and space work together to develop safe, functional, and attractive design solutions that meet client needs. Commercial designers work on large projects such as hotels and restaurants, while residential designers focus on private homes. Some designers are involved in the design and planning of architectural components, such as crown molding, built-in bookshelves, and building layouts. As such, interior designers often consult blueprints and have an understanding of building and

fire codes. All interior designers must work within a client's budget, charging customers for time, drawings, materials, and workroom labor.

Work Environment

Because interior designers spend much of their time with clients and vendors pricing individual aspects of each job, they are not constantly working in an office environment. Job functions outside of the office can include time spent shopping for necessary items and materials. When they are in their offices (or working from their homes), interior designers spend many hours placing orders, following up, and making creative decisions. Some designers work in a shop where the "storefront" displays gift-type items, with design services within for those interested clients; others work in furniture showrooms, which are open to the public.

Profile

Working Conditions: Work Indoors
Physical Strength: Light Work
Education Needs:
Technical/Community College,
Bachelor's Degree
Licensure/Certification:
Recommended
Physical Abilities Not Required: No
Heavy Work
Opportunities For Experience:
Internship, Part-Time Work
Holland Interest Score*: AES
* See Appendix A

Occupation Interest

Individuals attracted to the interior design profession need to be strategic in visualizing what a customer needs or envisions—creativity gives interior designers the ability to explain an idea or concept to a client and then sell it. They should take notice of their surroundings and have an interest in physical spaces and their functionality. Interior designers need patience, business sense, and the ability to use interpersonal communication to work with a team and manage client expectations. They should be willing to negotiate and mediate to solve problems, and be savvy shoppers with attention to detail. Because they are continually dealing with client budgets, interior designers need to be financially astute.

A Day in the Life—Duties and Responsibilities

Typical daily tasks of an interior designer include determining client needs, agreeing to a budget and deadlines, and understanding how a space will be used. Designers estimate costs and put together a plan, often using computer-aided design (CAD) software, which makes it easier to revise the plans as changes occur. Once the design concept is completed, interior designers coordinate with contractors' work schedules. They follow up on the whereabouts of furnishings or decorative items they are tracking, and communicate with workroom members about installation schedules. Interior designers must also communicate with clients about re-selection of items that may have become discontinued or unavailable for their deadline. They collaborate with everyone from electricians to builders for designs that are safe and meet construction requirements.

Interior designers might select everything required in a design plan, from fabric to paint to furniture, and/or work with other professionals such as drapery experts and carpet installers. They will also review catalogues and order samples, examine space and equipment requirements, and develop new business contacts. Interior designers must manage their time effectively, and when necessary, make customers aware of unavoidable problems that could delay a specific job, such as inaccurate orders or delays in product shipping.

Duties and Responsibilities

- Developing design plans based on function of a space and client's preferences
- Collecting and presenting fabric, material, and color samples
- Estimating costs and evaluating them in relation to client's budget
- Presenting detailed design plans for client approval
- Working with vendors to obtain required materials and labor
- Overseeing installation and/or application of design elements

WORK ENVIRONMENT

Physical Environment

In large design firms, interior design offices are typically in well-lit, comfortable settings that reflect the designer's style. Their hours of operation align with typical business hours. Smaller design firms or self-employed contractors adjust their workday to meet client needs, which means they may be on-site at a showroom or client location after the traditional workday. Although the bulk of interior design work is done indoors, interior designers may also be asked to design outdoor spaces such as covered entrances or patios and decks.

Transferable Skills and Abilities

Communication Skills
- Expressing thoughts and ideas clearly
- Speaking and writing effectively

Creative/Artistic Skills
- Being skilled in art or design

Interpersonal/Social Skills
- Cooperating with others
- Working as a member of a team

Organization & Management Skills
- Coordinating tasks
- Managing people/groups

Research & Planning Skills
- Researching ideas
- Solving problems
- Laying out a plan

Human Environment

An interior designer's work space is usually functional, aesthetically pleasing and busy, with creative and inspirational people who not only enjoy the job, but have a good working relationship with peers and colleagues, clients, and third-party contacts. Because personal tastes and preferences are involved, however, interior designers must be prepared to sometimes work with finicky or difficult clients.

Technological Environment

Interior designers use computer-aided software (such as computer-aided design and drafting, or CADD) to help with the actual design process. Designers are increasingly using computers and smartphones to view, price, and order products such as stocks of fabric from any location.

OCCUPATION SPECIALTIES

Kitchen and Bath Designers

Kitchen and Bath Designers specialize in kitchens and bathrooms and have expert knowledge of the variety of cabinets, fixtures, appliances, plumbing, and electrical solutions for these rooms.

Lighting Designers

Lighting Designers focus on the effect of lighting for home, office, and public spaces. For example, lighting designers may work on stage productions, in gallery and museum spaces, and in healthcare facilities, to find appropriate light fixtures and lighting effects for each space.

Sustainable Designers

Sustainable Designers use strategies to improve energy and water efficiencies and indoor air quality, and they specify environmentally preferable products, such as bamboo and cork for floors.

EDUCATION, TRAINING, AND ADVANCEMENT

High School/Secondary

Some high schools offer courses related to interior design. Otherwise, high school students interested in pursuing an interior design career should take basic art classes, learn about the color wheel and the use of different textiles, and work to develop basic business and math skills.

Students should maintain good study habits and participate in a related extracurricular activity, such as projects or clubs involving art, graphic design, or business. High school students should consider applying for interior design firm internships that may later qualify them for apprenticeships or lead to paid positions.

Suggested High School Subjects
- Applied Math
- Arts
- Blueprint Reading
- Clothing & Textiles
- English
- Family & Consumer Sciences
- Graphic Communications
- Interior Design
- Mechanical Drawing
- Merchandising

Famous First

The first notable interior decorating firm was Herter Brothers, founded in New York City after the Civil War. The brothers, Gustave and Christian, began operating an upholstery business and branched out from there into furniture making and cabinetry. Later they incorporated paneling and ceiling design into their business, and eventually offered everything from flooring, carpeting, and draperies to general furnishings. Among their most prominent clients were the Vanderbilts and Jay Gould.

Postsecondary

College students interested in an interior design career should take courses in art, design, business, and the sciences, which can help them in their understanding of the basics of textiles. (The subfield of textile design requires numerous chemistry classes.) Psychology classes can help students work more effectively with other people in the creative field. Many cities offer career-specific training programs at design schools or colleges. Upon completion of a bachelor's degree, interior designers are ready for a formal design apprenticeship program.

Postsecondary students will benefit from internships and volunteer opportunities at showrooms, interior design offices, or as assistants to designers who are constantly on the road. These activities can lead to entry-level employment with various companies.

Related College Majors
- Art, Architecture, and Decoration
- Fashion Design
- Interior Design
- Textile Design

Adult Job Seekers

Joining interior design professional industry organizations encourages networking, which can help adult job seekers without a college degree gain access to the interior design profession as assistants to working professionals. These organizations and associations generally list available job openings and offer mentoring services to help those new in the field plan their career and educational choices. Professional Certification and Licensure: Through the National Council for Interior Design Qualification (NCIDQ), interior designers can be accredited with licenses after testing that includes passing knowledge of computer-aided design, drawing, perspectives, spatial planning, color and fabrics, architecture, codes, measurements, lighting and building specifications, and ergonomics. Once they demonstrate sufficient knowledge to pass test requirements, interior designers advertise their new credentials.

Most often, however, professional certification and licensure is not required in the interior design field.

Additional Requirements

Interior designers need to be familiar with CADD software and be quick to react to changing trends. They should be able to adapt quickly when clients change their minds about a design element, and should understand basic customer service skills and concepts. In some cases, interior designers may have to absorb the cost of materials or items purchased that cannot be returned. They need to understand different aspects of the industry: clients, distributors, wholesale showrooms, builders, sales people, and architects. It is helpful for interior designers to have excellent collaborative skills, and to be comfortable working as members of a team.

EARNINGS AND ADVANCEMENT

Earnings of interior designers vary widely with the specialty, type of employer, number of years of experience, and reputation of the individual. Among salaried interior designers, those in large specialized design and architectural firms tend to earn higher and more stable salaries. Interior designers working in retail stores usually earn a commission, which can be irregular.

For residential design projects, self-employed interior designers and those working in smaller firms usually earn a per-hour consulting fee, plus a percentage of the total cost of furniture, lighting, artwork, and other design elements. For commercial projects, they might charge a per-hour consulting fee, charge by the square footage, or charge a flat fee for the whole project.

Mean annual earnings of interior designers were $52,970 in 2012. The lowest ten percent earned less than $25,670 and the highest ten percent earned more than $86,900.

Interior designers may receive paid vacations, holidays, and sick days; life and health insurance; and retirement benefits. These are usually paid by the employer. Self-employed interior designers have to provide their own benefits.

Metropolitan Areas with the Highest Employment Level in this Occupation

Metropolitan area	Employment[1]	Employment per thousand jobs	Hourly mean wage
New York-White Plains-Wayne, NY-NJ	2,540	0.49	$31.70
Los Angeles-Long Beach-Glendale, CA	1,820	0.47	$29.95
Atlanta-Sandy Springs-Marietta, GA	1,330	0.59	$23.27
Washington-Arlington-Alexandria, DC-VA-MD-WV	1,200	0.51	$31.14
Chicago-Joliet-Naperville, IL	1,150	0.32	$28.57
San Francisco-San Mateo-Redwood City, CA	1,140	1.13	$34.42
Dallas-Plano-Irving, TX	1,050	0.50	$25.38
Seattle-Bellevue-Everett, WA	950	0.68	$24.33

[1]Does not include self-employed. Source: Bureau of Labor Statistics

EMPLOYMENT AND OUTLOOK

Interior designers held about 55,000 jobs nationally in 2012. Employment of interior designers is expected to grow about as fast as the average for all occupations through the year 2022, which means employment is projected to increase 8 percent to 15 percent. Rising demand for the professional design of homes, offices, restaurants and other retail establishments, in addition to institutions like hospitals and nursing homes, should create job growth for interior designers. Although competition is strong, this field is expected to grow.

Employment Trend, Projected 2012–22

Interior Designers: 13%

Total, All Occupations: 11%

Arts, Design, and Entertainment Occupations: 7%

Note: "All Occupations" includes all occupations in the U.S. Economy. Source: U.S. Bureau of Labor Statistics, Employment Projections Program

Related Occupations
- Fashion Designer
- Florist
- Hotel & Motel Manager

Conversation With . . .
ROBYN ELIZABETH ENANY
Interior Designer, 14 years

1. What was your individual career path in terms of education/training, entry-level job, or other significant opportunity?

I studied child development in school but I've also always done design on the side. I was always very good with color. During my first marriage, we ran three insurance offices. I was then divorced and needed something that would give me a little bit more growth and financial security. I was approached by a doctor friend and got a job in the medical field. Still, I was doing interior design on the side. Along the way, I worked for a family furniture company doing their showcases, floor plans, and window displays. After I remarried, we moved to a manor house in Maryland. I did the whole house, top to bottom, as well as a 2600-square-foot rental. When we moved back to California three years later, I knew that design was my love and took classes at Long Beach Day College. I started my first gig through a contractor with a good-sized piece of property, met other contractors, and it just developed from there.

My tourism clients have included a few restaurants, mostly along Long Beach. Here, you're dealing with a whole different spectrum from typical clients; owners and investors dealing with millions of dollars, and contractors and architects. You have to keep designs user-friendly, think of all different sizes of people and accommodate not just seating but seating arrangements, both inside and out. Also consider the storefront: how inviting is it? And restaurants should include rooms for conferences or parties that need to be insulated from the rest of the space. Where's the bar? Where's the private space?

2. What are the most important skills and/or qualities for someone in your profession?

You have to be knowledgeable about design and have a good listening ear. If you're not comprehending the client's needs, your job won't go anywhere.

3. What do you wish you had known going into this profession?

Every job is a learning curve for me. I love it. I can do 20 kitchens and each will have a different hiccup. But there are some similarities, so you grab the best for the next job.

4. Are there many job opportunities in your profession?

Many. There are many people out there who don't know how to pull a paint palette together. So it's very beneficial for them to spend a day with me. They may just want the assurance of what furnishings to buy. Since many people are uncomfortable with or unsure of how to decorate their homes, there will always be a need for interior designers.

5. How do you see your profession changing in the next five years? What role will technology play in those changes, and what skills will be required?

Everything is CAD (computer-aided design) now. These programs are not cheap. I do 20-20 Design programs, and we get all the measurements—skylights, windows, everything—and at the end of the day the client is sent, say, an aerial view of their new kitchen, how it looks when the cabinets are opened up, what the cabinets contain, the entrances, the exits … everything. The more visual, the more people want it.

The thing is, you can be very computer literate but you don't want to limit your time to be onsite with clients. Technology notwithstanding, you still need to go out and meet clients, show them what you've done for other clients and give them a good visual.

You have to be a good listener and be on the side of your client. It's a process. They have to trust us.

6. What do you enjoy most about your job? What do you enjoy least?

I love working with people. I enjoy challenges, such as when I turn a dysfunctional kitchen turn into a downright gorgeous one.

What I enjoy least is when my material is on backorder, or when they assure me backorder is 6 to 8 weeks, then tell me the vendor doesn't make it anymore.

7. Can you suggest a valuable "try this" for students considering a career in your profession?

I bring students interested in interior design along to first consultations. They can see how you conduct yourself around clients. Seventy percent of this is public relations and etiquette; the client needs to trust you fully. I remember bringing a 19-year-old along. At the end of an hour and a half, two-hour consult with a client, we got in the car and she said, "You gave them so many options. Why don't you tell them what you want?" And I said: "Because this is not my home." I always give clients two or three layouts. Give clients a say in a particular project, they feel part of it. That is very important.

SELECTED SCHOOLS

Students interested in a career in interior design are generally advised to obtain an associates' degree or a bachelor's degree in the subject. There are over 200 bachelor's degree programs available, according to the Council for Interior Design Accreditation (CIDA). The CIDA website (see address below) provides a comprehensive listing by state, and is the best place to begin researching schools.

MORE INFORMATION

American Society of Interior Designers
608 Massachusetts Avenue, NE
Washington, D.C. 20002-6006
202.546.3480
www.asid.org

Association of Interior Design Professionals
113 N. Main Street
Kernersville, NC 27284
336.310.4819
www.aidponline.com

Council for Interior Design Accreditation
206 Grandville Avenue
Suite 350
Grand Rapids, MI 49503-4014
616.458.0400
accredit-id.org

National Council for Interior Design Qualification
1602 L Street NW
Suite 200
Washington, DC 20036-5681
202.721.0220
www.ncidq.org

Interior Design Educators Council
9100 Purdue Road
Suite 200
Indianapolis, IN 46268
317.328.4437
www.idec.org

Interior Design Society
164 S. Main Street
Suite 404
High Point, NC 27260
336.884.4437
www.interiordesignsociety.org

International Interior Design Association
222 Merchandise Mart, Suite 567
Chicago, IL 60654
888.799.4432
www.iida.org

Susan Williams/Editor

Jeweler & Precious Stone & Metal Worker

Snapshot

Career Cluster(s): Arts

Interests: Art, industrial design, product design

Earnings (Yearly Average): $37,060

Employment & Outlook: Decline expected

OVERVIEW

Sphere of Work

Jewelers, precious stone artisans, and metal workers are artisans who design, sell, and repair jewelry and other precious metal and stone items. The fields blend creative artistry with hands on technical skills needed to utilize the tools and techniques specific to the field. The popularity of jewels, precious stones, and precious metals varies with broader economic patterns as products in these categories are typically considered luxury items in the consumer market. Artisans working in these fields can be independently employed, serving clients through a private workshop or retail location, or may work for larger jewelry or metal working companies that employ

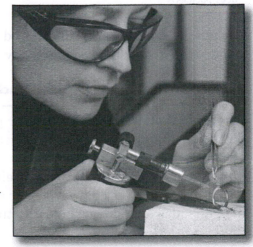

artisans. Jewelry making and precious metal working are difficult, time consuming activities that have a long and complicated history in human culture and the modern techniques, though enhanced with a variety of technological equipment, continue to rely on practices that have been part of the field for centuries.

Work Environment

Most precious stone, jewel, and precious metal workers work in workshops or factories and complete much of their work at a work table or bench equipped with specialized equipment. Artisans in these fields work with potentially dangerous tools and chemicals and safety equipment and procedures are necessary to work successfully. While some precious stone and metal workers work alone, others may work in groups under the management of a lead artisan, or may serve as managers themselves, overseeing the work of assistant artisans.

Profile

Working Conditions: Work Indoors
Physical Strength: Light to strenuous work
Education Needs: None, Trade School, Bachelor's Degree
Licensure/Certification: Not required
Opportunities For Experience: On-Job Training, Part-Time Work, Internship
Holland Interest Score*: RA

* See Appendix A

Occupation Interest

Individuals looking to become jewelers, precious stone artisans, or metal workers should have a strong interest in artistic expression and in working with their hands. Artisan work blends the lines between industrial design and artistry and workers in these fields should have an interest in both disciplines. In addition, artisans working with jewels and precious metals are part of an ancient tradition and will benefit from interest and knowledge of the history of artistry using precious materials.

A Day in the Life—Duties and Responsibilities

A typical day for a gem, jewelry, or precious metal worker will depend on the specific project that the artisan is working on. A precious stone or jeweler might spend all or part of a typical day examining gems or precious stones to determine their quality and how to use them in the creation of wearable jewelry or accessories. Precious materials artisans also spend time investigating and sourcing raw materials, meeting with vendors, and traveling to trade shows and wholesalers to purchase materials for new projects. Once the raw materials have been obtained, a jeweler or precious metal worker needs to clean and polish the stones or metals using grinders, hand tools, and chemical baths. Before beginning an original piece, an artisan will typically sketch or create a digital design of the product and might also create a prototype out of wax or another non-precious material. Using cleaned and prepared raw materials and templates or designs, the artisan uses a variety of hand tools, electric tools, and, in some cases, computer aided tools, to create original pieces of jewelry or accessories. Some shops that sell retail jewels and precious metals also offer repair services and the artisan may therefore spend time cleaning and polishing stones and metals, repairing pieces, or other maintenance/ repair activities. Services in this vein include altering the size of rings and resetting stones that have become loose from their settings.

Duties and Responsibilities

- **Research, source, and purchase materials.**
- **Clean, polish, and grade jewels and other materials**
- **Create designs and templates for jewelry and accessories**
- **Repair jewelry and accessories for customers**
- **Use welding, polishing, and shaping techniques to create jewelry**
- **Clean and refine jewels, stones, or metal pieces created by others**
- **Meet with clients to sell or repair jewelry and accessories**
- **Market and advertise services to potential clients**

OCCUPATION SPECIALTIES

Gemologists

Gemologists are mineralogical specialists who use a variety of instruments to examine, describe, certify, and analyze the qualities and characteristics of jewels and precious stones. Gemologists may work for academic organizations or companies involved in wholesale and retail sales of gems and/or other precious stones.

Precious Metal Workers

Precious metal workers use many of the same skills as artisans who work with non-precious metals like steel and iron, though also need to learn techniques specific to working with precious metals. Precious metal workers specialize in working with silver, gold, platinum and other rare metallic elements.

Jewelry Appraisers

Jewelry appraisers examine jewelry or gemstones to determine their market value and write appraisal documents for customers or jewelry makers. Appraisers must have a detailed knowledge of the factors influencing gem and stone value and also need to have detailed marketing and industry data on current prices. Appraisers can work for retailers, appraisal firms, second hand retailers, or insurance providers.

WORK ENVIRONMENT

Physical Environment

Jewelers, precious stone and precious metal workers tend to work in studios or workshop environments equipped with work benches or tables and a variety of other specialized tools. Working with jewels and precious metals can be time consuming and physically demanding, requiring both dexterity and endurance. Artisans working for larger firms or companies may instead work on a factory floor or in an office attached to a manufacturing facility. Roughly 40 percent of jewelers and precious metal workers were self-employed as of 2014-15. Of the remaining artisans employed by a company, 27 percent worked in clothing and accessory retail stores, while 16 percent worked for specialized jewelry manufacturing companies.

Relevant Skills and Abilities

Communication Skills

- Communicating with clients, customers, and tradespeople
- Interpreting written instructions or information

Interpersonal/Social Skills

- Working with clients, customers, and other workers
- Marketing work to potential clients

Organization & Management Skills

- Being goal oriented to meet deadlines
- Managing employees
- Creating and maintaining lists of vendors and materials

Research & Planning Skills

- Researching and helping to create design trends

Technical Skills

- Utilizing a variety of specialized electric and hand tools
- Using Computer Aided Design (CAD) and other software tools

Human Environment

Jewelry and metal working can be independent activities and some artists work alone most of the time, while others work alongside assistants, gemologists, sales specialists and managers, and other professionals. Jewelers and metal workers working in retail are often asked to meet directly with clients to discuss their needs. Some artisans spend considerable time speaking with potential customers or consulting with other professionals during the construction of an item and artisans should therefore be comfortable meeting with and negotiating with clients and customers. Artisans also often interact with individuals involved in procuring and selling gems and precious metals to artisans and jewelry makers.

Technological Environment

Computer Aided Design (CAD) programs have become increasingly common and important in many fields of artistic production. While an artisan can design and create jewelry or precious metal works without using digital technology, the advent of CAD and other design software streamlines the design and template making process. In some large companies, lasers and robots have become common features of jewelry and precious metal manufacturing, though independent artisans typically work with electric and hand tools rather than using automated equipment.

EDUCATION, TRAINING, AND ADVANCEMENT

High School/Secondary

There are no general education requirements for individuals looking to become gem and precious metal workers, though a balanced education and introduction to material art will be helpful for future professionals. High school students are advised to make use of craft and arts classes offered by their respective schools as well as studying basic sciences, physics, mathematics, and other subjects commonly used in material design.

Suggested High School Subjects

- English
- Art
- Sculpture
- Metal working
- Industrial Design
- Graphic Design
- Art History
- Geology/Earth Science
- Physics
- Mathematics

Famous First

Brothers Nathan and Oscar Heyman were the first artisans to found an internationally famous jewelry manufacturing company in the United States. Before immigrating to the US in 1906, the Heyman brothers trained in the prestigious Fabergé workshops in Paris, starting off as maintenance workers in the Fabergé workshop. In 1912, the Heyman brothers founded what would become the most prestigious jewelry manufacturing shop in the United States, manufacturing pieces for companies like Cartier, Tiffany & Co., and Marcus & Co. Pieces created by Oscar Heyman remain highly prized on the fine jewelry market and the company has endured into the 21st century, being run by descendants of the immigrant brothers who first started the firm.

College/Postsecondary

There are a number of trade and technical schools that offer training programs, that typically last from 6th months to a year, that introduce students to the tools and techniques used to work with gems and precious metals. Many colleges and universities also offer classes relevant to material arts work, such as minerology, geology, and material design. Some colleges and universities offer specialized degrees in metal sculpture and many of the skills developed in this discipline will overlap with the skills needed for precious metal working and jewelry design.

Related College Majors

- Geology
- Minerology
- Industrial Design
- Retail Design
- Fine Arts/Masters of Fine Arts
- Jewelry making
- Metal working and sculpture

Adult Job Seekers

Individuals looking for work as precious stone/metal worker can seek out technical or trade school programs offering training and/or can look for assistant or internship programs working under a professional jewelry or precious materials artisan. In some cases, individuals might be able to obtain work in sales and/or maintenance at a jewelry retailer or wholesaler and can then train under an artisan to advance to jewelry making or precious metal working as a profession.

Professional Certification and Licensure

There are no specific professional licenses needed to work professionally with jewels and precious materials, but aspiring professionals can choose to obtain certificates of achievement from technical and trade schools demonstrating their proficiency with tools and techniques used in the industry, such as CAD design, gemology, and precious materials appraisal. Those seeking to sell jewelry or precious materials in a retail capacity will need to adhere to guidelines for licensing businesses in their area.

Additional Requirements

Working with gems and precious metals requires a steady hand and good vision. Some of the technical work needed to fashion jewels or precious metals can be physically demanding and those seeking careers in the field should be detail oriented and comfortable with highly technical work. In addition, artisans need to have creativity and the ability to visualize completed products during their work, helping to guide their adjustments and subtle refinements in creating a finished piece of jewelry or accessory.

Fun Fact

Seventy-five percent of the periodic table's elements are metal, and, of all the elements, silver has the highest electrical and thermal conductivity.
Source: http://chemistry.about.com/od/metalsalloys

EARNINGS AND ADVANCEMENT

According to the Bureau of Labor Statistics (BLS), the median annual wage for artisans in the jewelry, precious stone, and precious metal working fields was $37,060 in 2015, with the lowest paid 10 percent earning an average of $10.40 per hour and the highest paid 10 percent earning over $32.00/hr. Wages were highest for those working in retail stores, such as those selling jewelry, luggage, or other high end goods. Some jewelry and precious goods artisans begin by participating in educational programs or by working in a factory, wholesaler, or as an assistant in a retail manufacturer. After obtaining the necessary skills and experience, an artisan in fine goods can consider opening his or her own boutique or marketing their creations independently to consumers.

Metropolitan Areas with the Highest
Employment Level in this Occupation

Metropolitan area	Employment	Employment per thousand jobs	Hourly mean wage
New York-Jersey City-White Plains, NY-NJ Metropolitan Division	5,640	0.87	$24.15
Los Angeles-Long Beach-Glendale, CA Metropolitan Division	1,260	0.31	$17.62
Dallas-Plano-Irving, TX Metropolitan Division	920	0.40	$22.56
Providence-Warwick, RI-MA	850	1.52	$20.41
Fort Worth-Arlington, TX Metropolitan Division	370	0.38	N/A
Austin-Round Rock, TX	360	0.38	$17.81
Warren-Troy-Farmington Hills, MI Metropolitan Division	350	0.30	$16.29
Anaheim-Santa Ana-Irvine, CA Metropolitan Division	320	0.21	$16.81
Nassau County-Suffolk County, NY Metropolitan Division	300	0.24	N/A
San Diego-Carlsbad, CA	280	0.21	$17.47

Source: Bureau of Labor Statistics

EMPLOYMENT AND OUTLOOK

The Bureau of Labor Statistics (BLS) estimates a probable decline of as much as 11 percent for employment of jewelry and precious materials artisans between 2014 and 2024 due to an increasing tendency for retailers and wholesalers to purchase jewelry and precious goods manufactured in other countries. Outsourcing and the increasing difficulty in obtaining raw materials also contributes to the overall reduction in job opportunities. Those skilled in repair and design are expected to have better prospects as jewelry repair is typically a local rather than international trade. In addition, experienced designers may find additional employment opportunities in designing products that are then manufactured overseas. Due to the lack of job growth, individuals interested in careers in the field should consider trade school certification and training, which can give candidates and advantage over candidates without educational experience.

Employment Trend, Projected 2014–24

Total, All Occupations: 7%

Production Occupations: -3%

Jewelers and Precious Stone and Metal Workers: -11%

Note: "All Occupations" includes all occupations in the U.S. Economy. Source: U.S. Bureau of Labor Statistics, Employment Projections Program

Related Occupations
- Craft and Fine Artists
- Fashion Designers
- Industrial Designers
- Retail Sales Workers
- Woodworkers
- Welders, Cutters, Solderers and Brazers
- Metal workers

Conversation With . . .
ROBIN HEPBURN

Owner/Jeweler, Orion Jewelry Studio
Pennington, New Jersey
Metalsmith, 35 years

1. What was your individual career path in terms of education/training, entry-level job, or other significant opportunity?

I was always involved in art. My father had been a silversmith before I was born, but I grew up with a collection of his work, which was handcrafted rings, earrings and brooches. To me, there was a certain mystery about it. The year after I graduated from high school, I had the opportunity to take an eight-week course in metalsmithing at the Hinkley School of Crafts in Maine, and I just loved it. I changed my interest from early childhood development to metalsmithing—jewelry making, design and fabrication—and went to art school in Portland, Maine, at what's now called Maine College of the Art to learn to make jewelry.

After graduating, I moved to Philadelphia and worked in a jewelry store repair shop for a year, then moved to St. Thomas, in the Virgin Islands, and worked for jewelry stores until I decided to open my own store in 1986. In 1990, after three hurricanes, I moved my store home to New Jersey.

I had done a few craft fairs, selling my work that way, but I made a conscious decision that I wanted my own space for my own work. I have developed my own style from trying a lot of different styles; it's eclectic, with roots in organic and abstract forms. My interest now is incorporating color gemstones into my work.

2. What are the most important skills and/or qualities for someone in your profession?

It's important to have a healthy mixture of business skills and creative skills. I think a lot of people who get into this don't have those business skills. I was lucky because my father had those skills and since I was so passionate about making a living from my jewelry, he pushed me to keep at it.

3. What do you wish you had known going into this profession?

Just how married to it I would become. A brick-and-mortar store requires many skills, such as marketing or displaying, in addition to jewelry making. I wish I could have investigated other options, but we didn't have the internet 30 years ago. Today, you could sell through Etsy or other websites, including your own.

4. Are there many job opportunities in your profession? In what specific areas?

Many. There are setters, gemologists, and designers who do CAD design and somebody else makes it. One student who worked for me went on to work at Tiffany's.

5. How do you see your profession changing in the next five years, what role will technology play in those changes, and what skills will be required?

I think the next step is 3D printers. Basically, you type in coordinates and information and it builds your piece in a 3D form. The artist won't have to create it by hand. That said, I work in new technology if somebody comes to me with a very specific idea—I can draw the design, give it to a CAD person, and fine-tune with the client—but I still make a lot by hand.

6. What do you enjoy most about your job? What do you enjoy least about your job?

I really love working with people and problem solving. How to fix something, how to build something, how to manifest their idea into a design. What I like least is the time and energy involved in running all aspects of a business.

7. Can you suggest a valuable "try this" for students considering a career in your profession?

Get out to local jewelry stores or find local artisans and pick their brains. Talk to goldsmiths and silversmiths. That's what I did. Be willing to ask for apprenticeships or jobs.

MORE INFORMATION

Gemological Institutes of America (GIA)
5345 Armada Drive
Carlsbad, CA 92008
760-603-4000
www.gia.edu

Jewelers of America
120 Broadway, Suite 2820
New York, NY 10271
800-223-0673
www.jewelers.org

Manufacturing Jewelers & Suppliers of America (MJSA)
8 Hayward St.
Attleboro, MA 02703
508-316-1429
www.mjsa.org

American Gem Society (AGS)
8881 W. Sahara Ave.
Las Vegas, NV 89117
866-805-6500
www.americangemsociety.org

International Precious Metals Institute (IPMI)
5101 North 12th Ave., Suite C
Pensacola, FL 32504
www.ipmi.org

Micah Issitt/Editor

Landscape Architect

Snapshot

Career Cluster: Architecture & Construction; Environment & Conservation

Interests: Environment, technology, design, communicating with others

Earnings (Yearly Average): $68,570

Employment & Outlook: Average Growth Expected

OVERVIEW

Sphere of Work

Landscape architects are designers of exterior space. Much of the work they do is both decorative and functional. They plan the surrounding landscape for new buildings, deciding where to place walkways, lawns, trees, gardens, retaining walls, fountains, reflecting pools, and other natural and manmade objects. They also design bike trails, golf courses, playgrounds, highway and waterfront beautification projects, and other public spaces. In addition to planning aesthetically pleasing environments, they prepare environmental impact statements, solve environmental problems such as flooding or mudslides, and restore habitats back to their original condition.

Work Environment

Landscape architects work in government and in the private sector. Many landscape architects are self-employed or work in small architectural firms. They interact with clients, architects, urban planners, engineers, and other professionals involved in construction and development. They also often supervise the contractors and gardeners who carry out their landscaping plans. They frequently work long or odd hours to meet deadlines.

Profile

Working Conditions: Work both Indoors and Outdoors
Physical Strength: Light Work
Education Needs: Bachelor's Degree, Master's Degree
Licensure/Certification: Required
Physical Abilities Not Required: No Heavy Labor
Opportunities For Experience: Internship, Apprenticeship, Volunteer Work, Part-Time Work
Holland Interest Score*: AIR

* See Appendix A

Occupation Interest

Landscape architecture attracts people who value the harmony between humans and nature that can be achieved through thoughtful planning and manipulating the environment. They are imaginative, artistic problem-solvers who are solidly grounded in science and technology. They are both detail-oriented and able to envision large-scale projects. Successful landscape architects use their excellent communication skills to convey their design ideas to others.

A Day in the Life—Duties and Responsibilities

The duties and responsibilities of landscape architects are many and varied. Larger jobs usually involve carrying out a preliminary assessment, or feasibility study, performed in collaboration with the architect, engineers, and environmental scientists. At that time, the landscape architect might take photographs or a video of the area to be developed. He or she might also have to submit applications to government agencies for zoning permits and environmental approval.

After a site has been approved, the landscape architect studies the area's topographic features. The landscape architect then offers suggestions on how best to situate the project's buildings, walkways and roadways, and natural elements based on environmental factors such as sunlight and drainage. He or she then designs the landscape to complement the design of the building, harmonize with the surrounding environment, and accommodate the spatial needs of various stakeholders. Much of the design work is done with a computer-aided design (CAD) program, but it may also be sketched by hand. The landscape architect might also prepare a video simulation or build a 3-D model of the design. He or she then puts together a proposal that also includes a cost analysis, written reports, permits, and other materials.

On large projects, the approval process typically involves many meetings with the developer over the course of several months. During this time, the landscape architect might give several presentations to a board of shareholders or a government commission. He or she also submits construction designs to local building commissioners for approval.

Once approved, the landscape architect refines the drawings and details specific construction guidelines. After construction begins, he or she may return to the site to oversee the work.

Duties and Responsibilities

- **Preparing site plans, working drawings, specifications and cost estimates for land developments**
- **Presenting design sketches to clients and community interest groups**
- **Outlining in detail the methods of construction**
- **Drawing up a list of necessary materials**
- **Inspecting construction work in progress to make sure specifications are followed**
- **Conferring with clients, engineering personnel and architects on overall programs for project**
- **Compiling and analyzing data on site conditions such as geographic location, soil, vegetation and rock features, drainage and location of structures**

WORK ENVIRONMENT

Physical Environment

Landscape architects work in offices but also spend much time at job sites. Undeveloped sites may have safety issues such as uneven terrain, mud, or plant and animal pests, while those under construction may involve loud noise, fumes, chemicals, or other hazards.

Relevant Skills and Abilities

Communication Skills
- Expressing thoughts and ideas clearly
- Speaking and writing effectively

Creative/Artistic Skills
- Being skilled in art or design

Organization & Management Skills
- Making decisions
- Paying attention to and handling details

Research & Planning Skills
- Using logical reasoning

Technical Skills
- Performing technical work

Human Environment

Unless they are self-employed, landscape architects usually work in firms or departments with other architects, assistants, and staff, under supervision by the head architect or director. They may supervise drafters, surveyors, gardeners, and other employees or contractors. Their clients range from homeowners to residential and commercial developers to boards of directors.

Technological Environment

Landscape architects use computers equipped with CAD software, word processing, geographic information systems (GIS), and spreadsheets, among other programs. They might also use photo imaging, illustration, modeling, and other computer graphics or design software. In addition to conventional office equipment, they use large format copiers and a variety of drafting and art tools and supplies. They may also use surveying equipment.

EDUCATION, TRAINING, AND ADVANCEMENT

High School/Secondary

A well-rounded college preparatory program that emphasizes math, science, and courses that introduce CAD, such as mechanical drawing or drafting, will provide the best foundation for a career in landscape design. Especially relevant courses include geometry, trigonometry, environmental science, biology, geology, and botany. Speech communication and English courses help develop communication skills, while drawing, sculpture, photography, computer graphics, and other art courses encourage creativity. Part-time jobs in gardening, lawn care, or construction, or volunteering at a nature center or arboretum can provide valuable hands-on work experience.

Suggested High School Subjects
- Applied Biology/Chemistry
- Applied Math
- Arts
- Blueprint Reading
- Drafting
- English
- Landscaping
- Mathematics
- Mechanical Drawing
- Ornamental Horticulture
- Photography

Famous First

The first American landscape architect of note was Frederick Law Olmstead (1822-1903), designer of Central Park and Prospect Park in New York City as well as numerous other notable municipal parks, state parks, and college campuses. Olmsted was also active in the conservation movement, and during the Civil War he headed the US Sanitary Commission, which oversaw care of sick and wounded soldiers.

College/Postsecondary

A bachelor's degree in landscape architecture is the minimum requirement for licensing as a landscape architect; some employers require an advanced degree. The undergraduate degree in landscape architecture often takes five years and includes courses in surveying, CAD and modeling, ecology, horticulture, earth sciences, landscape planning, design, and construction, and management. Some programs require, or strongly suggest, an internship and offer hands-on opportunities as part of the curriculum.

Related College Majors
- Architectural Environmental Design
- Landscape Architecture

Adult Job Seekers

Adults with a background in horticulture, gardening, botany, geology, urban planning, or another related discipline would have an advantage when entering this career. Those with a bachelor's degree in a related field may be able to enroll directly in a three-year master's degree program, thus saving time and money. Qualified landscape architects should consider membership in professional associations, which often provide opportunities for networking, job-finding, and professional development.

Advancement opportunities depend on the place of employment and its size. Experienced landscape architects are given more difficult and higher-profile jobs. They may become project managers, partners in their firms, or establish their own firms. Some move into consulting or academic positions.

Professional Certification and Licensure

All states license landscape architects. In most cases, candidates are required to have a bachelor's degree from a Landscape Architectural Accreditation Board (LAAB) accredited program as well as one to four years of experience and a passing score on the Landscape Architect Registration Examination (LARE). Some states also administer their own test and have slightly different requirements for experience and education. Continuing education is a common requirement for license renewal. Interested individuals should check the requirements of their home state.

Additional Requirements:

Landscape architects must be familiar with local zoning regulations and environmental codes. Those who wish to establish their own landscape design firms should have business skills and motivation as well as experience in the field.

Fun Fact

A tree shading an outdoor air conditioner unit can increase its efficiency by as much as ten percent.

Source: signatureconcretedesign.com

EARNINGS AND ADVANCEMENT

Earnings of landscape architects depend on the type, size, and geographic location of the employer and the individual's education and experience. Mean annual earnings for landscape architects were $68,570 in 2013. The lowest ten percent earned less than $39,000, and the highest ten percent earned more than $104,000. Landscape architects may receive paid vacations, holidays, and sick days; life and health insurance; and retirement benefits. These are usually paid by the employer.

Metropolitan Areas with the Highest Employment Level in This Occupation

Metropolitan area	Employment[1]	Employment per thousand jobs	Hourly mean wage
Seattle-Bellevue-Everett, WA	680	0.47	$30.19
Washington-Arlington-Alexandria, DC-VA-MD-WV	570	0.24	$39.84
Minneapolis-St. Paul-Bloomington, MN-WI	550	0.30	$26.51
Denver-Aurora-Broomfield, CO	530	0.42	$34.96
Santa Ana-Anaheim-Irvine, CA	440	0.30	$33.82
Boston-Cambridge-Quincy, MA	420	0.24	$43.54
Philadelphia, PA	420	0.23	$30.06
San Diego-Carlsbad-San Marcos, CA	410	0.32	$34.44
Oakland-Fremont-Hayward, CA	390	0.39	$42.97
Atlanta-Sandy Springs-Marietta, GA	350	0.15	$31.22

[1] Does not include self-employed. Source: Bureau of Labor Statistics

EMPLOYMENT AND OUTLOOK

There were approximately 24,000 landscape architects employed nationally in 2012. About one-fourth were self-employed. Employment of landscape architects is expected to grow about as fast as the average for all occupations through the year 2022, which means employment is projected to increase 10 percent to 16 percent. Employment will grow because of the expertise of landscape architects will be sought after in the planning and development of new construction. Growing interest in city and regional environmental planning, increased development of open space into recreation areas, wildlife refuges and parks and continued concern for the environment should also spur demand for landscape architects.

Employment Trend, Projected 2012–22

Architects, Surveyors, and Cartographers (All): 15%

Landscape Architects: 14%

Total, All Occupations: 11%

Note: "All Occupations" includes all occupations in the U.S. Economy. Source: U.S. Bureau of Labor Statistics, Employment Projections Program.

Related Occupations
- Architect
- Floral Designer
- Forester & Conservation Scientist
- Gardener & Groundskeeper
- Urban & Regional Planner

Conversation With . . .
JON CONNER

Vice President and Practice Leader
Landscape Architecture, JMT, Sparks MD
Landscape Architect, 28 years

1. What was your individual career path in terms of education/training, entry-level job, or other significant opportunity?

I started in the School of Architecture at the University of Maryland but after two years figured out that wasn't my cup of tea. I was more of a logical thinker and not quite so prepared for the artistic side of that profession. So, moving to design outside of buildings placed me in a design environment that was more scientifically-based. That's how I found my comfort level. I got my degree in horticulture with a landscape design option from the College of Agriculture. I was at my first job about five years and decided to get my Master's in Landscape Architecture at Morgan State University. I then moved here to JMT, which is historically a transportation engineering firm

Our projects range from conceptual planning to final design. We do many streetscape projects, which include not only planting design but also design for sidewalks, urban plazas and parks. We led the planning team to site stations in neighborhoods for the Baltimore City Red Line. We've done studies and reports and management plans for scenic byways, understanding what's particularly special about an historic road or corridor. I plan and design pedestrian and bicycle facilities.

In general, landscape architecture has historically suffered from an identity crisis because people tend to place emphasis on the word "landscape" and not the word "architecture." Landscape Architects can focus on ecological and stream restoration, historic preservation, parks and recreation, or even schools. I chose to pursue the transportation realm.

2. What are the most important skills and/or qualities for someone in your profession?

You need to be well-equipped in terms of graphic capabilities. You communicate with drawings, and you still need to be able to sketch something out to depict what you're thinking. As you get into the working world, you have to be a good communicator and comfortable presenting in front of people.

3. What do you wish you had known going into this profession?

I wish I had known that landscape architecture was more diverse. It would have allowed me to hone in more quickly on a niche that I was interested in pursuing.

4. Are there many job opportunities in your profession? In what specific areas?

Job prospects and the future are really bright because of the growing emphasis on sustainability and green solutions. Engineers, architects, and private institutions hire us because of our experience understanding how the built environment must co-exist with the natural environment. Many times we are brought in to serve as the quarterback for a project because we understand how the full range of project issues and systems fit into the overall ecosystem of an area.

5. How do you see your profession changing in the next five years? What role will technology play in those changes, and what skills will be required?

We'll see even more emphasis on sustainable solutions. Also, computer graphics are a big part of our production work, so being able to graphically depict views of what you want to build is important. Higher end software products that can depict ideas — something that's completely photorealistic — are used in higher levels of design. Any of the computer mapping and graphic applications are essential.

6. What do you enjoy most about your job? What do you enjoy least about your job?

My job is rewarding because in the broadest sense it gives me an opportunity to make a difference to improve places where people live, work, play and learn. One of my more rewarding projects came when we asked to re-invent Main Street in Rehoboth Beach, DE, a popular East Coast beach town. The main street was showing years of design decisions geared towards moving cars, and was not particularly attractive or safe for pedestrians and bicyclists. Much of the infrastructure was deteriorating and in need of replacement. It cost the city $35 million and took six years, but now there's a traffic circle when you come into town —with a replica of the local Cape Henlopen Lighthouse —that slows traffic down for pedestrians and bicyclists. It says, "I have arrived." The overhead utilities went underground as part of that project.

My least favorite thing, probably because most of our work is with the public sector, is the bureaucracy. It can be mind-numbing at times, and you see how much money gets wasted just trying to move designs to construction.

7. Can you suggest a valuable "try this" for students considering a career in your profession?

Think of one or more of your favorite places to go, go there, and think what is it about that place that makes it one of your favorite places. Is it the sheer natural beauty, or something designed? There's a full range: you might go to the Grand Canyon and be in awe of natural beauty, or you might go to Disney World, an artificial environment created by man.

Also look for opportunities such as the one offered by my company, which participates in the local chapter of the American Society of Landscape Architects' annual job shadow program. That lets students experience what we do. We take them out to a couple of job sites and look at projects that are under construction as well as reviewing designs that are "on the boards."

A good resource is ASLA.org, which has a section called "Become a Landscape Architect."

SELECTED SCHOOLS

Many colleges and universities have bachelor's degree programs in art and architecture, design, and related subjects; some offer concentrations in landscape architecture. The student may also gain an initial grounding in the field at an agricultural, technical, or community college. For advanced positions, a master's is commonly obtained. Below are listed some of the more prominent schools in this field.

Cal Poly, Pomona
3801 W. Temple Avenue
Pomona, CA 91768
909.869.7659
www.csupomona.edu

Cornell University
410 Thurston Avenue
Ithaca, NY 14850
607.255.5241
www.cornell.edu

Kansas State University
119 Anderson Hall
Manhattan, KS 66506
785.532.6250
www.k-state.edu

Louisiana State University
1146 Pleasant Hall
Baton Rouge, LA 70803
225.578.1175
www.lsu.edu

Purdue University
445 Stadium Mall
West Lafayette, IN 47907
765.494.1776
www.purdue.edu

Ohio State University
281 West Lane Avenue
Columbus, OH 43210
614.292.3980
www.osu.edu

Texas A&M University
PO Box 30014
College Station, TX 77842
978.845.1060
www.tamu.edu

University of Georgia
Terrell Hall
210 South Jackson Street
Athens, GA 30602
706.542.8776
www.uga.edu

University of Pennsylvania
1 College Hall, Room 1
Philadelphia, PA 19104
215.898.7507
www.upenn.edu

Virginia Tech
925 Prices Forks Road
Blacksburg, VA 24061
540.231.6267
www.vt.edu

MORE INFORMATION

American Institute of Architects
1735 New York Avenue NW
Washington, DC 20006-5292
800.242.3837
www.aia.org

**American Nursery and
Landscape Association**
1000 Vermont Avenue NW, Suite 300
Washington, DC 20005
202.789.2900
www.anla.org

**American Society of Landscape
Architects**
636 Eye Street NW
Washington, DC 20001-3736
888.999.2752
www.asla.org

**Association of Collegiate Schools
of Architecture**
1735 New York Avenue, NW
Washington, DC 20006
202.785.2324
www.acsa-arch.org

**Council of Landscape
Architectural Registration
Boards**
3949 Pender Drive, Suite 120
Fairfax, VA 22030
571.432.0332
www.clarb.org

**Landscape Architecture
Foundation**
818 18th Street NW, Suite 810
Washington, DC 20006
202.331.7070
www.lafoundation.org

**Society of American Registered
Architects**
14 E. 38th Street
New York, NY 10016
888.385.7272
www.sara-national.org

Sally Driscoll/Editor

Motion Picture/ Radio/TV Art Director

Snapshot

Career Cluster: Arts, A/V Technology & Communication, Business, Management & Administration

Interests: Set Design, Marketing & Advertising, Management, Art, IllustrationTechniques, Film Production

Earnings (Yearly Average): $85,468

Employment & Outlook: Average Growth Expected

OVERVIEW

Sphere of Work

Art directors for motion pictures, radio, and television work in collaboration with producers, writers, and directors to bring concepts from the page to the screen or airwaves. They oversee a studio's art department and typically play a major role in hiring the creative staff, which can include artists, graphic designers, model makers, and set builders. Sometimes known as production designers, they often directly assist in the construction of sets and props. Motion picture, radio, and television art directors

are also responsible for the management and allocation of the art department's budget, ensuring that the work performed on a given project stays within the production's overall financial framework. In addition, they are frequently called upon to assist in the marketing and advertisement of their projects.

Work Environment

Motion picture, radio, and television art directors commonly work in studios and sound stages that allow for little contact with individuals not involved in the production. Studios are busy locations in which many different working groups operate in concert with one another, so art directors should be comfortable interacting with others on a regular basis. Some art directors also spend a great deal of time in an office environment, working on advertising and marketing plans and designing sets. Frequently, art directors travel to off-site locations to scout filming or recording spots and must be prepared to encounter potentially unpleasant weather and climate conditions. Art directors often work irregular hours, particularly when working on a production set, but may work fewer and more consistent hours during pre-production periods prior to the start of shooting or recording. Due to the expectations of producers and directors to stay on schedule and within budget, art directors in the entertainment industry may experience work-related stress.

Profile

Working Conditions: Office/Production Studio Some Out Side Work
Physical Strength: Light To Moderate Work
Education Needs:
Technical/Community College
Bachelor's Degree
Licensure/Certification:
Recommended
Physical Abilities Not Required: No Strenuous Work
Opportunities For Experience:
Apprenticeship, Military Service
Volunteer Work, Part-Time Work
Holland Interest Score*: RCE

* See Appendix A

Occupation Interest

Art direction is a critical facet of the entertainment industry, and the seniority afforded by the position allows the art director creative input into the ways in which films, television programs, and radio shows are made and marketed. As such, this career attracts those who have a strong interest in the behind-the-scenes workings of media. The nature of the work requires that a large number of diverse responsibilities be managed simultaneously, so art directors are frequently masters of organization, leadership and delegation, and multitasking.

A Day in the Life—Duties and Responsibilities

Art directors are responsible for bringing the collective creative vision of producers, directors, and writers to life. They begin by meeting and consulting with these individuals during the pre-production stage, months in advance of shooting or recording. Using computer technologies as well as their own artistic abilities, they design set blueprints, present sketches and illustrations, and when applicable, conduct research on architectural styles to ensure historical accuracy. In addition to designing and building project-specific sets, they scout potential shooting or recording locations in both outdoor and indoor environments. Art directors also work with advertising managers to create a marketing strategy for the film, program, or show.

During the shoot or recording session, art directors assist in set building and design and in directing artists, model makers, and other members of the crew in accordance with the director and producer's desires. They often contribute to the design of costumes, makeup, lighting effects, and other aspects of the production. Art directors must also manage the internal operations of the art department, including establishing departmental budgets; hiring, training, and terminating team members; and monitoring individual assignments to ensure that the department is operating efficiently, on time, and within budget parameters.

In contrast, smaller stations frequently have few or no specialized technicians. Consequently, broadcast technicians working in these environments are often generalists, responsible for lights, sound, transmitters, and all other aspects of the station's technical systems.

Duties and Responsibilities

- Designing set blueprints and creating all visual elements
- Consulting with writers, producers and directors
- Supervising design staff
- Assisting in the marketing and advertising of products
- Managing budgets and ensuring that projects meet budget requirements

WORK ENVIRONMENT

Skills and Abilities

Communication Skills
- Speaking and writing effectively
- Describing visual elements to others

Creative/Artistic Skills
- Being skilled in art, music, or dance
- Creating ideas
- Translating ideas into concrete forms

Interpersonal/Social Skills
- Following instructions
- Paying attention to and handling details

Organization & Management Skills
- Coordinating tasks
- Managing people/groups
- Managing time
- Meeting goals and deadlines

Research & Planning Skil
- Researching subjects in art and architecture

Physical Environment

Motion picture, radio, and television art directors typically work in studios and office environments, which are generally well organized and highly controlled to ensure no interference from uninvolved individuals. They also work on location, which can either be an existing structure, such as a hotel, museum, or office building, or an outdoor setting, which can be remote and susceptible to various weather conditions.

Human Environment

Art directors work with and oversee a wide range of crew and cast members, including actors and extras, directors, producers, writers, creative directors, electricians, painters, construction crews, lighting and sound crews, unit publicists, camera operators, costume designers, and makeup artists. Therefore, they must have excellent interpersonal skills and the ability to work past any personality conflicts.

Technological Environment

Art directors must use a wide range of technologies. Off the set, they rely on many computer-based systems, including software devoted to computer-aided design (CAD), animation, graphic design, and special effects. On the set, they may use hand tools, photography and filming equipment, lighting systems, and sound recording equipment.

EDUCATION, TRAINING, AND ADVANCEMENT

High School/Secondary

High school students should study theater as well as explore the technical and creative arts through mechanical drawing, graphics, drafting, photography, and audio-visual courses. English, art history, the industrial arts, and mathematics are also highly useful for aspiring art directors. High school students can also gain experience in art direction through participation in school- or community-based theater and media productions

Suggested High School Subjects

- Arts
- Audio-Visual
- Drafting
- English
- Graphic Communications
- Industrial Arts
- Mathematics
- Mechanical Drawing
- Photography
- Theatre & Drama

Famous First

The first theater designed expressly for dance performances was Ted Shawn's theater at Jacob's Pillow in Becket, Mass. Opening in 1942, the space featured a large, smooth maple floor inside a pinewood building. Since that time the annual dance festival held there has become one of the largest and most respected venues of its kind.

College/Postsecondary

Art directors for motion pictures, radio, and television generally have a bachelor's degree in fine arts, theater, or a similar field. During postsecondary schooling, many aspiring art directors assemble a portfolio of their work, which can be used to fulfill the admission requirements for specialized undergraduate and graduate art programs that provide training in photography, graphic design, design, and other relevant fields. A strong portfolio also demonstrates the future art director's knowledge and skill to prospective employers. Students can gain practical experience and build a portfolio by participating in school-based or independent film, radio, and television productions.

Related College Majors
- Advertising
- Design & Visual Communications
- Graphic Design, Commercial Art & Illustration
- Studio Production
- Theater & Drama

Adult Job Seekers

The film, radio, and television job market is very competitive. While some individuals find work through placement offices at art schools or colleges, most art directors attain their positions after having acquired and worked in lower-level jobs within an art department. Internships, frequently unpaid, serve as a common entry point into the industry. Aspiring art directors can build their portfolios by working on commercials, independent film projects, and music videos, as well as through employment with entertainment-oriented advertising and marketing firms. As with many other entertainment careers, networking is essential.

Professional Certification and Licensure

No certification is required to work as a motion picture, radio, and television art director. Some art directors, however, may pursue voluntary certification in specialized areas, such as design, digital technology, and art direction. As with any voluntary certification process, it is beneficial to consult credible professional associations within the field and follow professional debate as to the relevancy and value of any certification program.

Additional Requirements

Motion picture, television, and radio art directors should be excellent communicators and managers. They must be creative and detail oriented, and they should possess strong computer and budgeting skills. In order to succeed in this fast-paced environment, art directors must be decisive and able to handle stressful situations.

EARNINGS AND ADVANCEMENT

People who have become art directors do so after acquiring much experience in the advertising field. Salaries and job opportunities depend on the size and geographic location of the employer and the individual's experience and ability.

Median annual earnings of motion picture, radio and television art directors were $85,468 in 2012. The lowest ten percent earned less than $45,410, and the highest ten percent earned more than $173,236. Art directors may receive paid vacations, holidays, and sick days; life and health insurance; and retirement benefits. These are usually paid by the employer.

Metropolitan Areas with the Highest
Employment Level in This Occupation

Metropolitan area	Employment[1]	Employment per thousand jobs	Hourly mean wage
New York-White Plains-Wayne, NY-NJ	5,940	1.15	$62.83
Los Angeles-Long Beach-Glendale, CA	2,830	0.73	$57.01
Chicago-Joliet-Naperville, IL	1,650	0.45	$38.67
Boston-Cambridge-Quincy, MA	1,010	0.59	$45.34
San Francisco-San Mateo-Redwood City, CA	970	0.96	$59.28
Minneapolis-St. Paul-Bloomington, MN-WI	730	0.42	$39.45
Seattle-Bellevue-Everett, WA	630	0.45	$48.69
Washington-Arlington-Alexandria, DC-VA-MD-WV	590	0.25	$40.97

[1] Includes all art directors, not only those employed in the motion picture/radio/television industry. Does not include self-employed Source: Bureau of Labor Statistics, 2012

EMPLOYMENT AND OUTLOOK

Art directors of all varieties (including those outside of the entertainment industry) held about 32,000 jobs nationally in 2012. Employment is expected to grow slower than the average for all occupations through the year 2020, which means employment is projected to increase up to 9 percent. Producers of information, goods and services will continue to place increased emphasis on visual appeal in product design, advertising, marketing and television. Competition for good jobs will be strong.

Employment Trend, Projected 2010–20

Total, All Occupations: 14%

Arts, Design, Entertainment, Sports, and Media: 13%

Art Directors: 9%

Note: "All Occupations" includes all occupations in the U.S. Economy Source: U.S. Bureau of Labor Statistics, Employment Projections Program

Related Occupations
- Advertising Director
- Art Director
- Cinematographer
- Photographer

Conversation With . . .
CHARLES E. MCCARRY
Motion Picture / Television Art Director
30 years in the profession

1. What was your individual career path in terms of education, entry-level job, or other significant opportunity?

I was always one of the kids who hung around the art room in high school and helped backstage with plays. I selected a college which had a very robust graduate theater program in my hometown of Philadelphia. I received a bachelor's of science degree. In a way I'm glad I didn't simply concentrate in theater. I always advise my college students, don't forget to go to college while you're here! Get as broad an education as possible. You need to know about the world.

By my sophomore year of college is was clear to me that I had an interest in design – creating the environment for theater productions. A faculty member endorsed me for a number of different jobs as scenic designer at small theaters around town. I did that for two years, then, with a nice portfolio of my work, moved to New York. That got me into a number of professional studios as an assistant and I had opportunities to work on quite a number of interesting and fairly sizeable Broadway shows. Some of them won Tony awards for scenic design, and I was part of that.

After a few years I was accepted into Yale School of Drama, concentrating in scenic drama. It was a three-year M.F.A. program. I got into film when I was asked to create the film sequence for the Broadway musical *City of Angels*, which is about Hollywood. I thought, I could do that for real and began looking for opportunities to work in film.

2. Are there many job opportunities in your profession? In what specific areas?

There are never any job opportunities and there are always lots of job opportunities. In the arts, that's pretty much the way it is. There are absolutely always opportunities for someone who is committed and well rounded and willing to work hard and willing to learn. You need to be completely prepared and then you need to locate yourself in a place where opportunity might knock. If you aspire to be a production designer in film or an art director on a network, you should probably be in New York or Los Angeles. Possibly Chicago, Washington, or Boston.

Union membership is important. I'm a member of United Scenic Artists Local 829.

3. What do you wish you had known going into this profession?

I wish I had known the critical importance of the social side of the profession. Never pass up an opportunity to have lunch with someone. Never pass up an opportunity to go to a reception or a gathering. It's entirely people based. It's who you know.

4. How do you see your profession changing in the next five years?

With the digital revolution, anything is possible now. Creating gaming environments is a rich area of opportunity for the kids coming up nowadays. There's also a blending of gaming environments with other areas of production design. The very nature of a "show" is changing, with the television networks dying off and Netflix, Hulu Plus and the like replacing them. And the delivery of the product is absolutely changing. I will often watch a movie on my laptop or on my television set in my living room instead of going to the movie theater.

Yet, as a production designer and art director I use exactly the same skills as always. These digital tools are just entering a centuries-old profession and being seamlessly integrated.

5. What role will technology play in those changes, and what skills will be required?

Twenty to 30 years ago, we would make a little model out of foam core and now that model might exist on a laptop, but it's essentially the same work. Any young person entering the profession at the very least needs to be familiar with Google SketchUp and possibly Vectorworks, and always, a pencil, pencil, pencil. You need to be able to present your visual ideas. The easiest way to do that at lunch with the director is to sketch it on a napkin and that will never change. And then you can open your laptop.

6. Do you have any general advice or additional professional insights to share with someone interested in your profession?

The most important word in our line of work is "collaborate." So, ask yourself if you enjoy collaborating. For someone who has a real comfort level with working with others and can bring strong, visual ideas to the table while being mindful of checking your ego at the door, then you're a good fit for this profession. If you're more of a loner, someone much more happy working in a studio on sculpture or a painting, then this is not your line of work.

7. Can you suggest a valuable "try this" for students considering a career in your profession?

Get involved with the shows at school and see if that floats your boat. By involved, I mean the collaboration. Be part of a situation where a day might consist of a lofty conversation about characters and motivation one moment, and a how many sheets of plywood you need the next. A high school drama club can sometimes be a clique, so if you're not comfortable with that, seek out other opportunities in community theater.

SELECTED SCHOOLS

Many colleges and universities offer bachelor's degree programs in the arts; some have programs in theater, film, and television production as well. The student may also gain initial training through enrollment at a community college. Below are listed some of the more prominent institutions in this field.

Art Center College of Design
1700 Lida Street
Pasadena, CA 91103
626.396.2200
www.artcenter.edu

Carnegie-Mellon University
5000 Forbes Avenue
Pittsburgh, PA 15213
412.268.2000
www.cmu.edu

Columbia University
116th Street and Broadway
New York, NY 10027
212.854.1754
www.columbia.edu

Loyola Marymount
1 Loyola Marymount University
Drive
Los Angeles, CA 90045
310.338.2700
www.lmu.edu

New York University
70 Washington Square S.
New York, NY 10012
212.998.1212
www.nyu.edu

Parsons The New School for Design
66 5th Avenue
New York, NY 10011
212.229.8900
www.newschool.edu/parsons

Pratt Institute
2000 Willoughby Avenue
Brooklyn, NY 11205
718.636.3600
www.pratt.edu

Rhode Island School of Design
2 College Street
Providence, RI 02903
401.454.6100
www.risd.edu

University of Southern California
Los Angeles, CA 90089
323.442.1130
www.usc.edu

University of Texas–Austin
110 Inner Campus Drive
Austin, TX 78712
512.471.3434
www.utexas.edu

MORE INFORMATION

Art Directors Club
106 West 29th Street
New York, NY 10001
212.643.1440
www.adcglobal.org

Art Directors Guild
11969 Ventura Boulevard, 2nd Floor
Studio City, CA 91604
818.762.9995
www.adg.org

**Association of Independent
Colleges of Art and Design**
236 Hope Street
Providence, RI 02906
401.270.5991
www.aicad.org

**National Association of
Broadcasters**
1771 N Street NW
Washington, DC 20036
202.429.5300
www.nab.org

**Set Decorators Society of
America**
7100 Tujunga Avenue, Suite A
North Hollywood, CA 91605
818.255.2425
www.setdecorators.org

Michael Auerbach/Editor

Multimedia Artist & Animator

Snapshot

Career Cluster: Arts, A/V Technology & Communications
Interests: Art, Illustration, Web Design, Cartooning
Earnings (Yearly Average): $62,021
Employment & Outlook: Slower Than Average Growth Expected

OVERVIEW

Sphere of Work

Multimedia artists and animators create visual effects and animations for television, movies, video games, and other media. They create two- and three-dimensional models and animations. They may be involved in the creation of media advertisements and other marketing campaigns, or create illustrations for websites, online magazines, and other forms of media. Some are self-employed, working from home offices, while others work for film, television, and video production companies of varying sizes.

Work Environment

Multimedia artists and animators often work in studio environments that are generally clean and comfortable, or they work in a home office/studio. Their hours vary based on the size and scope of the project on which they are working, as well as the time constraints established in a contract. Smaller companies and independent, self-employed artists tend to work longer hours to manage not only their projects but also the issues associated with running a small business.

Profile

Working Conditions: Office/Production Studio Some Out Side Work

Physical Strength: Light To Moderate Work

Education Needs:
Technical/Community College
Bachelor's Degree

Licensure/Certification:
Recommended

Physical Abilities Not Required: No Strenuous Work

Opportunities For Experience:
Apprenticeship, Military Service
Volunteer Work, Part-Time Work

Holland Interest Score*: RCE

* See Appendix A

Occupation Interest

Multimedia artists and animators must combine a talent for art and creative thinking with good research and communication skills, close attention to detail, and the ability to meet deadlines and work in a competitive atmosphere, all while remaining true to the needs of the client. They should be aware of general public attitudes and keep up with current trends. Many independent commercial artists set their own hours and act as small business entrepreneurs as well as creative artists.

A Day in the Life—Duties and Responsibilities

The duties and responsibilities of multimedia artists and animators vary based on the area and the size of the business in which they work. These artists may specialize in video games or animated movies, or they may create visual effects for television shows or online venues. They can further specialize in particular elements, such as characters or scenery or pieces that contribute to the overall look and feel of a digital production.

In general, multimedia artists and animators first confer with clients or supervisors to establish the preferred design approach, budget, and anything else that needs to be taken into account. They then develop the requested design, often showing samples to the client at different points in the process. The artist may work independently, or as part of a team overseen by an art director. In a team setting, the art director's job is to assign tasks, give the artists advice and feedback, and approve and present the final product.

Duties and Responsibilities

- **Conferring with clients, other artists, and directors to determine budgets and timelines**
- **Creating graphics and animations using computer programs**
- **Developing storyboards that lay out the main scenes in a production**
- **Editing and refining the work in response to feedback**

WORK ENVIRONMENT

Skills and Abilities

Communication Skills
- Expressing thoughts and ideas
- Understanding others' wishes

Creative/Artistic Skills
- Creating ideas
- Translating ideas into concrete forms

Interpersonal/Social Skills
- Respecting others' opinions
- Working as part of a team

Organization & Management Skills
- Adhering to time schedules
- Making decisions
- Paying attention to and handling details

Technical Skills
- Performing technical work using computer programs

Physical Environment

Multimedia artists and animators work primarily in video production firms, studios, or office spaces in film and television companies. These environments are well lit and well ventilated, with computers and other production and display technologies. Many artists/animators are independent consultants who work from studios and office spaces in their own private residences.

Human Environment

Depending on their areas of expertise, multimedia artists and animators meet and interact with a wide range of individuals. These parties include creative professionals, business executives, editors, designers, and other specialized commercial artists.

Technological Environment

Multimedia artists and animators might not only use computer programs in their work but also may be required to write programming code in order to create or mount their art.. For this reason a solid grounding in digital graphics technology is a must. Some animation studios have their own software and computer applications that they use to create films. They give workers on-the-job training to use this software.

EDUCATION, TRAINING, AND ADVANCEMENT

High School/Secondary

High school students should study art, including drawing, photography, and design; math, including geometry; and computer science, including graphic design and drafting. They should also take advantage of any subject areas of interest to them as artists; for example, future animators are advised to take cartooning and media classes.

Suggested High School Subjects
- Applied Math
- Arts
- Cartooning
- Computer Science
- Crafts
- Drafting
- English
- Graphic Communications
- Photography
- Web Design

Famous First

The first entirely computer-animated film was *Toy Story*, released in 1995. It was produced by Pixar Studios under the control of Walt Disney Pictures. The film was an "instant classic," garnering $300 million in its first year and spawning legions of toys, video games, theme-park attractions, and other spin-offs—including two sequels.

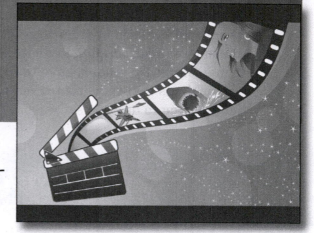

Postsecondary

Aspiring multimedia artists and animators may pursue a bachelor's degree in graphic art, design, computer graphics, or a similar field. Alternatively, they may enroll in art or design institutes for programs with more studio time and a greater focus on graphic design, digital imaging, or illustration. Further education may be warranted depending on how an artist chooses to specialize. For example, a prospective art director may also study management or art administration, while somebody interested in animation would be well served by specialist programs in that field.

Related College Majors

- Art, General
- Computer Graphics
- Educational/Instructional Media Design
- Educational/Instructional Media Technology
- Fine/Studio Arts
- Graphic Design/Commercial Art & Illustration
- Illustration
- Multimedia Production
- Visual & Performing Arts
- Web Design

Adult Job Seekers

An internship or apprenticeship is a good way to gain necessary experience. Individuals looking for work can apply directly to the art or advertising director of a particular company, and may also find opportunities through professional organizations such as the American Institute of Graphic Arts (now known as AIGA). Any potential commercial artist must have a portfolio showing his or her best work.

Professional Certification and Licensure

Some organizations provide certification programs to help multimedia artists and animators become specialists in their particular fields. Such certification can provide a competitive edge for job candidates.

Additional Requirements

Multimedia artists and animators should be both creative and extremely knowledgeable of the wide range of media options available to them to meet a client's needs. They should be willing to listen to and communicate with clients who may or may not agree with their ideas. Such artists must have self-discipline and a strong work ethic, especially in light of the fact that many are self-employed.

Fun Fact

In 1920, Walter Elias Disney, at 19 years old, started working in animation at the Kansas City Slide Company.

Source: http://www.arenamalleswaram.com/animation_facts.html

EARNINGS AND ADVANCEMENT

Earnings of multimedia artists and animators depend on skill, education, and the type, size, and geographic location of the employer. Earnings of freelance multimedia artists and animators may vary with the artists' individual fees and reputation, as well as the nature and amount of work sold.

Median annual earnings of salaried multimedia artists and animators were $62,021 in 2012. The lowest ten percent earned less than $35,870, and the highest ten percent earned more than $105,820.

Earnings for self-employed multimedia artists and animators vary widely. Those struggling to gain experience and build a reputation may be forced to charge only small fees for their work. Well-established free-lancers may earn much more than salaried artists.

Multimedia artists and animators may receive paid vacations, holidays, and sick days; life and health insurance; and retirement benefits. These are usually paid for by the employer.

Metropolitan Areas with the Highest Employment Level in This Occupation

Metropolitan area	Employment[1]	Employment per thousand jobs	Hourly mean wage
Los Angeles-Long Beach-Glendale, CA	5,730	1.48	$43.11
Seattle-Bellevue-Everett, WA	2,330	1.65	$33.17
New York-White Plains-Wayne, NY-NJ	2,280	0.44	$35.03
San Francisco-San Mateo-Redwood City, CA	1,050	1.05	$34.33
Bridgeport-Stamford-Norwalk, CT	850	2.05	(8)
Chicago-Joliet-Naperville, IL	810	0.22	$30.52
Atlanta-Sandy Springs-Marietta, GA	790	0.35	$27.18
Oakland-Fremont-Hayward, CA	750	0.78	$41.83

[1] Does not include self-employed Source: Bureau of Labor Statistics, 2012

EMPLOYMENT AND OUTLOOK

Nationally, there were approximately 30,000 multimedia artists and animators employed in 2012. Employment is expected to grow slower than the average for all occupations through the year 2020, which means employment is projected to increase about 8 percent. Multimedia artists and animators should have better job opportunities than other artists, but still will experience competition. Demand for these workers will increase as consumers continue to require more realistic video games, movie and television special effects, and 3-D animated movies. Additional job openings will arise from the growth of computer graphics in the increasing number of mobile technologies. However, job growth will be limited by companies sending animation work overseas where workers can be paid less than in the United States.

Employment Trend, Projected 2010–20

Total, All Occupations: 14%

Art and Design Workers: 10%

Multimedia Artists and Animators: 8%

Note: "All Occupations" includes all occupations in the U.S. Economy Source: U.S. Bureau of Labor Statistics, Employment Projections Program

Related Occupations
- Art Director
- Designer
- Graphic Designer & Illustrator
- Industrial Designer
- Medical & Scientific Illustrator
- Photographer
- Software Developer
- Web Developer

Related Military Occupations
- Graphic Designer & Illustrator

Conversation With . . .
TYLER NAUGLE
MTV Production Assistant
Freelance Animator, 2 years

1. What was your individual career path in terms of education, entry-level job, or other significant opportunity?

At Maryland Institute, College of Art (MICA) I majored in 2D Animation with a concentration in Video. After my junior year I was fortunate to get an internship with MTV's On-Air Design department. Shortly before my 2011 graduation, I received a call from my previous supervisor at MTV who offered me Production Assistant position. I accepted the position and started working at MTV full-time a few weeks after graduation. I work on different projects: it could be animating, it could be editing. Something called a "lower third" is a big thing we work on; it pops out from the corner of the screen and gives information about a show coming out and directs the viewer toward something. I've also done some freelance jobs in my free time.

2. Are there many job opportunities in your profession? In what specific areas?

Animation is a big industry with a lot of opportunities. Corporations, independent film makers, small companies trying to show people what they're about...people are willing to pay for motion graphics. There is no shortage of people looking for motion graphics or animation in general.

I focus in 2D Animation and there are an assortment of positions available (Key Artist, In-betweener, Background Artist, Effects Artist, Motion Designer). At MTV, I'm specifically in motion graphics. Work assignments are mainly elements for TV, and more subdued than what I do in my spare time, which is very character-based, usually revolving around humor, and much more manic.

3. What do you wish you had known going into this profession?

I wish that I had known more about negotiating pay. That is a topic that's only very briefly touched on in school and is a huge part of working as an artist.

4. How do you see your profession changing in the next five years?

I may be wrong, but it think animation is going toward a more graphic-based presentation even though there is always going to be a market for more experimental animation. Also, independents use Kickstarter. Outside the commercial side of things, that's where all the independent animation is going to be flourishing. That's where people should focus if they just want to do their own projects.

5. What role will technology play in those changes, and what skills will be required?

Technology is huge in the animation industry. Programs are constantly changing so you have to pay attention to what's new and what's being phased out. Depending on what you want to do, your toolkit could be completely different from your fellow animators. For example, I use mostly Flash and After Effects and edit in Premiere. There are people I know who use Toon Boom and edit in Final Cut. We end up with a similar product but how we each get there is completely different.

6. Do you have any general advice or additional professional insights to share with someone interested in your profession?

To work professionally as an animator is to essentially sell your abilities as a product and you need to be able to sell the product successfully. Being confident in your work and knowing what your abilities are worth is very important. Too many animators sell their abilities for way less than they are worth. This is a problem that I have found affects recent graduates more than any other group. It's something that a lot of people are uncomfortable talking about, and though pay varies depending on the type of job you're doing and the client that it's for, it's a good idea to talk about it with your peers to make sure that you're not getting taken advantage of.

7. Can you suggest a valuable "try this" for students considering a career in your profession?

Anyone wanting to go into animation should work with others as often as possible. Commercial animation requires you to work closely with peers. That's quite different from other fields within art and it's an aspect of the industry that some people might find difficult or unusual. Practicing that level of cooperation in school could be particularly useful; it has the potential to provide contacts that could be mutually beneficial in later years.

SELECTED SCHOOLS

A variety of colleges and universities offer bachelor's degree programs in graphic arts; some have programs in digital media and animation. The student may also gain initial training through enrollment at a community college. Below are listed some of the more prominent institutions in this field. stitutions in this field.

California State University, Fullerton
800 N. State College Boulevard
Fullerton, CA 92831
657.278.1600
www.fullerton.edu

City University of New York
535 E. 80th Street
New York, NY 10075
212.794.5555
www.cuny.edu

Drexel University
3141 Chestnut Street
Philadelphia, PA 19104
215.895.2000
www.drexel.edu
Emerson College

120 Boylston Street
Boston, MA 02116
617.824.8500
www.emerson.edu

Florida State University
600 W. College Avenue
Tallahassee, FL 32308
850.644.2525
www.fsu.edu

Lesley University
29 Everett Street
Cambridge, MA 02138
617.868.9600
www.lesley.edu

Louisiana State University
3357 Highland Road
Baton Rouge, LA 70802
225.578.3202
www.lsu.edu

North Carolina State University
2200 Hillsborough
Raleigh, NC 27695
919.515.2011
www.ncsu.edu

Syracuse University
900 S. Crouse Avenue
Syracuse, NY 13210
315.443.1870
syr.edu

University of Colorado, Denver
1250 14th Street
Denver, CO 80202
303.556.2400
www.ucdenver.edu

MORE INFORMATION

Association of Independent Colleges of Art and Design
236 Hope Street
Providence, RI 02906
401.270.5991
www.aicad.org

Computer Graphics Society
134 Gilbert Street
Adelaide, SA, 5000
AUSTRALIA
61.8.82128255
www.cgsociety.org

International Digital Media and Arts Association
P.O. Box 622
Agoura Hills, CA 91376
818.564.7898
idmaa.org

National Art Education Association
1806 Robert Fulton Drive, Suite 300
Reston, VA 20191-1590
703.860.8000
info@arteducators.org
www.naea-reston.org

Michael Auerbach/Editor

Music Director

Snapshot

Career Cluster(s): Arts; Fine, Visual, and Performing
Interests: Music, composition, management, artistic expression, performance
Earnings (Yearly Average): $49,820
Employment & Outlook: Slower than average

OVERVIEW

Sphere of Work

Music directors or conductors are musicians who lead orchestras and musical groups during recording session or performances. Some music directors are also composers, who write and arrange original pieces of music for solo or group performance, while most music directors work with arrangements created by other composers. The field of music direction blends creativity with managerial skills as music directors typically manage groups of musicians and other professionals involved in producing live performances and recordings but are also artists who express original ideas through their presentation and arrangement of musical compositions.

Work Environment

Most music directors do their work indoors, either in concert halls, recording studios, or other performance spaces. Many music directors are employed by religious organizations and so may spend much of their work time in churches or other religious centers. Other music directors are employed in educational institutions and so may in school auditoriums or offices. Travel is an important part of the job for many music directors, as they must travel to attend and direct performances or to music studios during recording sessions. While music director positions are found around the world, job opportunities tend to be concentrated in cities or regions with thriving music and performance industries.

Profile

Working Conditions: Work Indoor
Physical Strength: Light work
Education Needs: Bachelor's Degree,
  Master's Degree
Licensure/Certification: Not required
Opportunities For Experience:
  On-Job Training, Part-Time Work,
  Internship
Holland Interest Score*: AES

* See Appendix A

Occupation Interest

Music directors should have a strong interest in music and performance. High profile conductors may direct performances for large audiences and so become performing professionals in their own right as they serve as the public face for a performing orchestra, choir, or other ensemble. Music directors also should have a strong interest in creative work as they are often responsible for creating creative arrangements or productions using music and performance. In addition, music direction is a social field that involves frequent collaboration and the management of musicians and other professionals and prospective music directors should therefore have strong interests in team building and collaborative art.

A Day in the Life—Duties and Responsibilities

Leading up to a performance or recording session, a music director works with composers and other individuals involved in producing a performance or recording to select arrangements. Depending on the type of production, the director might also be responsible for selecting individuals to serve as soloists or to invite guest musicians to perform with the regular members of an ensemble. Directors are also typically involved in staffing, and may participate in auditioning new performers and hiring assistants and interns. Once the musical group is organized and the arrangements have been finalized, the music director oversees practices and rehearsals. During this stage, directors are responsible for working with individual musicians and groups and for giving feedback to musicians involved in a production. Musical directors are also typically involved in organizing funding for their productions and may therefore participate in fund drives and meet with philanthropic organizations and donors to secure funding for upcoming productions or performance seasons.

Duties and Responsibilities

- Select and evaluate compositions and arrangements
- Audition new musicians or members of a musical team
- Meet with performers, producers, and others involved in a production
- Conduct rehearsals and performances
- Choose and contact featured guests and soloists
- Manage technical aspects of a production
- Participate in the fund raising process for a performance or recording
- Attend professional conferences and research developments in the field

OCCUPATION SPECIALTIES

Music Supervisor

Music supervisors are music directors who work on film and television productions, integrating music with the scenes of the show or film. Music supervisors may also be composers, who create original film or television scores, or may work alongside composers, helping to integrate original or selected compositions into the finished product.

Orchestra Conductor

An orchestra conductor is a music director who works with a symphony orchestra or other orchestral group and may also be known as a "principal conductor." Orchestra conductors in high profile positions can become nationally famous celebrities, serving as the most-recognizable figure for a certain orchestra.

Choirmaster

A choirmaster is a music director who works with a choir or one who directs music at a cathedral or church. Choirmasters are typically former singers and work with members of the choir to arrange and perform chorale concerts.

Bandmaster or Bandleader

A bandmaster or bandleader is a music director or conductor that works with an institutional band or marching band. Bandmasters and bandleaders can work for sports organizations, schools and educational institutions, or for a branch of the military that maintains a military band or performance troupe.

WORK ENVIRONMENT

Relevant Skills and Abilities

Communication Skills
- Communicating with musicians and other production professionals
- Writing and transposing arrangements

Interpersonal/Social Skills
- Working in a group environment
- Interacting with the public, other managers, and employees

Organization & Management Skills
- Hiring and mentoring musicians and other employees
- Organizing performance, rehearsal, and recording schedules
- Giving feedback to musicians to refine performances

Research & Planning Skills
- Researching new music and possible collaborators/guest artists
- Creating and managing performance schedules

Technical Skills
- Utilizing digital recording and performance tools
- Using word processing, presentation, and digital communication tools

Physical Environment

Music directors tend to work indoors in offices or performance spaces. Those employed to lead choirs or religious music programs may complete most of their work in a church or other religious building, while conductors working with symphonies or other orchestras may work primarily within concert halls or similar venues. Those working on film/television or recordings typically work in recording studios. Many music directors need to travel, either to audition and meet with musicians or to conduct performances or recordings with artists or various ensembles.

Human Environment

Music direction is a managerial and collaborative discipline and music directors work closely with a variety of other professionals involved in staging musical productions or conducting recording sessions. In a managerial capacity, music directors are responsible for hiring and managing musicians and also for providing feedback, guidance, and mentoring to musicians and other members of a production staff. Music directors might also need to work with other types of directors and project managers for certain types of productions and may be asked to take part in fundraising and promotional endeavors for the production company or organization.

Technological Environment

Many modern musical productions utilize a variety of traditional tools as well as modern, digital technology. For instance, many modern music directors use computers or tablets to schedule and keep track of information for a production. Those using digital or electronic music might also need to be familiar with digital and MIDI interfaces used to play and record digital instruments. A variety of recording programs are also used, including popular music recording programs like Pro Tools and Logic, which are two of a wide variety of digital recording and post-recording programs. Finally, music directors may use digital communication and composition tools to arrange scores, create presentations, and to write documents related to a production.

EDUCATION, TRAINING, AND ADVANCEMENT

High School/Secondary

High school students interested in careers in musical direction can begin by studying music and music composition. In addition, as most musical directors enter the field with at least a postsecondary or undergraduate college degree, high school students interested in the field can pursue a general education towards the goal of entering higher education.

Suggested High School Subjects
- English
- Composition
- Music
- Music History
- Classical Music History
- Drama

- Art History
- Introduction to Computers

Famous First

Violinist and conductor Theodore Thomas (1835-1905) was the first American conductor to gain worldwide acclaim and was the first music director for the Chicago Symphony Orchestra. Born in Göttingen, Germany, Thomas began performing publically when he was six years old and, at age 10, relocated to the United States with his family. From New York, Thomas traveled around the country performing with orchestras and for some of the most famous operatic singers of the era. Thomas went on to conduct with the New York Philharmonic and the Brooklyn Philharmonic Society and, in 1891, became the music director for the Chicago Symphony. His contribution to Chicago culture has been memorialized with a statue, called the "Spirit of Music," in Chicago's Grant Park.

College/Postsecondary

Most music directors begin their careers by studying music theory and composition and most complete at least an undergraduate or basic postsecondary degree program. Organizations like the National Association of Schools of Music provide helpful information about postsecondary degree programs in musical disciplines. A music director should study composition, the history of music, recording, conducting, and music education. While there are no specific educational requirements to begin working in the field, individuals with bachelor's or higher level degrees will have an advantage in seeking employment. After obtaining a postsecondary degree, aspiring music directors can continue their education by seeking a master's or doctorate in music theory, composition, or conducting. A number of prestigious institutions offer degrees specifically in the art of conducting, in which students can also choose to subspecialize in specific types of conducting, such as strings, choir, wins & brass, or orchestral.

Related College Majors
- Orchestral Conducting

- Choral Conducting
- Music History/Theory
- Musical Performance
- Music Composition
- Music Education
- Master of Musical Arts
- Doctor of Musical Arts

Adult Job Seekers

Obtaining a position as a musical director typically requires a significant level of work experience. Prospective professionals can seek out assistant conductor or assistant director positions or can pursue an internship to work alongside an established production team. Director positions are typically considered upper management and so a prospective musical director might need to spend years working at lower levels before applying for positions in upper level directing.

Professional Certification and Licensure

There are no specific certificates or licenses required to become a music director. However, those who want to work in educational institutions will need to adhere to teacher's certification requirements in their area.

Additional Requirements

Musical directors need excellent interpersonal skills, a capability for leadership, and the ability to help promote their work. In addition, because musical directors are responsible for evaluating and organizing musical compositions and performances, directors need to have excellent hearing and need to develop their ability to evaluate music and the nuances of individual performances by ear.

Fun Fact

French composer Erik Satie wrote the longest piece of music in 1893. *Vexations* is comprised of 180 notes, repeated 845 times. Five pianists handed off playing duties all night when the piece was finally performed in New York in 1963.

Source: http://www.cbcmusic.ca/posts/12560/satie-vexations-calgary-honens

EARNINGS AND ADVANCEMENT

According to the Bureau of Labor Statistics (BLS), the median wage for both music directors and composers was $49,820 in 2015, with the lowest paid 10 percent earning less than $21,000 and the highest paid 10 percent earning over $100,000 annually. Estimates of wages in the industry are skewed by high wages earned by a small number of high profile composers and conductors, many of whom work for nationally famous symphony orchestras or compose and direct music for films and television. Advancing in the industry typically involves working as an assistant or in low-profile director positions as one develops his or her career with the goal of applying for positions in higher profile institutions or organizations.

Metropolitan Areas with the Highest Employment Level in this Occupation

Metropolitan area	Employment	Employment per thousand jobs	Hourly mean wage
New York-Jersey City-White Plains, NY-NJ Metropolitan Division	1,550	0.24	$40.62
Los Angeles-Long Beach-Glendale, CA Metropolitan Division	700	0.17	$29.71
Nassau County-Suffolk County, NY Metropolitan Division	560	0.44	N/A
Chicago-Naperville-Arlington Heights, IL Metropolitan Division	520	0.15	$31.30
Boston-Cambridge-Newton, MA NECTA Division	350	0.20	$33.16
Portland-Vancouver-Hillsboro, OR-WA	320	0.30	$18.74
Virginia Beach-Norfolk-Newport News, VA-NC	280	0.39	$28.20
Anaheim-Santa Ana-Irvine, CA Metropolitan Division	280	0.18	$28.44
Atlanta-Sandy Springs-Roswell, GA	280	0.11	$27.22
Washington-Arlington-Alexandria, DC-VA-MD-WV Metropolitan Division	270	0.11	$29.58

Source: Bureau of Labor Statistics

EMPLOYMENT AND OUTLOOK

The BLS estimates that job opportunities in the music direction industry will grow by only 3 percent between 2014 and 2024, marking slower than average growth compared to the estimated 6-7 percent average growth for all industries. Part of the reason for slow growth is a dearth of funding sources, with many public orchestral, educational, or other performance production programs funded primarily by public donations. However, positions for directors and composers in film and television productions is likely to increase at a more rapid rate due to an expansion of independent and streaming television and film productions. Because the field is expected to grow slowly, experts also expect that there will be strong competition for available positions. Individuals with diverse experience and advanced education will therefore have an advantage in the field.

Employment Trend, Projected 2014–24

Total, All Occupations: 7%

Entertainers and Performers, Sports and Related Workers: 6%

Music Directors and Composers: 3%

Note: "All Occupations" includes all occupations in the U.S. Economy. Source: U.S. Bureau of Labor Statistics, Employment Projections Program

Related Occupations
- Dancers and Choreographers
- Musicians and Singers
- Directors and Producers
- Writers and Authors
- Actors
- Postsecondary Teachers
- Middle School Teachers
- Kindergarten and Elementary School Teachers
- High School Teachers

Related Military Occupations
- Military Bandleader

Conversation With . . .
SCOTT SHEEHAN

Director of Bands & Music Department Chair
Hollidaysburg Area Senior High School
Hollidaysburg, Pennsylvania
Music teacher, 20 years

1. What was your individual career path in terms of education/training, entry-level job, or other significant opportunity?

I started playing trumpet at age 8 because my dad played. So, I knew how to make a sound before I actually started lessons in fourth grade. In high school, we got a new band director who influenced me and took us to a new level of musicianship, with competitions, out-of-town parades and concerts.

In music, there's something known as an aesthetic response, or out-of-body experience, that transports you to a different place. That happened to me in my junior year. I remember walking home from school, sad the moment had passed. That's when I knew I wanted to be a band director.

I received a bachelor's in music education from Clarion University in Pennsylvania. My parents were concerned that I might not find a job or be satisfied as a music teacher, so I double majored in music marketing. That helped me get my first job, at a rural junior-senior high school. The principal later told me they were hoping to build their band program and thought the marketing might help. A big part of being a high school band director is understanding the business and management part of your job: working with administrators and budgets, or promoting concerts.

Today, I teach and direct the band and music department at a larger, suburban school. I also conduct a summer community band and play occasionally for shows or with brass quintets. I serve as Eastern Division President of the National Association for Music Education.

2. What are the most important skills and/or qualities for someone in your profession?

Good communication—written, aural, oral, or musical—is the key to success. You also need leadership, a strong work ethic, charisma, honesty, creativity, and a willingness to be a life-long learner. You must enjoy working collaboratively with students and colleagues.

Personal musicianship is essential to teaching others music. A variety of music skills are necessary, including the ability to read standard musical notation, aural skills such as pitch and rhythm identification, internal pulse and a steady beat, and an interest in playing or teaching all instruments.

3. What do you wish you had known going into this profession?

I wish I had known more about teaching and playing instruments other than the trumpet, and that I had developed my aural discrimination skills sooner since you need to hear what is wrong during a rehearsal in order to offer suggestions to correct it.

I also wish I could play piano better. The piano encompasses all musical theory and therefore adds to one's understanding of the harmonies and theory behind the music.

4. Are there many job opportunities in your profession? In what specific areas?

The eastern U.S. tends to have more universities that offer music education programs compared to the west so there are more music positions available in the west. Positions are also available in urban and rural areas. Some schools are replacing retiring music teachers or expanding music programs.

5. How do you see your profession changing in the next five years, what role will technology play in those changes, and what skills will be required?

I think there will be a focus on reaching students through music outside of the traditional band, chorus, and orchestra settings, with new electives such as rock, rap, and hip hop, music technology, sound engineering, and composition. I also think there will be a focus on digital music and software. Teachers will need to stay informed about the newest technology and develop curricula that allow students to interact in new and creative ways.

I see our profession changing as we advocate for access to music education for students from all backgrounds and cultures and find ways to bridge the gap between traditional programs and what is culturally relevant to the students.

6. What do you enjoy most about your job? What do you enjoy least about your job?

I enjoy seeing my students accomplish goals that they thought were impossible. I'll never forget coming to this school and playing a recording of a jazz halftime show for the band. The trumpet player looked at me with big eyes and said, "Well that sounds awesome, but there's no way we are ever going to be able to play that." I said, "Yes, you can." After extensive rehearsals, they went out, played it, and got a standing ovation from 3,000 people.

I also enjoy seeing students grow as musicians and perform music with a high level of expression, meaning, and technical facility.

I don't enjoy seeing disappointment on students' faces; the reality that some students face outside of school; the politics of school bureaucracy; standardized testing; and tight budgets.

7. **Can you suggest a valuable "try this" for students considering a career in your profession?**

Shadow a music teacher in an elementary music classroom, a middle school setting, and a high school. It's important to understand how different, yet how important, each component of a music education program is to the next level, and how a sequential approach to learning musical concepts is critical.

MORE INFORMATION

National Association of Schools of Music
11250 Roger Bacon Drive, Suite 21
Reston, VA 20190
703-437-0700
www.nasm.arts-accredit.org

Future of Music Coalition
2217 14th Street NW, 2nd Floor
Washington, DC 20009
202-822-2051
www.futureofmusic.org

College Orchestra Directors Association (CODA)
540-654-1956
www.codaweb.org

American Choral Directors Association (ACDA)
545 Couch Drive
Oklahoma City, OK 73102
405-232-8161
www.acda.org

Conductors Guild
19350 Magnolia Grove, Sq., #301
Leesburg, VA 20176
646-335-2032
www.conductorsguild.org

Micah Issitt/Editor

Music Therapist

Snapshot

Career Cluster: Health Care; Human Services

Interests: Music, playing instruments, singing, patient rehabilitation, planning and organizing musical activities, therapeutic programs and services

Earnings (Yearly Average): $43,180

Employment & Outlook: Average Growth Expected

OVERVIEW

Sphere of Work

Music therapists are trained professionals who work within the health industry to help people manage pain, overcome an emotional issue, build self-esteem, facilitate communication and social interaction, and improve well-being. Music therapy treatments may include singing, playing instruments, or listening to music. Practitioners of musical therapy are considered recreational therapists, along with art, dance, and writing therapists.

Work Environment

Music therapists work in private practice and in hospitals, schools, nursing homes, mental health clinics, prisons, and other environments. They tend to specialize in clients with physical disabilities or illnesses, cognitive problems, or emotional issues. Some music therapists treat all conditions. Full-time therapists work about a forty-hour week, usually with some evenings, nights, and weekends. They might travel from site to site or work at one institution. They interact mostly with their clients and other professionals.

Profile

Working Conditions: Work Indoors
Physical Strength: Light Work
Education Needs: Bachelor's Degree
Licensure/Certification: Required
Physical Abilities Not Required: No Heavy Labor
Opportunities For Experience: Internship, Volunteer Work
Holland Interest Score*: ESI

* See Appendix A

Occupation Interest

People attracted to the music therapy profession are usually musicians who are passionate about music and enjoy putting their talents and skills to use to help others. The ability to sing and play instruments and a familiarity with music theory, notation, and various genres (including classical, jazz, and popular music) are crucial. In addition to musical ability, therapists are excellent communicators, empathetic, patient, creative, and mentally and emotionally strong.

A Day in the Life—Duties and Responsibilities

Music therapists spend most of their work time engaged in activities with clients. The first meeting with a client usually involves assessing his or her needs and setting goals.

If a client has been referred by a doctor or psychiatrist, as is often the case, the therapist begins by devising a treatment plan intended to meet the prescribed goals. For example, a child with autism may need to work on some cognitive issues, such as basic math skills or how to tie shoes, but is difficult to reach through normal methods of communication and traditional instructional techniques. The music therapist might select or compose songs to sing with the child that are both engaging and instructional.

Some music therapists work in hospices, where patients are often depressed and frightened of death. The therapist might play soothing tunes on an instrument, such as a guitar or harp, or sing songs that bring back positive memories.

Other common treatment plans include drumming sessions, songwriting, and dancing to music, which might be done in conjunction with a dance therapist. Music therapists also sometimes teach clients how to sing or play an instrument. Occasionally, they may organize concerts involving groups of patients.

As part of the treatment plan, the therapist takes notes that will help him or her to evaluate its success and prepares assessment documents. Most therapists are also responsible for maintaining instruments and audio equipment. Therapists who own their own practices have additional business responsibilities.

Duties and Responsibilities

- Planning musical activities for patients or groups
- Playing music for patients to soothe them or get them physically active
- Working with disabled patients
- Assessing the needs of patients, choosing the appropriate treatment and evaluating patients' progress
- Using rhythmic exercises with patients

WORK ENVIRONMENT

Physical Environment

Music therapists usually work inside, in recreation rooms, classrooms, studios, offices, or private homes, but they may choose to conduct sessions outside in good weather. Some locations may be soundproofed for noise and privacy reasons.

Human Environment

Music therapists spend most of their time interacting with their clients and collaborate regularly with other therapists, teachers, or health professionals. Unless self-employed, they report to a supervisor. They may oversee part-time employees or interns. Those who own their own practices may be responsible for scheduling or bookkeeping staff.

Relevant Skills and Abilities

Creative/Artistic Skills
- Being skilled in art, music or dance

Interpersonal/Social Skills
- Being patient
- Being sensitive to others
- Cooperating with others
- Providing support to others
- Working as a member of a team

Research & Planning Skills
- Creating ideas

Technological Environment

Music therapists work with a variety of audio equipment, including portable stereo systems and mp3 players. They may also use recording equipment, such as a computer outfitted with a microphone and interfaced with an electronic keyboard or electric guitar. They must also know how to play a variety of instruments.

EDUCATION, TRAINING, AND ADVANCEMENT

High School/Secondary

A college preparatory program strong in the sciences, health, English, social sciences, and music courses will provide the necessary foundation for further studies. Interested high school students should supplement their coursework with extracurricular music activities, such as orchestra or choral group. A student must be proficient on at least one instrument—ideally piano, guitar, or voice—for admission into a music therapy program. Volunteer experience in a school, hospital, or recreational center is also recommended.

Suggested High School Subjects
- Biology
- English
- Health Science Technology
- Instrumental & Vocal Music
- Psychology
- Sociology

Famous First

The first large-scale study of the effects of music therapy on children was done at the University of Pennsylvania in 1962. The project was begun under music professor Paul Nordoff, who eventually collaborated with Dr. Clive Robbins, a special education expert. The focus of their study was piano and vocal improvisation as applied to children on the autistic spectrum, but a variety of other musical forms and young subjects were examined as well. The Nordoff-Robbins approach soon became the standard in the field.

College/Postsecondary

A bachelor's degree in music therapy from an American Music Therapy Association (AMTA) approved program is the minimum requirement for board certification. The curriculum typically includes coursework in the social and behavioral sciences, biology, anatomy, music therapy, and music (theory, performance, piano, guitar, voice). These programs also require 1,200 hours of clinical training, including an internship.

A master's or doctorate degree is required for advancement to supervisory positions and also for teaching, research, or administrative work. Most music therapists who establish their own practices have an advanced degree and many years of experience.

Related College Majors
- Dance Therapy
- Music Therapy
- Psychology, General
- Sociology

Adult Job Seekers

Adults with a bachelor's degree or higher in another discipline may choose to complete the music therapy degree equivalency program. Program participants take only those courses that are necessary and fulfill internship and other clinical training requirements. Musicians and music teachers may find that music therapy fits well with their other interests and responsibilities.

Professional Certification and Licensure

State licensing requirements vary for music therapists. In some states, applicants are licensed as creative arts therapists or recreational therapists and may need a master's degree.

The Certification Board for Music Therapists (CBMT) offers national board certification for music therapists. To become a Music Therapist-Board Certified (MT-BC), an individual must hold a bachelor's degree in music therapy or degree equivalent, complete clinical training, and earn a passing grade on the examination. Certification renewal usually involves continuing education.

Additional Requirements

Some music therapists may need a driver's license. Those seeking employment in public schools need a teaching certificate. Music therapists must also abide by the CBMT Code of Professional Practice.

Advancement opportunities to supervisory or administrative positions limit the contact music therapists have with patients. Advancement is available in research, teaching, private practice, and consulting.

Fun Fact

Music therapy may sound a bit new age-y, but not only did Aristotle and Plato recognize the healing properties of music, and after both World Wars, amateur and professional musicians visited veterans' hospitals around the country. Doctors and nurses noticed that music truly was a salve for the soul, and insisted that staff musicians be hired.

Source: http://www.musictherapy.org/about/history/

EARNINGS AND ADVANCEMENT

Earnings are generally highest in the New England and Western states and lowest in the South Central states. Those employed in hospices or who specialize in gerontology tend to earn the least.

Median annual earnings of music therapists were $43,180 in 2013. The lowest ten percent earned less than $27,120, and the highest ten percent earned more than $68.950.

Music therapists may receive paid vacations, holidays, and sick days; life and health insurance; and retirement benefits. These are usually paid by the employer.

Metropolitan Areas with the Highest
Employment Level in this Occupation

Metropolitan area	Employment[1]	Employment per thousand jobs	Hourly mean wage
New York-White Plains-Wayne, NY-NJ	980	0.19	$25.67
Philadelphia, PA	580	0.32	$21.61
Chicago-Joliet-Naperville, IL	560	0.15	$21.94
Boston-Cambridge-Quincy, MA	510	0.29	$18.60
Nassau-Suffolk, NY	380	0.31	$23.94
Los Angeles-Long Beach-Glendale, CA	340	0.09	$30.24
Atlanta-Sandy Springs-Marietta, GA	320	0.14	$19.87
Washington-Arlington-Alexandria, DC-VA-MD-WV	300	0.13	$23.55
Warren-Troy-Farmington Hills, MI	260	0.23	$24.54
St. Louis, MO-IL	230	0.18	$20.05

[1]Does not include self-employed. Source: Bureau of Labor Statistics

EMPLOYMENT AND OUTLOOK

Recreational therapists, of whom music therapists are a part, held about 20,000 jobs nationally in 2012. Employment is expected to grow about as fast as the average for all occupations through the year 2022, which means employment is projected to increase 10 percent to 16 percent. Overall, the outlook for music therapists is growing as the older population increases. There are demands in nursing homes, rehabilitation centers, and extended care facilities. It is gaining acceptance and popularity as the medical profession and the public recognize the benefits of this alternative form of therapy in patient healing and recovery.

Employment Trend, Projected 2010–20

Health Diagnosing and Treating Practitioners: 20%

Recreational and Music Therapists: 13%

Total, All Occupations: 11%

Note: "All Occupations" includes all occupations in the U.S. Economy. Source: U.S. Bureau of Labor Statistics, Employment Projections Program

Related Occupations
- Art Therapist
- Occupational Therapist
- Recreational Therapist

Conversation With . . .
ANDREA YUN-SPRINGER

Music Therapist
Toneworks Music Therapy, Minneapolis, MN
Music therapist, 2 years

1. What was your individual career path in terms of education/training, entry-level job, or other significant opportunity?

When I first went to college, I was a psychology major and I got a job doing research. I realized that doing data collection and sitting behind a desk was not what I wanted to do. I had been a musician since I was 3 years old. My primary instruments are violin, piano and guitar, and I just kind of picked up the ukulele. A family friend had gotten her PhD in music therapy from the University of Minnesota Twin Cities (UMTC) and I decided to see what the program was about. I didn't really know what music therapy was about. When I realized it combined my two interests — music and helping people reach their potential — I decided to go back to school. At UMTC, if your first degree was not in music, you can't go into the master's program, so I got another bachelor's degree. After I graduated, I created Toneworks with my business partner, Lyndie Walker, who's also a music therapist. We go anywhere from assisted living facilities to early childhood centers.

2. What are the most important skills and/or qualities for someone in your profession?

First, you do have to be a competent musician, because if no one wants to hear you sing or play your instrument, you're not going to get anyone to connect. You have to have a strong learning base in how music therapy works and be interested in always knowing more about how it works. You don't have to be an extrovert necessarily, but you do develop long-term relationships with people. It's important to have a deep respect for people of all abilities and in all walks of life as you provide music therapy.

3. What do you wish you had known going into this profession?

I just wish I had known about it earlier, so that I could have gotten my bachelor's in music therapy the first time around! I wish I had known that anyone can be an advocate for anyone else. Sometimes you have to advocate for clients who are non-verbal or for caregivers who feel they can't ask for the resources they need.

Also, you shouldn't be intimidated by the idea of starting your own business. In a sense, even when you're going for a job interview, you're always pitching yourself.

4. Are there many job opportunities in your profession? In what specific areas?

Yes, there are jobs. Music therapy is a growing field. There are more opportunities in states that have less music therapists and are just gaining awareness, but have an increasing demand for services.

5. How do you see your profession changing in the next five years? What role will technology play in those changes, and what skills will be required?

I see the field growing in hospice settings. I see more opportunities for early intervention with little children who are, say, just diagnosed with autism. There's been a lot of press about music therapy lately and it's seen as less of an "out there" kind of thing. People can see how it actually works. As licensure requirements are enacted, I see the field growing. Technology has already played a role. Social media has helped spread the word; there were pictures of Gabby Giffords doing music therapy. There's an ethical issue with providing Skype sessions, but if it's in a rural area, that may be someone's only access. Already we record digitally with clients and make recordings with clients and show them how to share those recordings.

6. What do you enjoy most about your job? What do you enjoy least about your job?

I love seeing how music affects clients. Some of them can tell me how it affects them, and maybe write a song about how happy music makes them. Some of them smile; some sign me; some point to the happy face on their iPad. With a hospice patient, it might be slow, steady breathing instead of a look of pain on their face. What I enjoy least is going from place to place and driving around Minnesota.

7. Can you suggest a valuable "try this" for students considering a career in your profession?

Try searching for music therapists by state using Google or cbmt.org. Once you find one in your area, call and ask if you can volunteer in one of the groups. They may just have you help hand out instruments and sit in the circle, but you'll have an idea of what it's like.

SELECTED SCHOOLS

Many colleges and universities have bachelor's degree programs in recreational therapy or related subjects; a number of them have programs specifically in music therapy. The student may also gain an initial grounding at a technical or community college. Consult with your school guidance counselor or research post-secondary programs in your area. The online Therapeutic Recreation Directory (see below) contains a listing of accredited recreational therapy schools and programs; and the web site of the American Music Therapy Association has additional resources.

MORE INFORMATION

American Music Therapy Association
8455 Colesville Road, Suite 1000
Silver Spring, MD 20910
301.589.3300
www.musictherapy.org

Certification Board for Music Therapists
506 E. Lancaster Avenue, Suite 102
Downingtown, PA 19335
800.765.2268
www.cbmt.org

National Association of Schools of Music
11250 Roger Bacon Drive, Suite 21
Reston, VA 20190-5248
703.437.0700
info@arts-accredit.org
nasm.arts-accredit.org/index.jsp

National Council for Therapeutic Recreation Certification
7 Elmwood Drive
New City, NY 10956
845.639.1439
nctrc@nctrc.org
www.nctrc.org

National Federation of Music Clubs
1646 Smith Valley Road
Greenwood, IN 46142
317.882.4003
www.nfmc-music.org

Sally Driscoll/Editor

Musician

Snapshot

Career Cluster(s): Arts; Fine, Visual, and Performing

Interests: Music, composition, management, artistic expression, performance

Earnings (Yearly Average): N/A

Employment & Outlook: Slower than average

OVERVIEW

Sphere of Work

Musicians play instruments either solo or in ensembles, performing for audiences or playing in recording sessions. Some musicians specialize in certain genres, while others learn to perform in a variety of styles. Becoming a musician requires creativity and an intense amount of practice and musicians often spend years learning and perfecting their skills on one or more instruments. While there are thousands of professional musicians working in various capacities around the world, most musicians work part time or perform as a hobby rather than pursuing music as a full-time career. A very small percentage of professional musicians become stars or superstars

achieving national or international fame for their recordings and/or performances.

Work Environment

Musicians typically work indoors, but may work in a variety of different types of environments. When practicing or recording, musicians typically work in recording studios while performing musicians work on a variety of performance venues from small bars and clubs to massive amphitheaters. Performing musicians travel often, whether to various performing venues within their local area or even internationally to perform in concert venues around the world. Musicians may also work with composers, conductors or music directors, and a variety of other professionals involved in various parts of the musical performance or recording process.

Profile

Working Conditions: Work Indoors
Physical Strength: Light work
Education Needs: Secondary school, Bachelor's Degree, Master's Degree
Licensure/Certification: Not required
Opportunities For Experience: On-Job Training, Part-Time Work, Internship
Holland Interest Score*: AE

* See Appendix A

Occupation Interest

Musicians need strong interest in artistic expression and should be prepared to spend a considerable amount of time practicing and honing their craft. In addition, while some musicians perform as solo artists, a professional music career is typically collaborative and social and professional musicians should be interested or comfortable with frequent collaboration and interaction. In addition, learning about cultural and artistic history is beneficial for a musician in any genre and so musicians benefit from an interest in history.

A Day in the Life—Duties and Responsibilities

The daily activities for a musician will depend on the musician's current and future projects. A musician may spend part of each day practicing his or her skill on one or more instruments or practicing techniques for recording and post-recording production. Musicians looking for projects might also participate in auditions. Leading up to a performance, a musicians spends time working on specific compositions needed for the upcoming performance and might meet with other musicians to practice or rehearse. Performing musicians might also spend time traveling to performance venues and meeting with press/fans to promote his or her music or a certain production. Depending on the type of musician, a performer or recording artist might also spend time listening to other musicians or recordings to learn or evaluate new techniques for future performances. Finally, musicians perform in either live settings or during recording sessions.

Duties and Responsibilities

- Practice and refine musical techniques and instrumental skills
- Audition for performances or to join various musical ensembles
- Meet with producers, music directors, composers, and other musicians
- Schedule or participate in rehearsals and practices for group performance
- Research historic and current music to learn new techniques
- Travel to new venues for recording or performance
- Promote musical recordings and/or performances
- Audition musicians and other professionals for a production

---

OCCUPATION SPECIALTIES

Session Musician

Session musicians are instrumentalists or singers who work with recording artists in recording studios, performing background vocals or instrumental parts on various recordings. Session musicians can be employed directly by artists or may be one of a group of artists who typically work with the managers of a specific studio or production company.

Electronic Musician

An electronic musician manipulates recordings made by other musicians and recording artists to create new music and uses a variety of digital and electronic instruments to create original music. Dance DJs are a type of electronic musician who typically play music made by other individuals in dance clubs, at weddings, or at other venues.

Music Teacher

A music teacher is typically also a musician who spends part of their time teaching musical techniques. Music teachers may be employed by a school, while many work for instrument repair and retail shops that offer music lessons to beginning, intermediate, and advanced students. Other music teachers work independently, inviting students to their private offices or visiting students in their homes to conduct music lessons.

Singer/Songwriter

A singer/songwriter is a composer and musician who creates original musical compositions and performs or records his or her music. Singer/songwriters may work as independent recording or performing artists while others write songs to be performed by other musicians.

WORK ENVIRONMENT

Physical Environment

Musicians do most of their work indoors, working in recording studios and performance spaces when practicing and rehearsing, and then in recording studios or concert venues when performing or recording. Travel is an essential part of many musical careers as performing musicians must travel to different venues for performances or to participate in recordings. Orchestral musicians who are part of symphony or other orchestral groups, may perform primarily in a dedicated theater, which will also typically have spaces for practicing and/or recording.

Relevant Skills and Abilities

Communication Skills
- Writing and transposing arrangements
- Reading and writing music in standard notation

Interpersonal/Social Skills
- Working in a group environment
- Interacting with members of the audience or media representatives
- Communicating effectively with collaborators and industry professionals
- Auditioning for performing or collaborative positions

Organization & Management Skills
- Scheduling time for recording sessions, rehearsals, and practice
- Keeping records of recordings and potential songs for performance/recording
- Managing collaborators, other musicians, and assistants during performances

Research & Planning Skills
- Research new techniques and practice new instrumental/ singing skills
- Seek out opportunities for performances or collaboration

Technical Skills
- Using special instrumental skills
- Using microphones, tuning equipment, and other tools for performing/recording
- Working with digital recording, amplification, and modulation equipment

Human Environment

Even for solo musicians, a career in music is typically collaborative. Orchestra musicians and members of ensemble groups work closely with their fellow musicians as well as with musical directors, recording specialists, and other technical professionals to put on performances or to complete recordings. Solo musicians will also typically work with other professionals, such as booking agents, managers, studio technicians, and stage technicians when performing or recording. For ensemble, musicians must not only learn to perform themselves, but also to perform with other musicians.

Technological Environment

Some types of instruments have specific tools, such as strings for stringed instruments, reeds for wind instruments, and sticks or mallets for percussion instruments. In addition, musicians learn to work with stands, tablets, or other equipment for holding musical scores, metronomes and other tools for developing rhythm and timing, and microphones for both performance and recording. There are a variety of digital tools designed for musicians, including software for reading, writing, and transcribing music and for recording and for altering digital files for post-production. In addition, independent artists may need to become familiar with digital promotional tools, such as websites and various forms of social media, in an effort to promote themselves as performers or collaborators.

EDUCATION, TRAINING, AND ADVANCEMENT

High School/Secondary

High school students interested in becoming professional musicians can begin by taking advantage of any musical instruction or performance opportunities offered through their high school or secondary school. Many schools have school in various genres, such as a jazz band, marching band, and classical band. In addition, many schools offer classes in different types of instrumental performance as well as classes on music theory and/or history. In addition, while there are no specific educational requirements for professional musicians, aspiring musicians should consider obtaining at least an undergraduate degree and so should prepare to apply for postsecondary programs.

Suggested High School Subjects

- English
- Composition
- Music
- Music History
- Music Theory
- Jazz
- Marching Band
- Guitar
- Piano

Famous First

Singer and songwriter Michael Jackson, who first gained fame as a member of the ensemble music group, the Jackson Five, becoming the first African American musical superstar after the civil-rights era, and one of the best-selling pop artists of all time. As of 2017, Michael Jackson's *Thriller* is still listed as the best-selling album of all time, with between 46 and 65 million copies sold worldwide. Jackson also became one of the most award winning artists in history, garnering 26 American Music Awards, 13 Grammy Awards and a Grammy Lifetime Achievement Award, among hundreds of other national and international honors. In the 1980s, Jackson was also the first African American artist whose videos appeared on MTV, and his theatrical videos helped cement the popularity of the network, helping to define an era of musical and television entertainment.

College/Postsecondary

While it is not required, many aspiring musicians obtain postsecondary degrees in music theory or performance. Degree programs introduce students to both composition, recording, performing, and also provide an introduction to the commercial aspects of the music industry. In addition, musicians with advanced degrees can more easily supplement their income from performing/recording by teaching students. Becoming skilled as a musician also requires dedicated study, practice, and training, and participating in collegiate level music education helps aspiring musicians to develop routines for practicing, study, and collaboration that will be helpful in their later careers.

Related College Majors
- Music Performance
- Music History
- Music Education
- Music Composition
- Master of Fine Arts in Music
- Doctor of Music Education
- Doctor of Music History

Adult Job Seekers

Those with sufficient skill in music to perform as solo artists or with a group can apply for positions with existing bands or can audition to perform in a variety of venues. Opportunities for session musicians and collaborators can be found through a variety of sources, including advertisements and postings on various websites and job boards. Those who have participated in a college/postsecondary music program can often use resources provided through alumni networks to find performing or recording opportunities.

Professional Certification and Licensure

There are no specific licenses or certificates needed to work as a professional musician, though individuals interested in teaching students through accredited educational institutions need to adhere to licensing guidelines for teachers in their state.

Additional Requirements

Becoming proficient as a musician involves many hours of dedicated study and practice. While discussions about careers in music often focus on an individual's relative level of musical talent, practice and study are equally important to developing skills as a performer and instrumentalist. Musicians also need to have good hearing and to develop a musical ear that can allow them to evaluate their own performance and the performances of other musicians and collaborators.

Fun Fact

At the first GRAMMY awards 1959, Record of the Year went to Domenico Modugno, whose "Nel Blu Dipito Di Blu," better known as "Volare," bested Frank Sinatra's "Witchcraft."

Source: https://www.grammy.com/awards/

EARNINGS AND ADVANCEMENT

According to the Bureau of Labor Statistics, approximately 2 in 5 professional musicians were self-employed in 2015, and many working musicians work only part time or intermittently while maintaining other forms of employment. In addition, musicians tend to work off hours, as live performances typically occur at night or on weekends. According to the BLS, the median hourly wage for the industry was $24.20 in 2015, with those at the lowest-paid 10 percent earning under $9.20 per hour and those at the upper 10 percent earning over $68.00 per hour. Estimating pay for professional musicians is skewed by the high salaries of the world's star and superstar musicians. Advancing in the industry requires promotion and musicians often work with agents or managers to help them advertise, promote, and market their musical talents.

Metropolitan Areas with the Highest Employment Level in this Occupation

Metropolitan area	Employment	Employment per thousand jobs	Hourly mean wage
New York-Jersey City-White Plains, NY-NJ Metropolitan Division	4,470	0.69	$49.68
Los Angeles-Long Beach-Glendale, CA Metropolitan Division	2,810	0.68	$42.69
Nashville-Davidson--Murfreesboro--Franklin, TN	1,040	1.18	$41.24
Anaheim-Santa Ana-Irvine, CA Metropolitan Division	800	0.52	$39.87
Chicago-Naperville-Arlington Heights, IL Metropolitan Division	790	0.22	$30.88
Portland-Vancouver-Hillsboro, OR-WA	760	0.70	$22.82
Nassau County-Suffolk County, NY Metropolitan Division	720	0.57	$46.92
San Francisco-Redwood City-South San Francisco, CA Metropolitan Division	720	0.71	$32.91
Washington-Arlington-Alexandria, DC-VA-MD-WV Metropolitan Division	710	0.30	$27.94
Seattle-Bellevue-Everett, WA Metropolitan Division	620	0.40	$34.98

Source: Bureau of Labor Statistics

EMPLOYMENT AND OUTLOOK

Employment opportunities for musicians are expected to grow by 3 percent between 2014 and 2024, constituting slower than average growth than the 6-7 percent estimated for all U.S. industries. Industry analysts believe that there will be an increasing demand for live performances, due to the expansion of digital downloads and streaming music platforms, which have helped lesser-known musicians to advertise their work and build interest in possible live performances. Studio and session musicians are increasingly needed to perform in ensembles for television and film productions and this facet of the industry may also grow due to the expansion of streaming television and film productions. For musicians looking to work in orchestras, opera companies, and other traditional live performance venues, opportunities are not expected to increase substantially during this period and those looking for work in these venues should expect high competition. In general, competition tends to be high in the music industry due to the large number of aspiring artists in comparison to the number of opportunities for work in the field.

Employment Trend, Projected 2014–24

Total, All Occupations: 7%

Entertainers and Performers, Sports and Related Workers: 6%

Musicians and Singers: 3%

Note: "All Occupations" includes all occupations in the U.S. Economy. Source: U.S. Bureau of Labor Statistics, Employment Projections Program

Related Occupations

- Dancers and Choreographers
- Music Directors and Composers
- Directors and Producers
- Writers and Authors
- Actors
- Postsecondary Teachers

- Middle School Teachers
- Kindergarten and Elementary School Teachers
- High School Teachers

Related Military Occupations

- Military Band Musician

Conversation With . . . CORINNE WINTERS

International opera singer
Professional singer, 7 years

1. What was your individual career path in terms of education/training, entry-level job, or other significant opportunity?

I chose to go to a liberal arts college rather than music conservatory for undergraduate school. I wasn't totally sure I wanted to pursue opera performance (or if I even had enough talent for it) so I kept my options open. I started in pop and choral singing but studying classical voice was my only option as a voice major. The more I learned about opera, the more I loved it. I earned a B.S in Voice from Towson University in Maryland. As I gained recognition for my talent and hard work, my confidence improved. For graduate and post-graduate work I chose rigorous and competitive programs that would prepare me for the challenges of the business. I earned a Master of Music in vocal performance from the Peabody Conservatory in Baltimore, then became a resident artist at the Academy of Vocal Arts in Philadelphia. My first professional contracts hinged on two vital stepping stones: winning competitions and making connections with mentors.My first professional contract was understudying at the Metropolitan Opera after making the semi-finals of their competition and winning the Palm Beach Opera competition, which was judged by Met administrators. The following year, I auditioned for the title role in "La traviata" at the English National Opera under the recommendation of one of my mentors, conductor Stephen Lord. I sang well, but his endorsement gave ENO the confidence to take a chance on me. In addition to ENO, I have performed with the Royal Opera at the Royal Opera House Covent Garden; Opernhaus Zürich; Washington National Opera; Seattle Opera; and the Santa Fe Opera, among others.

2. What are the most important skills and/or qualities for someone in your profession?

Resilience, discipline, creativity, optimism, adaptability, charisma, aptitude for language, and of course an operatic voice.

3. What do you wish you had known going into this profession?

Talent is only ten to twenty percent of what it takes. The artists who make it long term are the ones who refuse to give up.

4. Are there many job opportunities in your profession? In what specific areas?

There are more opportunities in Europe than anywhere else, but every major city in the world has at least one opera company with roles that need to be cast at any given time. For those who possess the necessary qualities for success, as well as the X-factor that draws people to them, there are plenty of opportunities. It never hurts to have someone in a position of power supporting you, though – like any business, it's all about building relationships.

5. How do you see your profession changing in the next five years, what role will technology play in those changes, and what skills will be required?

Technology has already changed the opera world tremendously. It's essential to have a beautiful, user-friendly website and an active social media presence. One must be discerning with social media though – more is not necessarily better. My publicist, who excels in online media, has taken some of the technology burden off of my plate. She also helps me gauge which social media initiatives are most effective in building and connecting with my fan base. HD cinema broadcasts have been helpful in bringing opera to small towns and suburbs with less exposure to opera. While both have merit, live performance is a completely different medium than HD broadcasts. The cinema is fun, but there is no substitute for the power of the live, unamplified human voice.

6. What do you enjoy most about your job? What do you enjoy least about your job?

Expressing myself through words and music is the greatest joy and privilege of my life. I would happily do it for free if I could! My least favorite aspect of the job is the constant travel and being away from loved ones. I'd prefer to travel three months per year rather than nine, but travel is necessary for a diverse, thriving career.

7. Can you suggest a valuable "try this" for students considering a career in your profession?

Build a network of five people whose opinion you trust and respect – older singers, conductors, teachers, directors, administrators, peers – and only seek input from those people. Art is subjective and we encounter many conflicting opinions. If you get feedback that aligns with your values, great; if you get an opinion that rubs you the wrong way, let it go in one ear and out the other. The point of a solid (and small) network is to reflect our strengths and weaknesses back to us with loving support. Ultimately, the goal is to trust ourselves and the work we produce. That's when the magic happens.

MORE INFORMATION

National Association of Schools of Music
11250 Roger Bacon Drive, Suite 21
Reston, VA 20190
703-437-0700
www.nasm.arts-accredit.org

Future of Music Coalition
2217 14th Street NW, 2nd Floor
Washington, DC 20009
202-822-2051
www.futureofmusic.org

Recording Industry Association of America (RIAA)
1025 F St NW
Washington, DC 20004
202-775-0101
www.riaa.com

American Federation of Musicians
1501 Broadway, Suite 600
New York, NY 10036
212-869-1330
www.afm.org

National Association for Music Education (NAFME)
1806 Robert Fulton Drive
Reston, VA 20191
800-336-3768
www.nafme.org

Micah Issitt/Editor

Photographer

Snapshot

Career Cluster: Arts, A/V Technology & Communications
Interests: Photography, Art, Photojournalism, Media, Technology
Earnings (Yearly Average): $30,867
Employment & Outlook: Average Growth Expected

OVERVIEW

Sphere of Work

Photographers capture images of various objects, people, and events using a film or digital camera. They must exhibit a solid understanding of technical camera operation and the fundamental processes behind photography, lighting, and the composition of an image. Most photographers focus on one area of photographic specialty. Photographic specialties include news, portrait, commercial and industrial, scientific, and fine arts photography. Because their profession is based on choosing image composition and creating unique images, creativity is a trait common among all types of photographers regardless of their area of specialization.

Work Environment

A photographer's work environment depends primarily on his or her area of photographic specialty. Some photographers, such as those who take studio portraits of children and families, work primarily out of comfortable, well-lit, indoor studios. Other photographers work outside in a multitude of environments and are subject to various weather conditions. Photographers who work for the government, advertising agencies, or private companies frequently maintain a forty-hour week. Freelance and newspaper photographers, or photojournalists, generally work irregular hours, travel often, and are expected to be on-call for last-minute projects or emergency events.

Profile

Working Conditions: Work Both Indoors And Outdoors

Physical Strength: Light to Medium Work

Education Needs: On-The-Job Training, High School Diploma or GED, Apprenticeship, Some College

Licensure/Certification: Usually Not Required

Physical Abilities Not Required: No Strenuous Work

Opportunities For Experience: Internship, Apprenticeship, Military Service, Volunteer Work, Part-Time Work

Holland Interest Score*: AES, ESA, RIC, RSE, SRC

* See Appendix A

Occupation Interest

Potential photographers should demonstrate a passion for artistic creation. They should be compelled to tell stories through photographs and possess a deep desire to analyze, present, and offer a unique perspective on their photographic subjects. They should express a definitive opinion through their photographs, and that opinion should be easily discernible to an audience examining their photography. They should be able to lead and work with different types of people and personalities.

A Day in the Life—Duties and Responsibilities

Most photographers purchase and maintain their own camera equipment, lenses, and accessories, which can be costly at the outset. Photographers usually work independently or with an assistant. They are responsible for the physical positioning of subjects as well as the arrangement of lighting and camera angles. If the photographs are taken with film (which is increasingly rare), the photographer develops the film and prints in either a darkroom or printing facility. Digital photographs may be edited and retouched prior to publishing or printing.

Photographers' specialties determine what they photograph and how those images are used. Portrait photographers specialize in photographing people or groups of people. They are generally self-employed and often travel to various locations for special events like weddings, school functions, and other special ceremonies. Commercial and industrial photographers travel to various locations to photograph landscapes, buildings, and merchandise. Their photographs are usually published in books, advertisements, catalogs, or other media. Scientific photographers make a photographic record of objects or events related to science and medicine. These photographers usually have technical training in the sciences as well as the arts. News photographers, or photojournalists, take pictures of relevant people or events for publication in regular newspapers or periodicals. Fine arts photographers are usually highly technically proficient, and may display their photographs in museums, art galleries, or private art shows.

Self-employed and freelance photographers must perform business and administrative tasks in addition to their creative work. Such tasks might include managing employees, handling billing and payments, setting appointments, and obtaining licenses, copyrights, contracts, and other legal documents as needed. They must also arrange their own advertising, marketing campaigns, and self-promotion.

Duties and Responsibilities

- Composing subjects using distance, angle, and lighting
- Deciding on camera settings
- Using, lights, reflectors, screens and props
- Capturing subjects on film or in digital images
- Editing, printing, and publishing photographic images
- Marketing and advertising services to prospective clients
- Maintaining a professional portfolio

OCCUPATION SPECIALTIES

Aerial Photographers

Aerial Photographers photograph segments of earth and other subject material from aircraft.

Scientific Photographers

Scientific Photographers use specialized equipment to illustrate and record scientific phenomena.

Studio Photographers

Studio Photographers photograph subjects in formal studios or similar settings, and use a variety of accessories. They normally specialize in a particular area of photography, such as illustrative, fashion, or portrait.

Photojournalists

Photojournalists photograph newsworthy events, locations, people, or other illustrative and educational material for use in publications or telecasts, using a still camera.

Fine Arts Photographers

Fine Arts Photographers create photographs for sale as art.

Other Photographic Specialties

Other notable photographic specialties include: Architectural Photography, Forensic Photography, Landscape/Nature/Wildlife Photography, Sports Photography, and Wedding Photography.

WORK ENVIRONMENT

Physical Environment

A photographer's working conditions vary greatly depending on his or her specialty. Some photographers can work in clean, comfortable, well-ventilated studios. Others work in unpleasant or dangerous outdoor environments. Photographers regularly travel to and from photographic sites. Those who process film and prints, especially in a darkroom, are exposed to potentially harmful chemicals.

Skills and Abilities

Communication Skills
- Speaking effectively

Creative/Artistic Skills
- Being skilled in art or photography
- Having a good eye for identifying and capturing subjects
- Displaying a sensitivity to color, light, and shadow

Interpersonal/Social Skills
- Listening to clients
- Cooperating with others
- Working independently and as a member of a team

Organization & Management Skills
- Handling challenging situations
- Paying attention to and handling details
- Promoting one's work to potential clients

Technical Skills
- Operating camera equipment
- Using digital editing software
- Working in a darkroom (film development)

Human Environment

Photographers work with numerous clients, customers, and subjects. They must interact easily with others, and they should be comfortable directing, evaluating, and occasionally comforting their photographic subjects. Photographers sometimes collaborate with graphic designers, journalists, reporters, and editors. Some may report to a supervisor or direct an assistant.

Technological Environment

Photographers must learn how to operate camera equipment in order to be successful. To create a photograph, photographers use film and digital cameras, film, digital memory and storage devices, tripods, lenses and filters, floodlights, reflectors, light meters, and electronic flash units. Image processing may require computers, imaging and editing software, printers and scanners, photographic paper, darkroom equipment, and chemicals for developing film and prints from film.

EDUCATION, TRAINING, AND ADVANCEMENT

High School/Secondary

High school students interested in becoming photographers should devote time to the study of communications, computers, art, photography, and media. Aspiring photographers should also engage in extracurricular activities (like the school newspaper or yearbook) that allow them to practice taking pictures, editing their work, and posting or printing their best photographs. Interested students should pursue part-time work with a photographer or store and consider applying to postsecondary photography programs.

Suggested High School Subjects
- Arts
- Communications
- Computers & Digital Imaging
- Media Studies
- Photography

Famous First

The first photograph to be sent via satellite from one location to another was an image of President Dwight D. Eisenhower taken in 1960. The picture was transmitted as a wirephoto from Cedar Rapids, Iowa, bounced off the Echo I satellite, and received in Dallas, Texas. One year before that, the first photograph of the earth taken in space was transmitted by the Explorer 6 satellite to a NASA unit in Hawaii.

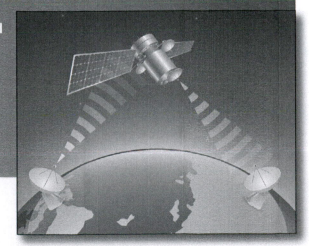

Photographer

Most photographers find it helpful to have an undergraduate degree or certificate in photography from a university, community college, private art school, or vocational institute. Many vocational education programs offer courses in visual imaging technology as well as in the fundamentals of photography. Other postsecondary programs teach students the practical and technical aspects of photography. Coursework may include the history of photography and cinema, camera maintenance, photojournalism, composition, color printing and print finishing, lighting, retouching, and other related subjects. Prospective freelance photographers may benefit from studying courses in business, including marketing, public relations, and business management.

Related College Majors
- Commercial Photography
- Digital Imaging
- Educational/Instructional Media Design
- Educational/Instructional Media Technology
- Fine/Studio Arts
- Photography

Adult Job Seekers

Many prospective photographers find positions as assistants to local, professional photographers after receiving their formal education. Assistants gain valuable technical experience, on-the-job training, and the practical skills needed to start their own businesses. Other job seekers apply for full- or part-time positions at camera shops, local newspapers, or photography studios. Candidates can also participate in apprenticeships, mentorships, or internships through their schools or photography training programs.

Many photographers subscribe to photography newsletters and magazines in order to make contacts in the industry. Networking, mentoring, and professional development opportunities are also frequently available through professional photographer associations.

Professional Certification and Licensure

Photographers are usually not required to obtain professional certification or licensure in their field; to an extent, this is because the work is highly visual, so photographers can easily provide samples of their work to others. Some professional photography organizations offer voluntary certifications, which may enhance a photographer's marketing and job-seeking efforts. To become a Certified Professional Photographer (CPP) through the Professional Photographers of America, candidates must pass a written exam and provide images for critique. Continuing education is typically required for certification renewal.

Additional Requirements

Photography is a well- respected form of artistic expression. Therefore, aspiring and professional photographers should be naturally artistic and able to understand the fundamentals of photographic composition. Because the field is intrinsically subjective, photographers should maintain the integrity and conviction necessary to present effective artwork and subject analysis, without reacting negatively to criticism. Photographers should be patient, have great eyesight, possess boundless imagination, and demonstrate impeccable communication skills when dealing with clients and subjects.

EARNINGS AND ADVANCEMENT

Earnings of photographers depend on geographic location, type of photographic specialty, number of hours worked, photographic skills and marketing ability. Most salaried photographers work full-time and earn more than the majority of self-employed photographers who usually work part-time, but some self-employed photographers have very high earnings. Unlike photojournalists and commercial photographers, very few fine arts photographers are successful enough to support themselves solely through this profession.

Median annual earnings of photographers were $30,867 in 2012. The lowest ten percent earned less than $18,388, and the highest ten percent earned more than $67,202.

Photographers may receive paid vacations, holidays, and sick days; life and health insurance; and retirement benefits. These are usually paid by the employer. Freelance and self-employed photographers must provide their own benefits.

Metropolitan Areas with the Highest Concentration of Jobs in this Occupation

Metropolitan area	Employment	Employment per thousand jobs	Hourly mean wage
New York-White Plains-Wayne, NY-NJ	3,100	0.60	$25.57
Chicago-Joliet-Naperville, IL	2,140	0.59	$24.93
Los Angeles-Long Beach-Glendale, CA	1,680	0.43	$28.68
Orlando-Kissimmee-Sanford, FL	1,500	1.48	$12.92
Atlanta-Sandy Springs-Marietta, GA	1,280	0.57	$14.21
Minneapolis-St. Paul-Bloomington, MN-WI	970	0.55	$23.88
Houston-Sugar Land-Baytown, TX	960	0.36	$15.91
Seattle-Bellevue-Everett, WA	900	0.64	$14.83

(1) Does not include self-employed. Source: Bureau of Labor Statistics, 2012

EMPLOYMENT AND OUTLOOK

There were approximately 56,000 photographers employed nationally in 2012. However, twice that many were self-employed. Some self-employed photographers have contracts with advertising agencies, magazine publishers, or other businesses to do individual projects for a set fee, while others operate portrait studios or provide photographs to stock-photo agencies. Most salaried photographers work in portrait or commercial photography studios; most of the others work for newspapers, magazines, and advertising agencies.

Employment is expected to grow about as fast as the average for all occupations through the year 2020, which means employment is projected to increase about 13 percent. Demand for portrait photography will increase as the population grows. As the number of electronic versions of magazines, journals and newspapers increases on the internet, commercial photographers will be needed to provide digital images.

Photography is a competitive field, and only those with the most skill and the best business ability will be able to find salaried positions or attract enough work to support themselves as self-employed photographers.

Employment Trend, Projected 2010–20

Total, All Occupations: 14%

Arts, Design, Entertainment, Sports, and Media Occupations: 13%

Photographers: 13%

Note: "All Occupations" includes all occupations in the U.S. Economy. Source: U.S. Bureau of Labor Statistics, Employment Projections Program

Related Occupations
- Art Director
- Camera Operator & Videographer
- Cinematographer
- Motion Picture/Radio/TV Art Director
- Photographic Process Worker

Related Military Occupations
- Audiovisual & Broadcast Technician
- Broadcast Journalist & Newswriter
- Photographic Specialist

Conversation With . . .
STEPHEN DONALDSON
Photographer, 18 years

1. What was your individual career path in terms of education, entry-level job, or other significant opportunity?

I got out of the business world after 13 years and am a self-taught, selfinstructed, self-managed photographer. I came from a profit-loss oriented place in sales, so when I got into this, I brought a sensibility and a skill set for selling my work. I always want to be mid-to-high level price-wise, then overdeliver the product. If you build and build, and consistently produce a good product, your photo business will eventually gain momentum that will carry you forward."

2. Are there many job opportunities in your profession? In what specific areas?

There are so many job opportunities in photography that intersect with other professions: sports photography, fashion, corporate, advertising, product, or tabletop photography. One of the things I do is have a lot of pokers in the fire. For instance, I also am a travel stock photographer and travel all over the planet on my own dime and photograph people, places, landmarks, towns, villages - everything that evokes a sense of the place. Directly or through my agent in New York, my photos get picked up and licensed for a cost for products such as educational books, encyclopedias, text books, calendars, even jigsaw puzzles.

3. What do you wish you had known going into this profession?

I had intermediate to advanced course instruction, mostly in high school. I often wish I had had more formal training as a photographer, and had a taken a more conventional path where I worked with another photographer and had more technical training – such as how to create certain lighting – that I wasn't able to do until I figured it out myself.

4. How do you see your profession changing in the next five years?

You've kind of seen early developments of it. Photography, to me, is going in the direction of television: everything is supernatural, hypersaturated, and doesn't look like what it looks like in the real world to the naked eye. Everything looks too perfect. But I do understand that's what people's expectations are gravitating to. That is part of what technology is making possible and driving, this unnatural representation of the natural world. In addition, royalty-free photography options are increasing. When people are in need of something very different, something that is going Photographer 13 to put their product in a different space, or service, that's where they will gravitate away from royalty free imagery.

5. What role will technology play in those changes, and what skills will be required?

Technology is creating and forcing certain changes regarding how to deliver theproduct. For instance, how long are coffee table - my published books – going to be marketable to the public? How much do I migrate from print work – framed – to digital copies of my work buyers can put on their TV screen on the wall, and how do I actually do that? How do I sell that file to them so they don't reproduce it or turn it over to five or six friends? Also, one of the strange conundrums for photographers: advances in technology have not made the equipment you use cheaper. When I started, a Nikon F5 was $1,800 to $2,000. Now, the top Nikon digital is $8,000. The price for professional level equipment has actually been rising as more technology goes into it, as opposed to dropping, like you see with computers and televisions.

6. Do you have any general advice or additional professional insights to share with someone interested in your profession?

You need to learn how to use a camera and become technically proficient. Young people now, their world is very woven into new forms of media, including social media. If they embrace the media and they study the media and how photography and imagery is being used in new media – for editorial, for news, for fashion – they will see how photography is being used in the here and now in the most cutting edge ways to say what they want to say with an image.

7. Can you suggest a valuable "try this" for students considering a career in your profession?

I would go into Facebook and create a photo page and post a picture a day or a week – maybe one out of 100 taken of a particular subject. For example, photograph the high school football team and put your best picture up and see if people like it. See how successful you are in building an audience, see what kind of comments and criticism you get. It's not always your friends – it's people who may be friends of friends and may not know you.

SELECTED SCHOOLS

Many colleges and universities offer bachelor's degree programs in the arts; some have majors or programs in photography. The student may also gain initial training through enrollment at a community college. Below are listed some of the more prominent institutions in this field.

Art Institute of Chicago
36 S. Wabash
Chicago, IL 60603
800.232.7242
www.saic.edu

California College of the Arts
5212 Broadway
Oakland, CA 94618
510.594.3600
www.cca.edu

California Institute of the Arts
24700 McBean Parkway
Valencia, CA 91355
661.255.1050
www.calarts.edu

Columbia College Chicago
600 S. Michigan Avenue
Chicago, IL 60605
312.369.1000
www.colum.edu

New York University
70 Washington Square S
New York, NY 10012
212.998.1212
www.nyu.edu

Rhode Island School of Design
2 College Street
Providence, RI 02903
800.364.7473
www.risd.edu

Rochester Institute of Technology
1 Lomb Memorial Drive
Rochester, NY 14623
585.475.2411
www.rit.edu

University of California, Los Angeles
405 Hilgard Avenue
Los Angeles, CA 90095
310.825.4321
www.ucla.edu

University of New Mexico
1 University Boulevard NE
Albuquerque, NM 87131
505.277.0111
www.unm.edu

Yale University
New Haven, CT 06520
203.432.4771
www.yale.edu

MORE INFORMATION

American Society of Media Photographers
150 North 2nd Street
Philadelphia, PA 19106
215.451.2767
www.asmp.org

American Society of Photographers
3120 N. Argonne Drive
Milwaukee, WI 53222
www.asofp.com

Association of Independent Colleges of Art and Design
236 Hope Street
Providence, RI 02906
401.270.5991
www.aicad.org

National Press Photographers Association, Inc.
3200 Croasdaile Drive, Suite 306
Durham, NC 27705
919.383.7246
www.nppa.org

North American Nature Photography Association
6382 Charleston Road
Alma, IL 62807
618.547.7616
www.nanpa.org

Professional Photographers of America, Inc.
229 Peachtree Street, NE, Suite 2200
Atlanta, GA 30303
800.786.6277
www.ppa.com
PPA Awards:
www.ppa.com/competitions/

Briana Nadeau/Editor

Woodworker

Snapshot

Career Cluster(s): Arts, manufacturing, industrial arts

Interests: Construction, artistry, technical skills, crafts, realistic skills

Earnings (Yearly Average): $32,130

Employment & Outlook: No growth expected

OVERVIEW

Sphere of Work

Woodworkers are artisans, craftspeople, and industrial workers who manufacture a variety of products using wood, laminates, and veneers. There are a variety of different jobs in the woodworking industry, from factory labor jobs assisting in the mass manufacture of wooden goods, to artisan craftsperson positions assisting in hand making cabinets, furniture, and other fine wooden items. Woodworking is also a technical trade with a variety of unique tools and techniques and, though most woodworking tools were traditionally hand tools, woodworkers increasingly used computer-aided machines to assist in their work.

Work Environment

Most woodworkers work indoors in either workshops or factories equipped with specialized equipment. Much of the equipment used in woodworking is potentially dangerous and woodworkers need to learn to safety use both hand and industrial tools to work in the field. Woodwork also involves using potentially harmful chemicals and workshops and factories must therefore be well ventilated. While some woodworkers work alone, many woodworkers work alongside other artisans or factory workers. Some woodworkers are also managers, managing a team of artisans or factory workers in the creation of wooden furniture or other wooden products for retail or wholesale markets.

Profile

Working Conditions: Work Indoors and outdoors
Physical Strength: Strenuous work
Education Needs: Secondary School, Trade school
Licensure/Certification: Not required
Opportunities For Experience: On-Job Training, Part-Time Work, Trade School
Holland Interest Score*: RC

* See Appendix A

Occupation Interest

Prospective woodworkers should have an interest in practical skills and knowledge, as woodworking is generally a functional trade that involves creating useful items for homes or businesses. However, depending on the type of woodworking, the field can also be artistic and creative and aspiring woodworkers might benefit from interest in the creative as well as practical arts. Specialists and artisans in the field will also benefit from an interest in the aesthetics of wood, helping to guide them in finding attractive ways to craft wooden items for customers.

A Day in the Life—Duties and Responsibilities

Woodworking begins with drawings, blueprints, and schematics and some woodworkers spend part of each day creating templates or drawings or using and interpreting existing plans to begin a project. Before a project can begin workers need to source and acquire materials, which may be in the form of raw lumber, processed and/or treated wood, or laminate wood, in addition to other needed materials that may include glue, nails and other fastening materials, and materials for sanding, finishing, and preserving a finished product.

Before working with wood, workers might spend time calibrating and setting up machines used in the woodworking process. From there, workers take pieces of wood through a variety of machining processes, using saws, milling machines, sanding machines and other tools to create pieces of a finished product. During the process, woodworkers must continually measure and evaluate their work to ensure that the product or parts of the product adhere to design specifications. Woodworkers may then use a variety of hand tools to refine the product and, depending on the type of woodworking, may also use tools like sprayers, brushes, and other tools to apply finishes and protective seals to the product. Depending on the type of woodworking shop or business, a woodworker might also spend time repairing or refinishing wooden furniture or other items build by other manufacturers.

Duties and Responsibilities

- Create or interpret detailed drawings and schematics
- Source and store materials for creating wooden items
- Prepare and calibrate machines and other tools
- Operate woodworking machines and use hand tools
- Ensure that products or parts meet specifications
- Refine and adjust parts before assembling a product
- Finish and preserve products
- Refinish or repair wooden furniture and other items

OCCUPATION SPECIALTIES

Cabinetmaker

Cabinetmakers are woodworkers who specialize in making parts for wooden cabinets and may work directly with consumers, building cabinets for a specific space in a customer's home or office. Cabinetmakers can work independently, in small custom cabinetry businesses, or for factories that mass product parts for cabinets.

Finish Carpenters

Finish carpenters are responsible for refining, finishing, and repairing damaged carpentry and furniture. Finish carpenters tend to be artisans, guided by an aesthetic as well as practical understanding of woodworking techniques. Products made by other carpenters or woodworkers are often given to finish carpenters to further refine, adjust, and decorate the finished product.

Woodworking Machine Specialists

Some woodworkers specialize in operating, fixing, and calibrating the numerous industrial tools used in modern woodworking. Some individuals have specific experience/expertise in Computer Numerical Control (CNC) tools, which are automated tools that perform tasks based on a programmed set of guidelines.

Marquetry Artisans

Marquetry is the process of using strips of veneer or wood to inlay a design into a product. Marquetry artisans are creative professionals that practice a variety of machine-oriented and manual woodworking tools and use creativity to create decorative designs to be inlaid in wood.

WORK ENVIRONMENT

Relevant Skills and Abilities

Communication Skills
- Interpreting drawings, designs, and schematics
- Creating woodworking designs and schematics

Interpersonal/Social Skills
- Working in a group environment
- Working with customers to design and build products

Organization & Management Skills
- Managing other woodworkers or members of a shop team
- Following instructions given by a team manager or leader
- Evaluating products against design specifications

Research & Planning Skills
- Organizing materials and equipment
- Following detailed plans and guidelines

Technical Skills
- Utilizing hand-operated tools
- Using computer-aided tools and equipment

Physical Environment

Woodworkers typically work in either workshops or factories, depending on the type of woodworking. Woodworkers encounter a variety of potentially dangerous chemicals and other materials in their work and so woodworking shops and factories need to be well ventilated and equipped with safety and first aid equipment. Most woodworking is done either as special stations where workers can use specific CNC or other industrial tools, or at work benches and other tables used to support wooden pieces while the woodworkers completes alterations. Many woodworking facilities are loud, due to the use of electronic machines and tools and woodworkers often wear safety equipment to protect their hearing as well as equipment to protect their eyes, respiratory system, and their hands.

Human Environment

While some woodworkers and woodworking artisans work alone, mass manufacturing and industrial woodworking are collaborative disciplines and woodworkers in these industries tend to be members of large teams that work on different aspects of a project. A woodworker might operate a single machine or complete one part of a process before passing his or her work onto another worker to complete another part of the process. In addition, woodworkers often work under shop or factory managers and may occasionally work with architects, designers, or customers when completing a job.

Technological Environment

While woodworking still relies on a variety of hand tools, such as saws, lathes, sanding blocks, hammers, chisels, and drills, increasingly woodworking uses computer-aided tools to product products. CNC or Computer Numerical Control tools are machines that complete a step in a woodworking process guided by a computer program. Woodworkers in factory and mass production facilities might therefore need specialized knowledge to operate computer-aided machines and tools used in the woodworking process.

EDUCATION, TRAINING, AND ADVANCEMENT

High School/Secondary

There are no specific educational requirements needed to become a woodworker, though high school/secondary school students can prepare for their career by taking classes that contribute to basic knowledge of design and construction, such as shop/woodworking, drafting, graphic design, mathematics, and physics. In addition, classes that teach basic computer use and or help refine a students ability to communicate and/or work with others will be helpful for those entering the field.

Suggested High School Subjects

- English
- Drafting/Industrial Drawing
- Drawing
- Mathematics
- Geometry

- Physics
- Woodworking
- Introduction to computers

Famous First

Norman Abram became one of the most famous woodworkers in the world thanks to his public television program *This Old House* from 1979, where he was billed as the series' "master carpenter." On the program, Abram introduced television audiences to traditional woodworking and carpentry techniques, influencing a generation of future woodworkers and inspiring a renaissance of interest in traditional carpentry techniques. Abram's spinoff show, *The New Yankee Workshop*, featured a variety of woodworking projects including furniture, gazebos, boats, and a variety of other items.

College/Postsecondary

Most employers hiring woodworkers look for students who have completed their secondary education. There are a variety of trade schools and technical schools offering certification in tools and techniques used in woodworking as well as those that offer specific programs tailored for woodworkers. Such certification, while not required to apply for jobs in the field, will give students an advantage. Postsecondary certification programs sometimes offer specialized training towards a specific facet of the industry, such as wood engineering, production management, finish carpentry, or furniture manufacturing.

Related College Majors
- Industrial design
- Sculpture
- Engineering

Adult Job Seekers

Individuals with a background in woodworking may consider applying for jobs in either a woodworking shop or a factory specializing in wooden materials. Whatever their educational background, woodworking is a skill that typically requires significant amounts of work experience and practice and individuals will typically begin in lower level positions before transitioning to more advanced work.

Professional Certification and Licensure

While there are no specific certification requirements for woodworking, individuals with trade or technical educational experience may have an advantage in seeking employment. Trade schools offer certification programs in different aspects of woodworking, including design and the use of computer-aided or CNC tools. There are national and local organizations that help aspiring woodworkers to find opportunities for education and employment in the field.

Additional Requirements

Woodworking can be a physically demanding and potentially dangerous disciplines. Woodworkers need considerable physical strength and endurance as well as physical coordination to avoid injury when working with tools and machines. In addition, woodworkers benefit from good eyesight and from the ability to evaluate the aesthetics and accuracy of their work.

Fun Fact

"Along the River during the Qingming Festival" is more than 40-feet-long, making it the world's largest wood carving. Made from a single tree trunk, the carving features 550 individually carved people as well as buildings, boats and bridges and took four years to complete.

Source: http://www.guinnessworldrecords.com/world-records/

EARNINGS AND ADVANCEMENT

According to the Bureau of Labor Statistics (BLS), the median annual wage in the industry was $28,990 in 2015, with those at the lowest 10 percent of the pay scale earning less than $18,000 annually and those at the upper end of the spectrum earning more than $50,000 per year. Hourly wages for workers range from just over $9.00 per hour to over $24.00. Advancing in the industry is largely a matter of gaining experience to take on high level tasks in a factory or woodshop or advancing to management level positions within a company.

Metropolitan Areas with the Highest Employment Level in this Occupation

Metropolitan area	Employment	Employment per thousand jobs	Hourly mean wage
Dallas-Plano-Irving, TX Metropolitan Division	250	0.11	$14.92
Houston-The Woodlands-Sugar Land, TX	200	0.07	$12.16
Los Angeles-Long Beach-Glendale, CA Metropolitan Division	190	0.05	$14.75
Elkhart-Goshen, IN	190	1.52	$14.23
Portland-Vancouver-Hillsboro, OR-WA	190	0.17	$14.14
New York-Jersey City-White Plains, NY-NJ Metropolitan Division	160	0.02	$21.87
Baltimore-Columbia-Towson, MD	110	0.08	$15.72
Seattle-Bellevue-Everett, WA Metropolitan Division	100	0.07	N/A
Oxnard-Thousand Oaks-Ventura, CA	80	0.28	$13.81
El Paso, TX	80	0.27	N/A

Source: Bureau of Labor Statistics

EMPLOYMENT AND OUTLOOK

The Bureau of Labor Statistics estimates that the woodworking field will see little growth between 2014 and 2024, compared to the average 6-7 percent growth expected in all U.S. industries over the same period. Any local or regional growth within the industry is expected to come from the need for repair and refinishing services more often than from the demand for new wooden products. The increasing tendency towards automation in the industry has resulted in an overall loss of job opportunities, though individuals with experience working with CNC and other computer-aided systems will likely have an advantage in applying for remaining jobs. The housing renovation market and the specialty woodworking markets are expected to have the strongest growth over the next decade and individuals with knowledge of finish carpentry and custom woodworking skills will find more opportunities in the field.

Employment Trend, Projected 2014–24

Total, All Occupations: 7%

Woodworkers: -1%

Production Occupations: -3%

Note: "All Occupations" includes all occupations in the U.S. Economy. Source: U.S. Bureau of Labor Statistics, Employment Projections Program

Related Occupations
- Social Workers
- Special Education Teachers
- Kindergarten and Elementary School Teachers
- Middle School Teachers
- High School Teachers
- School and Career Counselors
- Technical Education Teachers
- Curriculum Specialist

Related Military Occupations
- Military Foreign Language Instructor
- Language Department Lead

Conversation With . . .
ERIN HANLEY

Furniture maker,
Erin Hanley Fine Furniture, Burlington, Vermont
Woodworker, 7 years

1. What was your individual career path in terms of education/training, entry-level job, or other significant opportunity?

When I was 19, I worked for a short stint in a cabinet shop. While there, I met a fine furniture maker and became his apprentice for a couple of years. He was a one-man shop, and made mostly commissioned, one of a kind pieces, so I learned a lot. However, I didn't continue with furniture making once I stopped working for him. I worked for a few craftspeople, sewing clothes. I didn't go to college right away; in fact, not until I was 27. In between I did a number of things … working as a gardener, doing construction. I went to school to become a paralegal and did that for a couple of years. Then I went to college. After that, I worked in community development, and then worked for almost 10 years as an organic vegetable farmer. After I had a child and we moved to Boston, I decided to give up farming and enroll at the North Bennet Street School's Cabinet and Furniture Making Program in Boston. I graduated in 2007 and, for the past seven or eight years, have had shared a shop in Burlington, Vermont, with two other furniture makers. I'm interested in making furniture that's both beautiful and functional, with hand-cut joinery, richly colored woods and hand-applied finishes.

2. What are the most important skills and/or qualities for someone in your profession?

There are a number of skills you'll need to be a successful furniture maker. The first are the hand skills and technical skills to actually make the work, which you can get by going to school, taking workshops, or working for someone who can give you a foundation in how to construct furniture. In addition, you'll need business skills, mechanical skills to deal with equipment, and good people skills to deal with clients.

3. What do you wish you had known going into this profession?

I wish I'd known how hard it is to make a living!

4. **Are there many job opportunities in your profession? In what specific areas?**

Hard to know. Many people do appreciate fine, handcrafted things, but you have to know how to find these people, and you have to know how to appeal to them. There is a lot of mass produced furniture out there, and it's pretty inexpensive. Handmade furniture is not inexpensive. So, you need to find your customers: people who appreciate quality and are willing to invest in something that will become an heirloom.

5. **How do you see your profession changing in the next five years? What role will technology play in those changes, and what skills will be required?**

I'm not sure the profession will change much. It would be good for someone going into furniture making to have computer skills so they can use software to design pieces, and use computerized machines, like a CNC, to make things. I could imagine a use for 3-D printing in furniture making, possibly making parts, but certainly for making scale models of proposed pieces. But the most important technological skills may be prowess in using social media to market and promote your work. If you can get your stuff out to many pairs of eyes, you'll have an advantage over others.

6. **What do you enjoy most about your job? What do you enjoy least about your job?**

The thing I enjoy most is creating something new and following my inspiration to a new place. The thing I enjoy least is trying to figure out what to charge.

7. **Can you suggest a valuable "try this" for students considering a career in your profession?**

I'd suggest that students find a way to begin working with their hands and see how they like it. And maybe shadow someone who is successful in their business to see what all the aspects are like: dealing with customers, refining a design, dealing with business regulations and employees, buying materials, maintaining machines, building pieces, finishing, shipping, etc.

MORE INFORMATION

Teachers of English to Speakers of Other Languages, Inc. (TESOL)
1925 Ballenger Avenue, Suite 550
Alexandria, Virginia 22314
www.tesol.org

National Association for Bilingual Education (NABE)
11006 Viers Mills Road, L-1
Wheaton, MD 20902
www.nabe.org

National Council of Teachers of English (NCTE)
1111 W. Kenyon Road
Urbana, Illinois, 61801
www.ncte.org

American Association for Applied Linguistics (AAAL)
1827 Powers Ferry Road, Building 14
Suite 100
Atlanta, Georgia, 30339
www.aaal.org

American Council on the Teaching of Foreign Languages (ACTFL)
1001 N. Fairfax Street, Suite 200
Alexandria, Virginia, 22314
www.actfl.org

International Language Testing Assocation (ILTA)
3416 Primm Lane
Birmingham, Alabama 35216
www.iltaonline.com

Micah Issitt/Editor

Writer & Editor

Snapshot

Career Cluster: Arts, Media & Communications, Business Management

Interests: Language, Grammar, Writing, Publishing

Earnings (Yearly Average): $56,652

Employment & Outlook: Slower Than Average Growth Expected

OVERVIEW

Sphere of Work

Writers and editors are employed in all realms of business and industry. In addition to journalism, publishing, and media (i.e., radio and television), employment for writers can be found in government, marketing, law, entertainment, and sales. Writers employed by local, state, or federal governments may craft legislation or produce speeches and press releases for elected representatives. Every industrial sector, be it the automobile industry, healthcare, education, retail, agriculture, or mining, utilizes writers to communicate

with colleagues and clients and develop messaging regarding their productivity and business plan. Freelance writing and editing—that is, writing and editing under temporary contract—is common. Many freelancers work for online publishers, producing content for clients that adheres to specific guidelines. In general, writers create original content and editors review and revise that content; but there is significant overlap between these two roles.

Work Environment

Most writers and editors work in an office environment. Writers and editors in the media often work in the field, gathering data and interviewing people for news reports. Many freelance writers and editors work from a home office. Some freelance writers work at rented office spaces.

Profile

Working Conditions: Work Indoors
Physical Strength: Light Work
Education Needs: Bachelor's Degree
Licensure/Certification: Usually Not Required
Physical Abilities Not Required: No Heavy Labor
Opportunities For Experience: IInternship, Apprenticeship, Military Service, Volunteer Work, Part-Time Work
Holland Interest Score*: AES, SEA

* See Appendix A

Occupation Interest

Writers and editors enjoy working with language and ideas. They enjoy the challenge of communicating complex ideas in a way that is readily digestible to a specific audience. Writers and editors have a penchant for grammar and the intricacies of publishing formats and editorial guidelines. Those who are employed by a specific industry or business sector should have a passion for that area of communication and commerce. For examples, sports writers need to be knowledgeable about a particular sport's rules and regulations, teams, and players. Individuals interested in writing public policy or producing content for the news media should be interested in government, politics, and current events.

A Day in the Life—Duties and Responsibilities

The daily life of a writer/editor is highly dependent upon the field in which he or she is employed. For example, writers and editors employed in a marketing department—copywriters—may research a particular product line before beginning to write about it for a particular client or consumer market. Speechwriters and those working in the legal or political field will research archival material and conduct interviews with voters and policy makers. Other writing and editing work is more routinized. Writers and editors working for publishing companies traditionally follow a product development schedule, whether the product is a book, magazine, newspaper, or online publication. Technical writers produce product manuals, assembly instructions, or troubleshooting guidelines. The work of a freelance writer and editor will vary day-to-day depending on the project. In some cases a writer/editor is involved in the planning and preparation of a product and may have a hand not only in developing the text but also in choosing photos, illustrations, and other elements. sometimes include website maintenance, depending on the client's expectations.

Duties and Responsibilities

- Selecting a topic or being assigned one
- Researching the topic through library study, interviews, or observation
- Selecting and organizing information and writing about the information to achieve the desired effect
- Revising or rewriting for the best organization or the right phrasing
- Acquiring or contracting for original content from outside writers
- Evaluating manuscripts to determine their editorial needs
- Ensuring that manuscripts cover their topics and address their audiences
- Contributing to the planning of a publication, including text, photos, and illustrations
- Checking or proofreading a publication prior to its release

OCCUPATION SPECIALTIES

Copywriters

Copywriters prepare advertisements to promote the sale of a good or service. They often work with a client to produce advertising themes, jingles, and slogans.

Copy Editors & Proofreaders

Copy Editors review copy for errors in grammar, punctuation, and spelling and check the copy for readability, style, and agreement with editorial policy. They also may confirm sources and verify facts. Proofreaders check typeset pages for any remaining errors.

Staff Writers & Editors

Staff Writers and Editors prepare material for newspapers, magazine, books, or news broadcasts. They generally work under an executive or managing editor. They draft or receive copy and may suggest or choose graphics and images to accompany it. Depending on their seniority, they may be responsible for a particular subject area or type of editorial project.

Executive & Managing Editors

Executive Editors plan the contents and budget of publications and supervise their preparation. In most cases, they decide what gets published and what does not. Managing Editors, similarly, work with executives, department heads, and editorial staff to formulate policies, coordinate department activities, establish production schedules, solve publication problems, and make organizational changes.

Contributing Editors

Contributing Editors are professional authors who contribute original articles to magazines or newspapers on a regular or semi-regular basis.

Fiction and Nonfiction Writers

Fiction and Nonfiction Writers are professional authors who write original material for publication and seek to develop a readership for their work.

Screen Writers

Screen Writers are authors who write scripts for motion pictures or television. They may produce original stories, characters, and dialogue or turn a book into a movie or television script. Some may produce content for radio broadcasts and other types of performance.

WORK ENVIRONMENT

Relevant Skills and Abilities

Analytical Skills
- Analyzing information
- Reading with a critical eye

Communication Skills
- Expressing thoughts and ideas clearly
- Speaking and writing effectively

Creative Skills
- Creating ideas
- Appealing to an audience/readership

Interpersonal/Social Skills
- Being able to work both independently and as a member of a team
- Cooperating with others

Organization & Management Skills
- Managing time
- Meeting goals and deadlines
- Paying attention to and handling details

Planning & Research Skills
- Making an outline
- Researching a topic

Physical Environment

Freelance or contract writers and editors work primarily from home offices or in designated sections of their homes. Freelance work has no set hours or specified work schedule, and freelancers often work atypical hours and on weekends. Some long-term contracts require that writers or editors work at the company who is hiring them, which would require the writer or editor to work in an office setting during regular business hours for the length of the project they have been hired to complete.

Writers or editors who are hired as full-time employees for a company or organization work in office settings and during standard business hours and days.

Human Environment

Writers and editors interact frequently with clients and colleagues and good communication skills are essential to their work. While many writers and editors work alone, nearly all communicate regularly with colleagues and clients about project-specific guidelines and goals.

EDUCATION, TRAINING, AND ADVANCEMENT

High School/Secondary

High school students can best prepare for a career as a writer or editor by completing coursework in English, history, social studies, the arts, and science. Advanced coursework in a field of particular interest can prepare students for writing knowledgably and coherently about that field. Participation in extracurricular activities such as debate clubs, school papers, or school television and radio programs can also help students develop the skills needed for a career in writing and editing.

Suggested High School Subjects
- Applied Communication
- College Preparatory
- Composition
- Computer Science
- English
- History
- Journalism
- Keyboarding
- Literature
- Social Studies
- Science & Technology Studies
- Speech

College/Postsecondary

Postsecondary education is often a requirement for vacancies in the writing and editing field. Postsecondary coursework that can contribute to the numerous skills and vast frame of reference required of writers and editors includes education, literature, history, government, international business, economics, politics, and government.

Famous First

The first magazine to be edited by a woman was the *Ladies' Magazine*, published in Boston between 1828 and 1837 and edited by Sarah Josepha Hale (author of "*Mary Had a Little Lamb*"). The magazine was absorbed into the popular *Godey's Lady's Book*, and Hale moved to Philadelphia to oversee that publication. She stayed at the helm at *Godey's* for another 40 years.

Related College Majors

- Advertising
- Broadcast Journalism
- Business Communications
- Communications, General
- Creative Writing
- English
- Journalism
- Playwriting & Screenwriting

Adult Job Seekers

There are selected opportunities for adult job seekers interested in writing and editing. Working knowledge or experience in a particular field, such as education, marketing, or retail, represent skills that can be transferable to writing and editing work. Editors and writers working in one area, such as newspapers, can also sometimes cross over into another, such as book publishing. Oftentimes, however, the best way to make the switch is to seek a temporary or part-time assignment first.

Professional Certification and Licensure

Certification or licensure is not required to be employed as an editor or writer. The majority of hiring companies and organizations require that applicants have at least an undergraduate degree with a concentration in either English or another field that pertains to the position needing to be filled.

Additional Requirements

Writers and editors must possess a love of the language and a commitment to quality writing. Writers and editors often work alone or from their homes, so individuals who want to explore this line of work should be comfortable in solitary settings.

EARNINGS AND ADVANCEMENT

Advancement for writers and editors is achieved by being successful within an organization or by moving to another firm. Larger firms usually give writing and editing responsibilities only after a period of entry-level research, fact checking and proofreading. Smaller firms give major duties right away, and competence is expected.

Median annual earnings of writers were $58,745 in 2012. The lowest ten percent earned less than $30,327, and the highest ten percent earned more than $116,006.

Median annual earnings of editors were $54,558 in 2012. The lowest ten percent earned less than $30,613, and the highest ten percent earned more than $102,608.

Writers and editors may receive paid vacations, holidays, and sick days; life and health insurance; and retirement benefits. These are usually paid by the employer. In addition, many writers and editors freelance to supplement their salaries.

Metropolitan Areas with the Highest Employment Level in This Occupation

Metropolitan area	Employment[1]	Employment per thousand jobs	Hourly mean wage
New York-White Plains-Wayne, NY-NJ	23,5100	2.28	$40.08
Los Angeles-Long Beach-Glendale, CA	8,260	1.07	$44.80
Washington-Arlington-Alexandria, DC-VA-MD-WV	6,750	1.44	$36.34
Chicago-Joliet-Naperville, IL	5,110	0.70	$28.85
Minneapolis-St. Paul-Bloomington, MN-WI	3,780	1.09	$26.69
Boston-Cambridge-Quincy, MA	3,680	1.08	$35.46
San Francisco-San Mateo-Redwood City, CA	3,100	1.55	$30.33
Seattle-Bellevue-Everett, WA	2,660	0.95	$36.12

(1) Does not include self-employed. Source: Bureau of Labor Statistics, 2012

EMPLOYMENT AND OUTLOOK

Writers and editors held about 140,000 jobs nationally in 2012. Nearly the same number were self-employed. Most staff editors worked full-time, but about one-fourth of staff writers worked part-time. Employment is expected to grow slower than the average for all occupations through the year 2020, which means employment is projected to increase approximately 1 percent to 5 percent. Online publications and services continue to grow, creating demand for writers and editors with Web and multimedia experience while limiting the growth of more traditional jobs in the publishing industry. Lower costs for self-publishing and the increasing popularity of electronic books will allow more freelance writers to have their work published.

Employment Trend, Projected 2010–20

Total, All Occupations: 14%

Media and Communication Workers: 13%

Writers and Authors: 6%

Note: "All Occupations" includes all occupations in the U.S. Economy Source: U.S. Bureau of Labor Statistics, Employment Projections Program

Employment Trend, Projected 2010–20

Total, All Occupations: 14%

Media and Communication Workers: 13%

Editors: 1%

Note: "All Occupations" includes all occupations in the U.S. Economy Source: U.S. Bureau of Labor Statistics, Employment Projections Program

Related Occupations
- Copywriter
- Journalist
- Radio/TV Announcer & Newscaster

- Technical Writer

Related Military Occupations
- Public Information Officer

Conversation With . . .
Veronica Towers
Writer & Editor, 30 years

1. What was your individual career path in terms of education, entry-level job, or other significant opportunity?

As I worked my way through graduate school at Columbia University, I discovered that I very much enjoyed working as a research assistant but that I did not enjoy my teaching assistantship. Since my program was essentially designed to produce college professors, I decided that I needed to carve out a new career path. Thanks to a friend of a friend, I slipped into publishing and immediately felt at home. I was extremely fortunate that my first job was with a very small publisher. Although the company had already been acquired by the much larger Prentice-Hall (which itself would soon be acquired by Simon & Schuster), we were pretty much left to ourselves. I began as a production editor, then moved over to the editorial side. Because we were so small, I received intensive training from colleagues and had many more opportunities to stretch than would have been the case at a larger house.

Once Simon & Schuster stepped in, I found myself unemployed. On the coattails of a colleague, I became an in-house freelancer at Macmillan Educational, copyediting early-education classroom continuity units. I then went on contract at Macmillan Educational as copy chief for an entirely new edition of the *Golden Book Encyclopedia for Children*—my introduction to soup-to-nuts encyclopedia work. Once that task was completed, I was hired by Grolier, Inc., as humanities editor of the *Encyclopedia Americana*. There I remained for some 18 years, until the Internet upended encyclopedia publishing. After that I transitioned into reference book publishing, which is still my field.

2. Are there many job opportunities in your profession? In what specific areas?

It used to be said that if you wanted a raise in publishing, it was time to change jobs. No one would take that approach now. All in all, the opportunities seem erratic. Candidates experienced at managing social media for an employer definitely have an edge. Production and editorial administration seem distinctly better paths to employment.

3. What do you wish you had known going into this profession?

I started in an age of expansion, when opportunities seemed readily available. It would have been wise to be more proactive about seizing or creating opportunities.

4. How do you see your profession changing in the next five years?

E-publishing—because it allows authors to cut out traditional publishers—seems to pose a fundamental challenge to the industry. Also posing a challenge, perhaps more radically, is the ever more ephemeral nature of content. Publishing generally is in search of a new business model.

In terms of educational and reference publishing, I think publishing timetables will continue to accelerate as the market demands more and more information faster and faster. "Retail" publishing (for example, gearing an electronically published textbook specifically to a professor's particular course) seems likely to increase. Another challenge is the proliferation of blogs and all sorts of other unmediated content and commentary on the Internet. This has had a kind of flattening effect, undermining long-established notions of authoritativeness, the essential value-added argument for editorial departments everywhere. I do see some push-back against the flattening trend: readers are looking for help sorting it all out, and this is where publishing has to make its stand. Recently I have constantly been encountering the word curated, applied to everything from restaurant menus to boutique offerings. Perhaps we'll all become "curators" rather than editors.

5. What role will technology play in those changes, and what skills will be required?

I think editors will increasingly manage content from various sources across multiple platforms rather than engage in intensive developmental work and rigorous traditional editing. Editors will have to be conversant with social media. Already I find that some of my younger correspondents have difficulty responding to communications much longer than an average tweet.

6. Do you have any general advice or additional professional insights to share with someone interested in your profession?

Because of the barrage of information we must cope with, critical thinking skills are more important than ever. Mastery of grammar and style demonstrates competence: since both are essentially logic tools, and therefore the tools of critical thinking as well as writing, they are not to be regarded merely as niceties. Look over the major publishing style guides—*Chicago Manual of Style*, *Associated Press Stylebook*, the Modern Language Association's *MLA Style Guide*, *Publication Manual* of the American Psychological Association—not so much to "learn" the styles as to see how they hone in on the needs of their distinct audiences. Consistency is the essential virtue of style. Think about why. Read Strunk and White's brief *Elements of Style* for fun and profit.

Hone your presentation skills; seek out opportunities to learn new skills, especially technological skills; keep in mind that publishing is at base a business like any other; learn from and value your colleagues.

7. Can you suggest a valuable "try this" for students considering a career in your profession?

A student might take a substantial (but not overlong) feature story and rewrite it as an informative but succinct and engaging press release, or go over a mailer from a research or advocacy group looking for errors and ways of making the presentation more effective and concise. My experience suggests that errors are there to be found and that the writing in such communications can just about always be improved.

SELECTED SCHOOLS

Hundreds of colleges and universities offer degree programs in English and the liberal arts, both of which are good foundations for building a career in writing and editing. The student can also gain initial training at a community college. Below are listed some of the more prominent four-year institutions in this field.

Cornell University
410 Thurston Avenue
Ithaca, NY 14850
607.255.5242
www.cornell.edu

Columbia University
535 W. 116th Street
New York, NY 10027
212.854.1754
www.columbia.edu

Duke University
450 Research Drive
e-commerce, NC 27750
919.684.8111
www.duke.edu

Harvard University
1350 Massachusetts Avenue
Cambridge, MA 02138
617.495.1000
www.harvard.edu

Princeton University
Princeton, NJ 08544
609.258.3000
www.princeton.edu

Stanford University
450 Serra Mall
Stanford, CA 94305
650.723.2300
www.stanford.edu

University of California, Berkeley
101 Sproul Hall
Berkeley, CA 94704
510.642.6000
www.berkeley.edu

University of Chicago
5801 S. Ellis Avenue
Chicago, IL 60637
773.702.1234
www.uchicago.edu

University of Pennsylvania
3451 Walnut Street
Philadelphia, PA 19104
215.898.5000
www.upenn.edu

Yale University
P.O. Box 208234
New Haven, CT 06520
203.432.4771
www.yale.edu

MORE INFORMATION

American Copy Editors Society
7 Avenida Vista Grande, Suite B7
#467
Santa Fe, NM 87508
www.copydesk.org

**American Society of Journalists
and Authors**
Times Square
1501 Broadway, Suite 403
New York, NY 10036
212.997.0947
www.asja.org

**American Society of Magazine
Editors**
810 Seventh Avenue, 24th Floor
New York, NY 10019
212.872.3700
www.magazine.org/editorial/asme

**Association for Women in
Communications**
3337 Duke Street
Alexandria, VA 22314
703.370.7436
www.womcom.org

**Association of American
Publishers**
455 Massachusetts Avenue NW
Washington, DC 20001
202.347.3375
www.publishers.org

Editorial Freelancers Association
71 West 23rd Street, 4th Floor
New York, NY 10010-4102
212.929.5400
www.the-efa.org

**International Association of
Business Communicators**
601 Montgomery Street, Suite 1900
San Francisco, CA 94111
800.776.4222
www.iabc.com

**National Association of Science
Writers**
P.O. Box 7905
Berkeley, CA 94707
510.647.9500
www.nasw.org

National Newspaper Association
P.O. Box 7540
Columbia, MO 65205-7540
800.829.4662
www.nnaweb.org

**Newspaper Association of
America**
4401 Wilson Boulevard, Suite 900
Arlington, VA 22203-1867
571.366.1000
www.naa.org

**Society for Technical
Communication**
9401 Lee Highway, Suite 300
Fairfax, VA 22031
703.522.4114
www.stc.org

Price Grisham/Editor

What Are Your Career Interests?

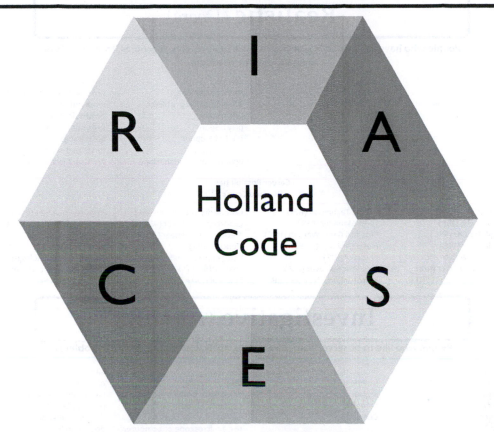

This is based on Dr. John Holland's theory that people and work environments can be loosely classified into six different groups. Each of the letters above corresponds to one of the six groups described in the following pages.

Different people's personalities may find different environments more to their liking. While you may have some interests in and similarities to several of the six groups, you may be attracted primarily to two or three of the areas. These two or three letters are your "Holland Code." For example, with a code of "RES" you would most resemble the Realistic type, somewhat less resemble the Enterprising type, and resemble the Social type even less. The types that are not in your code are the types you resemble least of all.

Most people, and most jobs, are best represented by some combination of two or three of the Holland interest areas. In addition, most people are most satisfied if there is some degree of fit between their personality and their work environment.

The rest of the pages in this booklet further explain each type and provide some examples of career possibilities, areas of study at MU, and co-curricular activities for each code. To take a more in-depth look at your Holland Code, take a self-assessment such as the SDS, Discover, or a card sort at the MU Career Center with a Career Specialist.

This hexagonal model of RIASEC occupations is the copyrighted work of Dr. John Holland, and is used with his permission. The Holland Game is adapted from Richard Bolles' "Quick Job Hunting Map." Copyright 1995, 1998 by the MU Career Center, University of Missouri-Columbia.

Realistic *(Doers)*

People who have athletic ability, prefer to work with objects, machines, tools, plants or animals, or to be outdoors.

Are you?
practical
straightforward/frank
mechanically inclined
stable
concrete
reserved
self-controlled

independent
ambitious
systematic

Can you?
fix electrical things
solve electrical problems
pitch a tent
play a sport
read a blueprint
plant a garden
operate tools and machine

Like to?
tinker with machines/vehicles
work outdoors
be physically active
use your hands
build things
tend/train animals
work on electronic equipment

**Career Possibilities
(Holland Code):**

Air Traffic Controller (SER)
Archaeologist (IRE)
Athletic Trainer (SRE)
Cartographer (IRE)
Commercial Airline Pilot (RIE)
Commercial Drafter (IRE)
Corrections Officer (SER)

Dental Technician (REI)
Farm Manager (ESR)
Fish and Game Warden (RES)
Floral Designer (RAE)
Forester (RIS)
Geodetic Surveyor (IRE)
Industrial Arts Teacher (IER)

Laboratory Technician (RIE)
Landscape Architect (AIR)
Mechanical Engineer (RIS)
Optician (REI)
Petroleum Geologist (RIE)
Police Officer (SER)
Practical Nurse (SER)

Property Manager (ESR)
Recreation Manager (SER)
Service Manager (ERS)
Software Technician (RCI)
Ultrasound Technologist (RSI)
Vocational Rehabilitation
   Consultant (ESR)

Investigative *(Thinkers)*

People who like to observe, learn, investigate, analyze, evaluate, or solve problems.

Are you?
inquisitive
analytical
scientific
observant/precise
scholarly
cautious

intellectually self-confident
Independent
logical
complex
Curious

Can you?
think abstractly
solve math problems
understand scientific theories
do complex calculations
use a microscope or computer
interpret formulas

Like to?
explore a variety of ideas
work independently
perform lab experiments
deal with abstractions
do research
be challenged

**Career Possibilities
(Holland Code):**

Actuary (ISE)
Agronomist (IRS)
Anesthesiologist (IRS)
Anthropologist (IRE)
Archaeologist (IRE)
Biochemist (IRS)
Biologist (ISR)

Chemical Engineer (IRE)
Chemist (IRE)
Computer Systems Analyst (IER)
Dentist (ISR)
Ecologist (IRE)
Economist (IAS)
Electrical Engineer (IRE)

Geologist (IRE)
Horticulturist (IRS)
Mathematician (IER)
Medical Technologist (ISA)
Meteorologist (IRS)
Nurse Practitioner (ISA)
Pharmacist (IES)

Physician, General Practice (ISE)
Psychologist (IES)
Research Analyst (IRC)
Statistician (IRE)
Surgeon (IRA)
Technical Writer (IRS)
Veterinarian (IRS)

Artistic *(Creators)*

People who have artistic, innovating, or intuitional abilities and like to work in unstructured situations using their imagination and creativity.

Are you?
creative
imaginative
innovative
unconventional
emotional
independent
Expressive

original
introspective
impulsive
sensitive
courageous
complicated
idealistic
nonconforming

Can you?
sketch, draw, paint
play a musical instrument
write stories, poetry, music
sing, act, dance
design fashions or interiors

Like to?
attend concerts, theatre, art
  exhibits
read fiction, plays, and poetry
work on crafts
take photography
express yourself creatively
deal with ambiguous ideas

**Career Possibilities
(Holland Code):**

Actor (AES)
Advertising Art Director (AES)
Advertising Manager (ASE)
Architect (AIR)
Art Teacher (ASE)
Artist (ASI)

Copy Writer (ASI)
Dance Instructor (AER)
Drama Coach (ASE)
English Teacher (ASE)
Entertainer/Performer (AES)
Fashion Illustrator (ASR)

Interior Designer (AES)
Intelligence Research Specialist
  (AEI)
Journalist/Reporter (ASE)
Landscape Architect (AIR)
Librarian (SAI)

Medical Illustrator (AIE)
Museum Curator (AES)
Music Teacher (ASI)
Photographer (AES)
Writer (ASI)
Graphic Designer (AES)

Social *(Helpers)*

People who like to work with people to enlighten, inform, help, train, or cure them, or are skilled with words.

Are you?
friendly
helpful
idealistic
insightful
outgoing
understanding

cooperative
generous
responsible
forgiving
patient
kind

Can you?
teach/train others
express yourself clearly
lead a group discussion
mediate disputes
plan and supervise an activity
cooperate well with others

Like to?
work in groups
help people with problems
do volunteer work
work with young people
serve others

**Career Possibilities
(Holland Code):**

City Manager (SEC)
Clinical Dietitian (SIE)
College/University Faculty (SEI)
Community Org. Director
  (SEA)
Consumer Affairs Director
  (SER)Counselor/Therapist
  (SAE)

Historian (SEI)
Hospital Administrator (SER)
Psychologist (SEI)
Insurance Claims Examiner
  (SIE)
Librarian (SAI)
Medical Assistant (SCR)
Minister/Priest/Rabbi (SAI)
Paralegal (SCE)

Park Naturalist (SEI)
Physical Therapist (SIE)
Police Officer (SER)
Probation and Parole Officer
  (SEC)
Real Estate Appraiser (SCE)
Recreation Director (SER)
Registered Nurse (SIA)

Teacher (SAE)
Social Worker (SEA)
Speech Pathologist (SAI)
Vocational-Rehab. Counselor
  (SEC)
Volunteer Services Director
  (SEC)

Enterprising *(Persuaders)*

People who like to work with people, influencing, persuading, leading or managing for organizational goals or economic gain.

Are you?
self-confident
assertive
persuasive
energetic
adventurous
popular

ambitious
agreeable
talkative
extroverted
spontaneous
optimistic

Can you?
initiate projects
convince people to do things
    your way
sell things
give talks or speeches
organize activities
lead a group
persuade others

Like to?
make decisions
be elected to office
start your own business
campaign politically
meet important people
have power or status

**Career Possibilities
(Holland Code):**

Advertising Executive (ESA)
Advertising Sales Rep (ESR)
Banker/Financial Planner (ESR)
Branch Manager (ESA)
Business Manager (ESC)
Buyer (ESA)
Chamber of Commerce Exec
    (ESA)

Credit Analyst (EAS)
Customer Service Manager
    (ESA)
Education & Training Manager
    (EIS)
Emergency Medical Technician
    (ESI)
Entrepreneur (ESA)

Foreign Service Officer (ESA)
Funeral Director (ESR)
Insurance Manager (ESC)
Interpreter (ESA)
Lawyer/Attorney (ESA)
Lobbyist (ESA)
Office Manager (ESR)
Personnel Recruiter (ESR)

Politician (ESA)
Public Relations Rep (EAS)
Retail Store Manager (ESR)
Sales Manager (ESA)
Sales Representative (ERS)
Social Service Director (ESA)
Stockbroker (ESI)
Tax Accountant (ECS)

Conventional *(Organizers)*

People who like to work with data, have clerical or numerical ability, carry out tasks in detail, or follow through on others' instructions.

Are you?
well-organized
accurate
numerically inclined
methodical
conscientious
efficient
conforming

practical
thrifty
systematic
structured
polite
ambitious
obedient
persistent

Can you?
work well within a system
do a lot of paper work in a short
    time
keep accurate records
use a computer terminal
write effective business letters

Like to?
follow clearly defined
    procedures
use data processing equipment
work with numbers
type or take shorthand
be responsible for details
collect or organize things

**Career Possibilities
(Holland Code):**

Abstractor (CSI)
Accountant (CSE)
Administrative Assistant (ESC)
Budget Analyst (CER)
Business Manager (ESC)
Business Programmer (CRI)
Business Teacher (CSE)
Catalog Librarian (CSE)

Claims Adjuster (SEC)
Computer Operator (CSR)
Congressional-District Aide (CES)
Cost Accountant (CES)
Court Reporter (CSE)
Credit Manager (ESC)
Customs Inspector (CEI)
Editorial Assistant (CSI)

Elementary School Teacher
    (SEC)
Financial Analyst (CSI)
Insurance Manager (ESC)
Insurance Underwriter (CSE)
Internal Auditor (ICR)
Kindergarten Teacher (ESC)

Medical Records Technician
    (CSE)
Museum Registrar (CSE)
Paralegal (SCE)
Safety Inspector (RCS)
Tax Accountant (ECS)
Tax Consultant (CES)
Travel Agent (ECS)

BIBLIOGRAPHY

Boslaugh, Sarah. *Careers and Occupations*. Gale Cengage, 2015. Print.

Burdick, Jan E. *Creative Careers in Museums*. New York: Constable & Robinson, 2012. Internet resource.

Career As a Florist: Floral Designer: Use Your Artistic Talent to Own Your Own Business. Chicago: Institute for Career Research, 2010. Internet resource.

Careers in Focus. New York: Ferguson's, 2012. Print.

Careers in Popular Music: Perfomers, Recording Artists, Writers. Chicago: Institute for Career Research, 2006. Internet resource.

Careers in Writing. Paw Prints, 2010. Print.

Congdon, Lisa, Meg M. Ilasco, and Jonathan Fields. *Art, Inc: The Essential Guide for Building Your Career As an Artist*., 2014. Print.

Fine Art As a Career: Painter, Sculptor, Printmaker: Portrait of the Artist As an Intriguing Individual. Chicago, Ill: Institute for Career Research, 2005. Internet resource.

Inkson, Kerr, Nicky Dries, and John Arnold. *Understanding Careers*. Los Angeles: Sage, 2015. Print.

Mathieu, Chris. *Careers in Creative Industries*. New York: Routledge, 2015. Print.

Melber, Leah M., ed. *Teaching the Museum: Careers in Museum Education*. New York: Routledge, 2009.

Occupational Employment Statistics. Washington, D.C: U.S. Dept. of Labor, Bureau of Labor Statistics; for sale by the Supt. of Docs., U.S. G.P.O, 1966. Print.

Schlatter, N. Elizabeth. *Museum Careers: A Practical Guide for Students and Novices*.

Shally-Jensen, Michael. *Careers in Communications & Media*., 2014. Print.

Washington, DC: American Alliance of Museums, 2014.

INDEX